the
BLUFF

the BLUFF

EMMA ST. CLAIR

This book is dedicated to all the readers who read these dedications.
I SEE YOU.
And I really like you.

BLUFF:
an action such as a call or raise intended to deceive others about the cards a player has in hand; a lie told to others or to oneself

CHAPTER 1

James

I'M STANDING on the deserted sidewalk of a town ridiculously named Sheet Cake, staring at a run-down warehouse. Not just any building, but one I'm supposed to magically turn into a successful brewery in a matter of months. It is ground zero in a cascading number of bad decisions I've made lately.

This is why I don't listen to other people. It's why I work alone, why I shouldn't care if my family teases me about being a control freak. Because when I loosen up, even a little, I end up here on my thirtieth birthday, questioning all my life choices in a tiny Texas town.

But even as I'm running through potential solutions as well as exit strategies, another bad decision appears, this one in human form. I hear the sound of her heels from halfway up the block. Who wears high heels on a street with more potholes than pavement, anyway? SHE does.

Stopping right next to me, close enough to make my skin itch, she mirrors my stance, arms crossed over her chest, facing the building. I refuse to look. If I ignore her, maybe she'll go away.

Doubtful.

Winchester Boyd is a hangnail on my soul. The current bane of my existence. And as of today at nine a.m., my employee.

I glance at my watch. Nine-oh-one. I heave a sigh.

Winnie says nothing, and I continue pretending she isn't there, even as every cell in my body seems to have swung her way like tiny, malfunctioning satellites. Being around her is like being massaged with rough-grit sandpaper.

Clenching my jaw, I force my attention to the empty warehouse and attached grain elevators. All metal, mostly corrugated. A lot rusted. While Winnie and I stand in tense silence, an orange cat with only one eye shimmies under the fence and saunters by like the place is his and we're the trespassers. On the plus side, a cat problem means there isn't a rat problem.

My current bar for positive thinking is at an all-time low.

The cat blinks its yellow eye at me, then sits down and begins to give himself a bath, starting between his legs. Because of course it does.

"It's a bit of a hot mess, isn't it?" Winnie asks. "But—"

"Nice attitude." I can't help bristling at her words. I think I was already pretty well bristled by just her presence before Winnie spoke.

Why AM I so irritated by her? It's the sassy, sarcastic mouth and maybe something deeper on a chemical level. She and I are like magnets with the same pole facing out, creating

2

this invisible yet palpable push between us. From the first moment we met, she seemed completely wary of me for no good reason, like I offended her before even speaking. Which in turn offended me.

The thing is, I don't disagree with her assessment about the building. This place is a hot mess, but it's MY hot mess. At least, after some convincing from Tank and Pat, it's mine. And maybe I'm questioning the wisdom in all of this—the move to Sheet Cake, expanding from a smaller home brewing system to a ten-thousand-barrel operation and tasting room, and using this massive, rusted-out building—but I won't admit it.

I *will* make this work. Because if Dark Horse Brewing fails, it's not just my own savings on the line. THAT I could handle. But my family doesn't just have a lot of nosy opinions about the business—they've invested financially. And I won't fail *them*.

"I hadn't finished," Winnie says. "It's a bit of a hot mess but—"

"I got the gist."

I feel Winnie's eyes on me, but I refuse to turn her way. Now I'm wondering what she had planned to say before I cut in. The need to know burns, making my fingers twitch.

But WHAT, Winnie?

She's silent for a few long beats. Then I see her nodding from my peripheral vision. "I was wondering how our workplace dynamic would be. I get it now."

"Do tell."

"You like your employees to toe the company line. Not to speak the truth, especially if it hurts. Am I getting warm?"

This woman will be the death of me. Literally, figuratively, maybe both.

"Ice. Cold."

I turn to face her now, which only makes everything worse. Because, despite the way she can irritate me in an instant, all of Winnie's individual parts work to create a tantalizing whole: silky blond hair, dark blue eyes behind black-framed glasses, lips painted a red that begs to be kissed off that smart mouth. Her style, not that I really *get* style, is edgy pin-up girl: a button-down blouse tucked into a belted knee-length skirt, heels with a little cut-out for the toes, a high ponytail with a scarf tied around it. For reasons I can't explain, the lack of visible skin is somehow sexier than if she were wearing less. The hint of her tattoos peeking out from her rolled-up sleeves makes me want to see more.

My attraction to her is a reflex, one I plan to eradicate. So far, it's like trying to stop myself from sneezing.

Any day now, the things I dislike about her will sour the attraction. Any. Day. Now.

Today would be preferable. Right this second would be perfect.

"Why don't you enlighten me, *boss*—what do you want in an employee?"

I don't hold back the snarl in my voice. "Someone who knows their place and stays in it."

Wow. I sound like a domineering jerk. A terrible boss. Not the kind of man I want to be. Not the man I *am*.

I may have the reputation of a grump, but it's only in contrast to the rest of my family. Pat is bright, loud sunshine, and my dad, whom we all call Tank from his football days, is hardly ever without a smile and booming laugh. Collin is more serious and uptight, but still warm and kind.

Only my sister, Harper, shares my intensity and doesn't pass out smiles like parade candy. But no one ever calls *her* a grouch. After losing Mom, we all closed ranks around our younger sister, and are way too protective to be critical of her.

In Winnie's presence, I become what they tease me about —only worse. I'm a cartoon version of myself with a tiny storm cloud rumbling over my head. I'm a surly curmudgeon. My life is the lawn, and I'm yelling at Winnie to get off it.

She whistles, long and low. "Is part of my job fetching you coffee? Because you clearly haven't had enough this morning."

I drag a hand through my hair, irked by the idea of Winnie doing anything so personal as fixing my coffee. "You won't be getting me coffee. Or picking up my dry cleaning."

Winnie eyes my worn jeans and motorcycle boots. "Good. Because I can't imagine your dry-cleaning bill for the month. Must be enormous."

Coming from anyone else, this might elicit a chuckle. But it comes from her, so I bite the inside of my cheek. One thing I'll say for Winnie—she's whip-smart. At least conversationally. We'll have to see how this translates to her job.

"I just want someone who will work hard. No drama." I eye her, hoping she catches my implied meaning: *Stop baiting me. Stop with the smart remarks.*

"Got it, boss. Be neither seen nor heard while completing my non-coffee, non-dry-cleaning jobs."

She gives me a jaunty salute which contains all the attitude of a middle finger. I am a bear, and she's standing there, grinning and poking. So much for low drama.

"Is this how it's going to be?" I ask, giving her a long look. Not the best idea, especially when I find my gaze snagging on her red lips. I jerk my attention back to the warehouse. "Not the best first impression."

"Right back at you." She gestures to the open gate in front of us. "I mean, not even a *Welcome to Your First Day* banner?"

"Sorry. I disbanded the party-planning committee."

Winnie spins to face me, hands on her hips. I try not to look—*I do*—but it's impossible. I turn to face her, mimicking her pose the way she did earlier. She blinks several times, then laughs. Head thrown back, ponytail swinging, the gentle curve of her throat exposed.

I swallow. I glare. I wait.

My whole body feels hot by the time Winnie's laughter dissolves into giggles. She lifts her glasses, wipes tears from her deep blue eyes. I don't move.

"Was that a reference to *The Office?*" she asks finally, a smile lifting one side of her mouth.

"No."

It totally was, but I'll deny it until my deathbed. I do not make jokes outside of my family. Even then, it's rare.

This was … an anomaly. A glitch. A *mistake*. Not the tone I want to set on day one. I turn away, and the orange cat stares up at me with its one yellow eye like he totally sees through me. Another cat, this one black, hops up on a nearby stack of wood pallets, and now it feels like Winnie and I are performing in front of a studio audience.

I make a mental note to add *Get rid of cats* to my already long to-do list. Then fight back a grin as I mentally add *Get rid of cats* to Winnie's to-do list.

"Too bad," Winnie says. "I thought for a moment you had a sense of humor hiding under all that."

She waves a hand over my body, her gaze sweeping from my head down to my boots, then back up. My pulse kicks up, definitely without my permission. I shouldn't like the way she's looking at me. But I do, and I want *more*, even as I tell myself it's a bad idea.

Her every word today seemed designed to get a reaction out of me. Might as well give her a taste of the same.

"Under all *what?*"

For the first time, Winnie loses her composure. A tiny slip, but I see the way she shifts on her feet. I hear the way her breath hitches. I love watching her squirm.

"*You* know," she says. When I don't respond, she groans. "Ugh. I have to say it? It's surprising to find humor underneath the grumpy demeanor. The boots. The whole—everything. You're the living embodiment of a fictional bad boy, ready to steal hearts and make ovaries explode."

Did she say something about *ovaries*? I frown. "Make ... *what?*"

Winnie covers her face with one hand and groans. "Please, please forget I said any of that."

Gladly. For the first time, I realize she has a turquoise envelope in her free hand. "What's that?"

Winnie uncovers her eyes, then looks down like she forgot she was even holding what appears to be a greeting card. Immediately, she tucks it behind her back. "Nothing."

I continue to stare.

Giving a frustrated huff, she holds out the envelope, shaking it when I don't move. Finally, she slaps it against my chest. "Take it."

I do, and when my fingers brush hers, my whole body feels electrified, like I've mistakenly grabbed a live wire. It is a wholly unfamiliar feeling, and I can't decide if I like or hate it. Winnie snatches her hand back, rubbing it, as though she felt it too.

I turn the envelope over in my hands. It's sealed and has nothing written on the outside. "Should I open it now?"

"Up to you. You're the boss."

I would rather open it without her gaze on me. I get the feeling Winnie sees too much. But I can't wait. I tear into the envelope, my pulse beating loud in my ears as I do so. Which is ridiculous. She got me a card on my birthday. Big deal. I hate birthdays. If she knew me for five minutes, she'd know that and she never would have gotten me anything.

Or maybe ... that's exactly why she DID get me something.

When I pull out the card, something smaller than a penny falls to the ground. Winnie quickly bends to retrieve it, but doesn't give it back, closing it in her fist. I'll ask about it in a minute, but I look at the card first.

The front has a picture of a cartoon plant, roots burrowing deep underground, a happy face on the thin stalk framed by green leaves. It reads, *Here's to planting the seeds...* I open it, finishing the rest: *of a fruitful partnership.* The cursive is written over an apple, which also has a smiley face.

Okay, so NOT a birthday card. Winnie has written something underneath, and it takes me a moment to read it because her handwriting is worse than a toddler's.

"Here's to a great *waltzing partnership?*" I arch a brow. "Dancing isn't in your job description."

"My handwriting isn't that bad!" she snaps. "It clearly says *working*—a working partnership."

Winnie snatches the card from my hand. But I grab it right back, holding it above my head when her grabby hands reach for it again. I half expect her to jump for it, which would fully transport us to an elementary school playground, but she only hangs her head, muttering something under her breath.

"What was that?" I tuck the card in my back pocket, out of sight and out of reach.

"Nothing." She holds out whatever fell from the card. "Here."

Instead of taking it from her fingers, I hold out my palm, not wanting to risk another stupid reaction to her touch. She drops a tiny, black object in my hand.

"It's a seed," she says, speaking slowly like she thinks I won't understand.

"I've heard of seeds. And what am I supposed to do with it?"

Winnie throws her hands up, and I bite back a smile at how flustered she is. "Plant it! Throw it away! Eat it. I don't care. It was a gesture. Clearly a misguided one. Whatever. Forget the whole thing and tell me what I'm supposed to do —job expectations and all that. What's my first task?"

I close the seed in my palm, torn between wanting to apologize and wanting to tell Winnie this job thing isn't going to work after all. We aren't going to have a waltzing partnership *or* a working one. There's just too much EVERY-THING between us.

Instead, I clear my throat. "Work on the website. That's what you're good at, right?"

It's the only reason I agreed to hire her when Pat begged, and then when Lindy, his wife and Winnie's friend, begged some more. I'm barely getting off the ground and don't need to take on a bunch of employees. But I also can't build a website myself, so it's part of the reason I said yes to her being a very temporary temp.

The other reason I said yes is guilt. Up until Tank purchased the town—because, yes, that is a thing even outside of shows like *Schitt's Creek*—Winnie worked for the crooked mayor who sold the downtown property, took the money, and ran. With him gone, the city council eliminated Winnie's position while they prepare for a special mayoral election, timeframe yet to be determined.

Winnie smirks, regaining her cool composure. "One of many things I'm good at."

I try to keep my brain from chasing down that rabbit trail,

wondering what the other things are. *Don't need to know. Don't care.*

"Great. We don't have Wi-Fi set up yet, so work from home or wherever." I wave a hand, dismissing her.

She frowns. "So, that's it? Work remotely and build a website?"

"Yep."

"No instructions first? No team meeting?"

"We aren't a team."

"I see."

I hope she's starting to. This won't be a warm and fuzzy work environment. We aren't partners, and I'm certainly not winning boss of the year.

Winnie is and needs to stay temporary in every sense of the word.

"Is that all? I could build a site for you in my sleep, assuming I know what you want. But I have no idea what you envision for the site. Branding, colors—"

"Whatever you do will be fine."

"Somehow, I doubt it. I get the sense you want control of every aspect of every detail. So, why not sit down with me and talk through what you want?"

I hate how well Winnie reads me. I can't let her know how right she is. Or how much my whole life has been spinning out of control lately, leaving me in a near-constant state of worry.

"No time."

Which is actually true. I've got a contractor coming tomorrow afternoon so we can start mapping out the renovations to the interior. But the building is still half-filled with junk and I'll be lucky if I can get enough done for a proper walk-through. The electrician will be coming later this week, and then the plumber. I have the proper permits filed, so at least the paperwork part is done. But I'm anxious about all the things left to do, most of which aren't things I care about at all. I'm eager to get to my main thing: brewing. Unfortunately, installing the equipment and the brew kettles can't happen until almost everything else is done. Winnie interrupts my thoughts, which were starting to sound like an angry mob.

"When do I check in? How should I contact you?"

"Text is fine."

"Let me guess—you don't like talking on the phone?" she asks with a smile.

I don't answer. I don't need to, apparently, as my closed-off expression somehow reads to Winnie like an open book. I need to do something about that.

We exchange numbers, and almost immediately, my phone buzzes with a text from her. It's a gif of Michael Scott.

I frown. She grins. I'm going to regret making that reference to *The Office*. I'm also going to regret giving her my number.

"And as for my hours—should I just make a spreadsheet?"

"That's fine." I don't tell her I hate spreadsheets. Harper is always getting after me about them. I know they're a necessary evil for business, but if I never had to look at another one again, it would be too soon.

"Well, if that's it, I guess I'll head out and do my thing." She starts to shift away.

An unfamiliar sense of desperation makes my mouth go dry. As much as I want Winnie gone, I also hate for her to leave. I make a split-second decision, one I regret even as the words leave my mouth. "Tomorrow, be here at eight thirty." I look her up and down. "Dressed prepared to work."

Winnie's hands go to her hips, and when her glasses slide

down her nose, I barely resist the urge to reach over and push them back up. "I'm prepared to work now."

"Not to do hard labor or heavy lifting, you're not. Wouldn't want you to break a heel or a fingernail cleaning out the building."

Winnie laughs, a sound that clutches my heart like a fist. "Oh, James. This is going to be so much fun."

Fun is the very last word I would consider to describe what working with Winnie will be like. *Torture* is a more apt choice.

She pats me twice on the shoulder, then winks, making the heat rise up my neck all the way to my scalp. I am not a man who blushes, but my temperature spikes to an unsafe level under the surface of my skin.

"I'll come prepared, *boss*."

The way she puts emphasis on the word boss puts me on edge. Because I like the way it sounds when she calls me boss, and I can't have that. I *won't* have that. I simply nod in response, a rough jerk of my head.

"See you tomorrow," Winnie calls as she walks away.

Tomorrow. When I start work on this building I don't fully believe in, located inside a town I don't want to live in, with one employee I don't want to work with. The orange cat meows, and I glance over, seeing several more cats who have joined him. All looking rough, all looking at me like they're daring me to take over their home.

I smile, knowing tomorrow I'll get to tell Winnie her other job is to get rid of the cats. Something to look forward to.

Happy birthday to me.

CHAPTER 2

Winnie

"That's it? You're *fine* with us breaking up?" I ask, unable to keep down the sharp pitch of my voice. "*Fine* is the word you want to use?"

Dale's sigh makes me want to throw my phone against the wall of Val's art studio. "What would be a more acceptable word choice, Winnie?"

Val catches the look on my face and winces, then lifts her brows, silently asking if I'm okay. I wave a dismissive hand before I step outside. The November air holds the slightest chill and I shiver, wrapping an arm around my waist. The main house where Val's aunt Mari lives is dark, but I hear the thump-thump-thump as one of the dogs wags its tail from the porch. I appreciate the show of solidarity.

I take a deep breath and do what I do best when nervous or upset. I don my snarky armor and pick up my sarcasm sword. Just like I did earlier today when I made a fool out of myself in front of James.

I had every intention of starting the new job off well. I brought him a card and a symbolic seed, which now makes me cringe. So juvenile! I envisioned the two of us discussing his website over coffee at Mari's diner, sitting on the same side of the booth while looking at colors and layout options on my laptop. I'd be the model employee.

Instead, James looked at me like I was gum on the bottom of his shoe. No—lower. I'm the dirt stuck in the gum on the bottom of his shoe. I lost confidence and got snappy, covering my vulnerability with dry humor and sarcasm.

The way I am right now.

"We've been together for a year, Dale. I'd expect a reaction other than just *fine*."

"You're the one breaking up with *me*. Do you want me to beg? To cry?"

I want you to feel something. I want to feel something.

And that's the exact problem. This plain oatmeal kind of breakup is the very reason *for* the breakup. I felt more this morning arguing with my surly boss than I do right here and now, ending a yearlong relationship.

And that's why I'm doing it. Not *because* of James, the too-handsome, too-muscly, dark-haired grump. Nope. I'm not touching that man with a ten-foot pole even while wearing a hazmat suit.

That said, being around James only highlighted what I've known and avoided for months—Dale and I have zero passion, zero chemistry between us.

Our relationship is … *fine*.

Our breakup is … also *fine*.

Fine, fine, fine.

I'm not upset about things ending between us, but by

14

Dale's ho-hum reaction. Which really isn't fair. I'm fully aware of this. But his complete lack of emotional response stings. His *fine*ness just makes me feel somehow very NOT fine. Not worthy. Not wanted.

I cared more when the heel broke off my favorite pair of red peep-toe pumps than Dale seems to care about this breakup. I actually stood over the trash can, debating about whether I should try some kind of glue or locate a shoe professional. (Is that a thing?) Meanwhile, Dale is simply shrugging and tossing me in a dumpster. I am less than a pair of broken heels to him.

Maybe if Dale did fight for me, if he showed an ounce of care, this relationship would be something worth salvaging. Dale sighs again. He's clearly been infected by some kind of sighing virus. Or else this breakup is THAT tedious.

"The truth is, I was going to break up with you this week," he says. "I met someone."

So much for salvaging. Our relationship is a junkyard car about to go in one of those big car-crushing things, to be flattened and spit out into a metal pancake. Except … I'm the one being crushed.

My breath is trapped somewhere between my trachea and my lungs. Everything feels tight. I try very hard to let the logical part of my brain captain the ship. I was breaking up with *him*. Who cares if he met someone? I don't want to be with him anyway. It's *fine*.

Except it absolutely isn't. Knowing he met someone else takes my mind places I don't want to go. How long ago did he meet her? Did he cheat? I can't let myself think about these things or I'll crumble.

"Are you okay, Winnie?"

"I'm *fine*."

We're both quiet for a long moment, and then he says, "I wish you well."

I wish you'd take a long walk off a short pier, Dale. And by the way, your name sucks.

I hang up, and then I *do* toss my phone. Just into the yard, not into a wall. Because even if I am throwing a tiny temper tantrum, I'm practical. I can't afford a new phone right now. Hopefully the grass is soft enough that the screen didn't crack.

For now, I leave it and walk back into the garage. Val works in her aunt Mari's garage and lives in the tiny apartment space above. Mari moved from Costa Rica to raise Val and her sisters after their mom ran off. Sofia and Camila didn't come back to Sheet Cake after college, but Val, like me and Lindy, couldn't seem to stay away.

Val has a space heater near the door but turned it off a bit ago. She's working on a large painting, so she's on her feet, moving back and forth in front of the canvas like a dancer. Since I left to talk to Dale, Val has stripped down into a tank top and boy-shorts underwear. Blue and green streaks cover her bare arms, a bright contrast to her rich brown skin.

I never want to interrupt when Val hits a zone, plus I'm not ready to discuss Dale, so I sink quietly onto a stool. It's therapeutic, watching her work. I try to let the ugly of my conversation slip away, losing myself in the color and the sound of the brush moving over canvas. The sting begins to ease as Val works.

Art like this is beyond my understanding, which is why I love seeing Val at work. It's nothing short of inspired. I can do graphic design, but I work with concrete images and shapes. Val's ability to drip and splatter and mix colors onto a canvas in a meaningful yet abstract way is beyond me. I

16

also love the way Val loses herself in her work, like she has right now. I don't think she even realizes I came back inside.

I haven't yet found the thing I can lose myself in, and boy, have I tried. Graphic design, web design, mixology, a brief foray into book blogging. I thought maybe I'd finally found my passion with app development. As proud as I am of the Neighborly app, which I built and actively tested in Sheet Cake, I'm already bored. I can't bring myself to finalize the updates that would make it ready to sell. If I didn't get such a kick out of Sheet Cake gossip, I'd already have shut the thing down. Moderating people's comments on the internet is enough to suck the soul out of anyone.

The ache in my chest grows as Val makes clean, sure strokes on the canvas. I need to find my own thing, something that I feel passionate about.

*Or some*one.

This brings me back to Dale. Or, not Dale specifically, but the fact I haven't met a man who makes me feel half of what I see in Val as she paints. My yearlong, just-fine relationship ended in a brief phone conversation, and now, only a few minutes later, I already have so much clarity.

I didn't love Dale. I'm not even sure how much I *liked* him.

So … why was I with him? The answer is immediate, and I don't like it one bit. I was with Dale because he was *safe*. Just like working as a receptionist for the mayor rather than trying to find a vocational passion—also *safe*.

I may long for what Val has—for passion and purpose— but I keep on choosing the low- or no-risk options.

A few minutes later, Val steps back, tilting her head to examine the canvas. It looks finished to me, but she groans and drops the brush in a mason jar. Turning around, she blinks when she spots me, as though she totally forgot I was ever here.

"Oh, hey." Her eyes soften. "How'd the breakup go?"

I shrug. "It was a fitting, anticlimactic end to the most boring relationship in history. One I should have ended months ago."

"I'm sorry? I mean, I'm not, but if you're sad, I am." Val forces her features into what I think is a valiant attempt at sympathy, which misses the mark completely. She looks like she just licked a toad. "*Are* you sad?"

"Nope."

I'm not sad, but I am *something*. What I am is a creeping, heavy kind of feeling I've never been able to identify by name. It hits me every so often, not always for reasons I can name, though today its origin is obvious. I call it feeling oily, and mostly, I do a good job hiding it from everyone else.

"Then, I guess I'm not sorry," Val says, hopping up on the stool nearest me. "Is that okay? I never liked Dale."

She and Lindy have made it pretty clear they weren't Dale's biggest fans. Or fans at all. Ugh. I absolutely should always listen to my friends.

Val's expression turns a little wicked. "Now you're freed up for a little workplace romance."

Forget what I said. I should absolutely NEVER listen to my friends.

"Rebound much?"

Val waves this off. "Nah. You'd have needed to really like Dale for James to be a rebound. If we're going to be totally honest here, I think you were just with Dale because you're scared to let yourself fall in love. So, you dated someone you knew you'd never fall for."

I want to protest, but isn't that essentially what I just admitted to myself? What's wrong with me? Why am I building a safe life? Why am I not seeking a job or a man I'm passionate about?

Val leans over, giving my arm a squeeze. "Are you feeling okay though? I mean, it's still a breakup. You need to process."

"Weirdly, I'm really okay. I care more that Dale *didn't* care."

Val frowns. "He wasn't upset? Because, let's be honest, you're way out of his league, chica."

"Aw, thanks. But nope. When I told him I wanted to end things, he just said *fine*. And then he told me he was planning to break up with me because he met someone."

"He *cheated*?" Steam practically explodes out of Val's ears.

"I … don't know. He didn't specify."

And honestly, I'd rather not know. Cheating is never good. But I have my own reasons for being even more upset by the idea. Ones I don't want to think about, much less discuss with Val.

"Then I won't specify all the ways I'll kill him if he did," she says.

"You can only kill someone once, Valentina."

"Minor detail. Enough about Dale." She swipes her palms together. "Let's brush him off. Come on, chica. Brush, brush, brush."

I roll my eyes. "Do I have to do hand motions?"

"Yes. The connection between mind and body is important. Brush him off, Winnie."

"Are you sure we shouldn't be shaking him off?"

Val glares. "*Brush*."

Though Val usually isn't pushy, when she is, it's best not to push back. So, feeling ridiculous, I dramatically brush my hands together along with Val. I'm giggling by the time I'm done, and she grins broadly.

"See? Much better. Next time, you will choose more wisely. You need someone you can really care about. Someone who makes you *feel*."

I hate the way an image of James, glaring at me, pops right into mind. *Wrong kind of feeling, brain.*

"You need passion. You want *love*."

I make the sound of a buzzer. "I want … nothing. Solitude. Celibacy. Peace."

"Bor-ing. Also, that doesn't sound like you, chica. You're a *fire*, but you've been hiding it. Or hiding from it. You need someone who burns as brightly as you." Val jumps to her feet, dark eyes bright.

"Fire sounds dangerous."

"Fire sounds like *life*," Val says, spinning in a circle, hair lifting and fluttering around her. "Don't you want to *live*?"

Yeah, okay. Maybe a little cozy fire would be nice. If it stays in the fireplace, where it belongs. A contained and controlled fire, able to be managed with one of those iron pokers and hidden behind a metal screen when it gets to be too much.

That's not the fire you want, and you know it.

If my mind zips straight to James again, it's only because the man inspires a different kind of fire in me. Irritation, for one. And a newly kindled fire of curiosity, which has me wanting to figure out the man behind the grouch. It's not the kind of passion Val is talking about. It's definitely not, and will never be, love.

"Can I drop you off at the birthday party?" Val asks.

Speaking of my surly boss … Today is his birthday. Which I definitely didn't know when I gave him a decidedly NOT-birthday card. I wondered about the strange look on his face, but thought it was just because giving your boss a card on your first day is, well, *strange*. Thinking back to this morning and how I behaved makes me want to crawl into a storm drain. Of all the dumb ideas, gifting my boss a first-day-of-work card (and let's not forget the seed) on his actual birthday ranks pretty high.

I only found out it was James's birthday when my brother texted me about the party. Chevy got the invite directly from Tank, who asked him to pass it on to me. I know James had nothing to do with it. He'd probably skip out on his own party if he knew I'd be there.

Which, honestly, is part of the appeal of going. Even after I made myself look like a fool this morning, giving the man a *seed*.

"It's already started."

"Better late than never."

I have a feeling if it were up to James, my presence would be better never than late. Or at all.

I give Val a pouty face. "You're not going?"

She shakes her head, then glances at her painting. "Nah. I'm itching to work."

"You don't mind driving me?"

"It's fine," she says. "Let me get these brushes clean and we can go."

My car is back at Chevy's house, where I'm crashing until I get my financials under control. Val picked me up for dinner, then had the sudden urge to paint while I had the sudden urge to break up with my boyfriend. We came here, then planned to hit the party together. Lindy, our other best friend and the third part of our Bermuda Triangle, is our link to the Grahams. It still feels a little strange without her bridging the gap. She and Pat, James's youngest brother, left for their honeymoon last night. Which means I'll be on my own.

I should just have Val drop me back at Chevy's. But the

curiosity about how James Graham celebrates his birthday is too great. I need to see if my suspicion is correct and James will grumble through the whole party, then turn in early like an old man trapped in a very young, very hot body.

While Val cleans her brushes, I hunt for my phone in the grass. I stuff it in my purse and grab James's gift, the one whose purchase I'm still questioning. I clear my throat loudly as Val emerges, whistling and twirling her car keys around her finger.

"What?" she asks, seeing my raised eyebrows.

I nod down at her lower half. "Pants."

Val looks down at her boy shorts above bare, paint-marked legs and laughs. "If I'm not getting out of the car, do I really *need* pants?"

"What if Chevy pulls you over for speeding?"

Since we were teenagers, Val has had a massive crush on my brother, who is definitely not good enough for her. I mean, I love Chevy, but he dates truly terrible women and has never even seemed to notice Val's interest. Still, the idea of him pulling her over and seeing her pantless has Val scurrying back inside, emerging moments later wearing coveralls, the top half unzipped down to her waist. Val is the only one I know who can still manage to look hot while sporting mechanic chic.

"So, what did you get James?" Val asks, nodding toward the bag in my lap.

I realize I'm holding it the way you might hold a Faberge egg, even though it's actually a coffee mug. The reality is that I shouldn't have gotten James anything at all. I wouldn't be shocked if he refused to take it and shoved it back at me with a single gruff *NO*.

"Just a coffee mug."

Val says nothing, but she gives me a smirk I do not like. "But you did find time today to get him a gift."

Not only did I *find* time, I drove all the way to Austin— something I'm definitely not admitting to Val. It may be just a coffee mug, but a very specific one I couldn't find anywhere in Sheet Cake.

"Not a big deal."

"And how was your first day with Mr. Hot Boss?"

"Mr. Grumpy Boss is more accurate, and might I remind you that I literally *just* broke up with my boyfriend? I'm not looking for another one."

"You had like five percent feelings for Dale."

"More like three or four percent."

In middle school, Val developed her own system for crushes in percents, arbitrarily assigning them as she saw fit. One hundred percent feelings would be love. Only Lindy has gotten there so far. Val and I have stayed pretty low on the percent scale, unless we're counting the feelings she never wants to talk about regarding Chevy.

"I told you when I met James he looks like trouble, and I stand by that assessment." Val looks ready to argue, but I jump into a subject that will shut her up. "I heard Tank found someone to open a gallery downtown. Are you going to submit some pieces?"

After purchasing Sheet Cake, the Grahams have made quick work of trying to revitalize the mostly dead downtown. The plan is to have most of the businesses open for the Sheet Cake Festival in a few months. Dark Horse Brewery being one of those, as well as a few boutiques, a coffee shop, and the latest, an art gallery. Tank has a Christmas lighting planned for early December as a kind of soft opening, but I'm not sure what will be up and running by then.

"We'll see."

Val presses her lips closed, and I thankfully escape any more questions about James. She pulls up out front of Mari's diner, and I don't miss the way she eyes Chevy's patrol car longingly.

"You sure you don't want to come in just for a few minutes?" I ask. "Say hi to your aunt, get some cake?"

Val shakes her head. "I'm a mess."

"A beautiful mess."

"Whatever. Anyway, I figured out the rest of the painting on the drive over. I'm going back to finish. Do you have a ride home?"

"Chevy will take me. Night, Val."

She waves once more before pulling away. I stand outside the diner for a minute, gathering my breath, gathering my wits, gathering my courage. I'm not sure why I feel so devoid of the third, but it has something to do with the gift bag in my hands. I already made a fool of myself once today. Am I really about to do it again?

"In for a penny, in for a pound," I say out loud before I take a deep breath and walk inside the diner.

CHAPTER 3

James

I keep my eyes fixed on the lit candles on the cake in front of me as I'm serenaded by the happy birthday song. It seems to take way longer than it should. How many verses are there? Did they add another two lines of happy birthdays?

Tank may have promised to keep tonight small and low-key, but the birthday not-quite surprise party at Mari's diner is still too much for me. Guests include my family (minus Pat and Lindy, who are somewhere in Europe) plus a dozen or so Sheeters, as they call themselves. It's about a dozen people too many.

Yes, I hate birthdays *and* parties. And sometimes people.

No, I don't want to talk about it.

My five-year-old niece, Jo, is perched on my lap at the diner counter. I give her a quick squeeze. "Want to blow out my candles, little one?"

"I'm not sure I can," Jo says with a tiny grin. "There are a *lot*."

I find the ticklish spot on her side. "Are you saying I'm old?"

Jo giggles. "Not THAT old."

I hear several snorts and look around to find Collin covering his mouth. Harper is biting her lip, and my dad's booming laughter fills the diner. Chase has ducked behind my sister, probably to hide his smile. At least he still views me with a healthy dose of fear.

Chevy, who clearly doesn't fear for his life nearly enough, laughs almost as loudly as my dad. The deputy seems intent on inserting himself into our family. Despite arresting all of us the night we met, he has somehow become Pat's new best friend. I'm sure Tank invited him to this party I didn't want to have in the first place, but as far as I'm concerned, Chevy can go.

Did I mention he's also Winnie's brother?

"The place is going to go up in flames if you don't hurry," Collin calls, and I glare before turning back to Jo.

"Fine. I'm old," I concede. "On three, we'll do it together."

I count down, then together Jo and I blow out the thirty candles. Another decade gone. *Thirty.* I'm supposed to feel something, right? I used to consider every birthday in light of how many years I've lived without Mom. But once I turned twenty-seven and officially existed longer without her in my life, it got too depressing to think about. One more reason to hate celebrating today.

"What was your wish?" Jo asks.

My mind blanks. "If I tell you, it won't come true."

She rolls her eyes and flashes her secret weapon: her single dimple. "Come on, Uncle James! I won't tell."

I would tell Jo. I would. But her question hits me like a gut punch, making me realize I don't have a wish to make. Not even now that I have a moment to think about it.

The last wish I had was to go pro. And when I injured my knee in one of my last college games, instantly ending my football career, I stopped wishing for anything at all.

"He probably wished for everything to fall into place with Dark Horse," Collin says.

It's an easy out. Because I do want things to fall into place. But it's not my wish, not my dream.

I nod to Jo and put a finger to my lips. "What he said. But don't tell."

"I promise," she says.

Mari slides the cake down the counter for Mo to cut and serve. Someone cranks the music back up, and Tank lifts Jo from my lap, putting her on his shoulders. The man was built to be a grandpa. I'm not sure I've seen him this happy in years, and it fills me with a deep ache I can't quite explain.

The tightness in my shoulders eases as people's attention shifts away from me. Big Mo sets down a piece of cake in front of me with a smile and I'm happy for the distraction.

"Thanks," I tell him, picking up the fork. It looks like chocolate heaven and will without a doubt be the best part of my evening until I'm alone again.

Mo walks away without saying *happy birthday*, like he can tell I'm already over it. Chevy plops down on the stool beside me. He's in uniform, so I assume he's on duty later tonight. Maybe even now—it's not like there's much trouble in Sheet Cake. Without being asked, Mari pours him a mug of coffee.

"Shouldn't you be out writing speeding tickets?" I ask.

"All in due time. How'd my sister do on her first day of work?" Chevy asks, adding enough sugar in his coffee to put someone in a coma.

I didn't see Winnie again after this morning, though the effect of our heated exchange clung to me all day like camp-fire smoke. I don't have the faintest clue how to answer this question.

Chevy takes a sip of coffee, barely hiding a smile. "That bad, huh?"

"It was fine."

Chevy chuckles, eyes shining as Mo puts a slice of cake in front of him. "Says the man with the murderous look in his eyes."

"Are you gonna arrest me again?"

"Not for a look." Chevy's jovial expression turns deadly so quickly I almost choke on my bite of cake. "But if you hurt so much as one hair on her head or even her smallest feeling, it will be a different story."

"We'll get along."

"Good." Chevy's cheerful expression returns as he takes a bite of cake. "Just don't be surprised if she antagonizes you. She's that way with me too. Always pushing buttons like it's her life's mission."

I don't like thinking of Winnie treating me the same way she treats her brother. Not even a little bit. And I definitely don't want to examine exactly why the idea bothers me so much.

"Winnie will do a great job as far as the work goes. She just might drive you to drink along the way. Guess it's a good thing you own a brewery." He chuckles. "Speaking of—need my help tomorrow? I can swing by in the afternoon. Winnie said you were clearing out the warehouse."

Oh, did she, now?

My fists clench reflexively. I don't know what came over me when I asked Winnie to help tomorrow. I've regretted it all day. And now she's inviting other people?

"She asked you to come?" I do my best to hide the irritation in my tone but clearly don't succeed.

Chevy laughs again. "She'll do that too—insert herself in your life. Especially in places you don't want her to be. Like a splinter you can't ever dig out." He winks. "So, tomorrow? You need a few extra hands? I really don't mind."

I almost tell Chevy no—that's how much I hate accepting help, even when freely offered. But the warehouse still has a bunch of junk I'd really like cleared out. More hands means quicker work, even though the idea of other people traipsing through the property makes me twitchy. I could have asked my family, but Pat's gone, Tank is helping with Jo, and Harper, Chase, and Collin all have jobs in Austin. Even if I were better about asking for help, it's abundantly clear that Dark Horse's success rests on one set of shoulders—mine.

"That'd be great." Chevy raises an eyebrow at my tone, which admittedly doesn't sound enthusiastic. "Thanks," I add.

Big Mo slides a second piece of cake in front of me. I hadn't realized I finished the first. Usually I don't have much of a sweet tooth, but I'm not mad at this cake. Not at all.

"Is this a new recipe, Mo?" Chevy licks icing from the tines of his fork with a groan. "It's delicious. And a little spicy."

"I'm working on variations for the festival. This is chocolate cayenne with a milk stout chocolate ganache," Big Mo says, his smile bright in contrast to his long, dark beard. "In honor of our brewmaster here."

I lift my eyebrows. "That's—wow." That's more trouble than anyone should go to for me. Especially a man I hardly know. Mo and I have only had brief conversations, usually when I'm picking up food from the diner. "Thanks. It's the best cake I've eaten."

"I hope so. I used your milk stout." Mo's grin widens, and I rear back in surprise at his thoughtfulness.

My beer is only sold on tap at a few bars in Austin, which means it's not easy to come by. I'd be willing to bet Tank brought him some from my private collection. I started brewing a few years ago out of a shed at the back of Tank's property. Pat jokingly calls it my she shed, and unfortunately, that name stuck—with my family anyway. To me, it's my me shed.

The fifteen-gallon brewing system I purchased does everything within one tank from the mash to the fermentation, saving space and making the process pretty simple. Because I don't have a system for bottling, almost everything goes straight into kegs. Bottles are done by hand and reserved for my family. And now, Big Mo.

Honestly, with icing this good, I'd happily supply him with more.

I take another bite, trying to pick up on the flavor—*my* flavor—I should have recognized. There it is. Subtle, but present.

"What's milk stout?" Jo asks, climbing up on the stool next to me. Chevy reaches around my back to give her a fist bump.

"Nothing you'll like yet," Big Mo says. "But I've got a special one just for you." He hands her a cupcake with white icing and sprinkles.

"Funfetti!" she says and quickly goes silent as she takes a big bite, icing going everywhere. Jo is so well-spoken and so brilliant that she usually seems far older than her age. And then there are times like this, where she is absolutely a typical five-year-old, stuffing a cupcake in her face.

Collin appears behind me, grabbing me by the shoulders. "Tell us when you want to open presents, birthday boy."

"I don't need presents."

Collin rolls his eyes. "Birthday presents are not about *need*. Come on—can't you put the grouch back in his trash can for just one night?"

I turn to snap at him, but as the bells over the door chime and Winnie strides into the diner, I forget my response. I forget Collin exists altogether.

What's *she* doing here? And does she have … a gift?

Her eyes meet mine, just before Tank reaches her and wraps her in a hug.

Now my dad is on hugging terms with Winnie? Her brother was right—she really is a splinter.

Chevy stands and stretches, then gives me a hearty slap on the back. "Happy birthday, man. I better get back out there. See you tomorrow at the warehouse."

"What's happening tomorrow?" Collin asks.

Great. I hadn't mentioned the workday to my family. Mostly, they "help" by way of unsolicited advice. It's the hands-off, noses-in approach. Harper bugs me about proper bookkeeping. Collin likes to give me business startup advice, as though opening a gym is anything like a brewery. Pat—well, I never know what will come out of his mouth, only that it's usually not helpful. And Tank asks the kinds of probing parental questions that never fail to make me feel like a teenager caught sneaking out halfway through the window.

In short, other than the financial investment—which was hard enough to get me to agree to—my family isn't involved.

"It's nothing," I say, just as Winnie settles next to me on the stool her brother just vacated.

"Tomorrow is a workday at the warehouse," Winnie says to Collin, ignoring my glare. "Aren't you going to be there?"

I wait for him to beg off and almost choke on my cake when Collin says, "What kind of workday?"

"Like you'd come work," I scoff.

"It's heavy lifting and cleaning," Winnie says, then catches my dark look. "Allegedly."

Collin huffs, then lifts his shirtsleeve and flexes. "I can do heavy lifting."

I shove him, catching Winnie trying to hold back a laugh. At least she doesn't look all doe-eyed and impressed by Collin showing off.

"Is Tank coming?" Collin asks. "What about Harper and Chase?"

"He's busy watching Jo this week. And I assume Chase and Harper are doing their jobs, so I didn't ask."

"Well, I can be here. I'll check with everyone else."

Before I can stop him from getting everyone involved, Mari appears and passes a slice of cake to Winnie. Only, Winnie doesn't start eating. Instead, she steps farther over the very solid line she just crossed.

"Mari, could you take over Jo duty tomorrow so Tank could come help James?" she asks.

"Of course," Mari says, brushing a hand through her white hair with a smile. "We're all helping watch Jojo. It takes a town."

"I think you mean a village," Winnie says with a smile.

Mari only laughs. "Town, village, city. Whatever. I can certainly help tomorrow."

"I don't need help," I say, but Mari is already walking Jo back to the kitchen, presumably to help wipe the icing off her face. The rest of my family is deep in conversation a few feet away, probably talking about me not telling them about tomorrow. Harper shoots me a disapproving look. Yep. They're definitely discussing me.

32

And this is why I don't like involving all of them in this or any of my business. Because they get *involved*.

"Why don't you want your family to help you?" Winnie asks. "If you don't mind me asking."

Speaking of getting involved …

"I do mind." Because it's none of her business. Just like inviting other people wasn't her business.

Winnie takes a big bite of cake. I can't help but wonder if she did so in order to keep from saying something she'd regret. But then she groans and her eyes roll back in her head. Maybe she just really likes cake.

Whatever the case, I shouldn't be watching her as she licks her lips, groaning again and wiggling on her stool. My thoughts are no longer on her crossing lines or on my family. I am completely focused on the last woman I should be focused on.

"Do I taste beer in this frosting?" Winnie asks, wiping her mouth with a napkin. The red lipstick she wore this morning has been replaced by a soft pink shade. The smallest speck of chocolate remains in the corner of her lips, and I have the ridiculous urge to wipe it away with my thumb.

Now, THAT thought needs to die. I scoot a little farther away from Winnie, training my eyes on the counter, where there's a coffee stain resembling a three-legged elephant.

Mo, collecting empty plates, tilts his head toward me. "It's from Dark Horse. Ask James."

Winnie spins on her stool to face me, leaning one elbow on the counter. Her knees brush my thighs and I slowly inch my legs out of reach.

"I haven't tried any of your beer, you know."

"It's not sold here."

"I have an in with a guy who could probably procure me some," Winnie says, tapping her lips in mock thoughtfulness.

"Though he doesn't seem like the kind of man who likes sharing."

"I share just fine. With people I like."

This makes her throw back her head and laugh. Why does that sound make something inside me shift? I should probably leave. But I don't move a muscle.

Winnie nudges me with her elbow. "All two of them? Or is it one?"

"I like lots of people."

"Sure you do, boss. Anyway, back to your beer. I should probably have some familiarity with my new company's product."

I grunt, which is more polite than the words on the top of my tongue. Words which would remind Winnie it's not *her* company. She's a glorified temp, and I don't care if she knows anything about my beer. I realize also that sharing with her, letting her taste the recipes I spent hours and a lot of failures developing would feel much too personal. If anything, Winnie and I need to be less personal.

"Maybe you could set up a private tasting? You, me, and your beer?"

I really need to NOT have that idea in my head. "No."

Before she can argue or throw some sharp retort my way, a big hand lands on my shoulder and squeezes.

"What time do you want us tomorrow, son?" Tank asks. I'm grateful for the interruption, even though I can tell by Dad's tone he's not happy I didn't tell him or anyone else about the workday.

"Eight thirty," Winnie answers before I can. She shrugs when I give her a look. "Right? That's the time you told me."

"Eight thirty is fine."

"I can stop by between the breakfast and lunch crowds," Big Mo says.

At this point, we might as well put a post up on the Neighborly app, Sheet Cake's go-to gossip source. Then again, most of the town hates the fact we're here at all. The city council hasn't made any of this easy. If someone posts about it publicly, we'd probably have a picket line forming.

"I promised you we'd keep this party short, so we're headed out. I'll see you tomorrow, son. And next time?" Tank gives my shoulder a last, borderline-painful squeeze. "I better hear about something like this directly from *you*."

I want to shake my head, to shake off my discomfort at the idea of everyone and their brother showing up tomorrow. It *will* be easier with more people. My irritation gives way to a little bit of relief.

See? It's not so hard to accept help, I tell myself.

But the words don't stick. They haven't for a long time. I can trace this tendency back to a very specific period in my life. One I'd prefer not to think about, where the idea took root that if I'm not fully in control, everything will fall apart. Trying to trust other people, even my own family sometimes, reminds me of physical therapy after my knee surgery. My own body felt *wrong*.

Winnie, the catalyst for all of this, bumps her shoulder into mine. "Living in a small town is like living in a nosy family."

"I've already got a nosy family," I grumble. "Next time, check with me before asking people to get involved."

Winnie actually looks chastised. "I'm sorry."

An apology is the last thing I expected. More like a smart retort or a teasing comment. An uncomfortable sensation tugs roughly at something inside my chest.

"It's fine."

Jo appears, the perfect distraction, climbing up in my lap to give me a hug. She's tiny in my arms and smells like cupcakes. Probably because she's still got a little icing in her hair.

"Happy birthday, Uncle James," she says through a yawn, and I catch Winnie watching us with an expression I can't quite read. I look away, feeling more exposed than I have all night, which is saying something.

"Thank you, little one," I say, just as Tank scoops Jo from my arms.

"Goodnight, birthday boy," Tank says. "Don't party too hard." He grins even before I roll my eyes.

"Even if there were somewhere in this small town to party, you'd be at home alone anyway, wouldn't you?" Harper teases, giving me a pat on the shoulder.

She's not wrong.

"Goodnight, old man," Collin says, slapping me on the back. "Better take some aspirin tonight so you don't wake up with a sore back."

"Has this turned into a roast instead of a birthday party?" I ask.

"We'd need a lot more time for that, brother." Collin darts out of reach as I take a playful swing. With Pat gone, Collin seems to be stepping into a more light-hearted role. Or maybe it's just that his very uptight new girlfriend, the one none of us can stand, isn't here so he's letting loose while he can.

When I turn back to the counter after saying my good-byes, Winnie deposits a small gift bag in front of me. "Happy birthday, boss."

I stare. The bag is pink with a photo of a pug wearing a pointy birthday hat. A rainbow of tissue paper peeks out from the top. It's offensive on every level, which I think is the point.

I want to knock the obnoxious gift bag right off the counter so I don't have to look at it. But I also want to rip right into it to see what kind of gift Winnie chose.

The bag is too small for things like cologne or a shirt, the kinds of gifts I get every Christmas from my family. Exactly what I ask for, no surprises. This morning, Winnie gave me a seed, which is still in my pocket because what am I supposed to do with it? I don't want to plant it, and I feel bad throwing it away.

A gift card? Too boring.

Cash? Ditto.

The pug stares back with its bugged-out eyes, mocking me. I want to look away, but I can't meet Winnie's gaze right now. "You didn't need to do this."

"I know. But I did, and there are no take-backs."

I'm still fishing for a response when Winnie stands and heads for the door, moving faster than seems possible wearing high heels. Probably better I say nothing.

She's gone, leaving only the gift bag and a napkin with her pink lipstick as proof she was ever here. The rest of the party disbands, thankfully, and I'm left carrying a few cards, a box wrapped in newspaper from Harper, and Winnie's gift bag, which I hold with two fingers like it's a snake.

I wait until I'm at Pat's loft, showered and ready for bed, before opening her gift. My heart thumps a crooked rhythm as I pull out layers of pink and purple and lime green tissue paper I just *know* Winnie picked to mess with me. I can almost imagine her standing in whatever aisle of whatever store sells tissue paper, a finger tapping her lips as she wonders what color combination I'd hate most.

I finally extricate a coffee mug reading World's Best Boss, just like the one Michael Scott has on his desk in *The Office*. Is it just because I am her boss? Or did she buy this today, after hearing my one reference to the show?

I stare at the mug for a solid minute before stuffing it back in the bag and hiding the whole thing under the sink in the guest bathroom where I can pretend it doesn't exist.

CHAPTER 4

Winnie

COUCH SURFING IS for the birds. Bad birds, like seagulls or pigeons. It's a way of life for college kids living on the ramen diet. Not the fifteen-dollars-a-bowl ramen I love when I can afford it. (And when I'm not in Sheet Cake, as clearly, we do not have that kind of food here.) I'm talking the multiple packages for a dollar kind of ramen.

Though I'm not technically on a couch, my current life-style of crashing with my brother is not for me: a twenty-seven-year-old independent woman. Except I'm flat-broke, and my budget is definitely more on the packaged ramen side of things.

On the plus side: I kind of want to marry the mattress on Chevy's guest room bed. It is the absolute best.

Still, it's not *my* bed. And I'm living out of bags, my poor clothes smushed into hanging bags and duffels. My portable steamer is my new BFF.

"Knock knock." Chevy's words come with actual knocking.

That's the other downside to my living situation. The nosy older brother.

I groan and grab the closest thing to me, which is a romance novel. "Go away! I'm sleeping." I punctuate this by tossing the book at the door. I hear the gasp of book lovers everywhere, but I picked this one up at the thrift store for ninety-seven cents and it's already missing the back cover.

Chevy cracks the door open slowly. Upon seeing me still in bed, he opens the door all the way and leans on the frame. "No you're not. I could hear you thinking from out there. Or —overthinking?"

I fluff the pillows and settle deeper into the bed. "Nah. Life is grand. The living is easy. What's there to overthink?"

I shouldn't have asked. Chevy's lips twitch and he rubs a hand over his jaw. Big mistake—I just opened up a figurative door by asking a question, however sarcastic, about my life. And my brother, who isn't afraid to be overbearing, is waltzing inside. On his way in the literal door, he bends to pick up the book I threw, his eyebrows shooting up as he examines the cover.

There's no man-chest on this one or a passionate embrace with invisible winds tossing hair around, but the sexy man in a suit says it all. Capital-R Romance.

"This is what you're reading?"

I refuse to be embarrassed about reading romance novels. "Yup. Maybe you should try it instead of judging."

"Calm down. I'm not judging. Just … surprised."

I get it. I'm not the typical romantic. Flowers—meh. Chocolate—I mean, I won't turn it down just because

CHOCOLATE, but it doesn't scream love to me. But real boyfriends suck. See: Dale. Whereas fictional ones never let me down. They come complete with a grand gesture and an HEA every dang time.

Chevy shakes his head, setting the book carefully back on my bedside table like he's afraid touching it for too long might rub off on the self-proclaimed forever-bachelor.

"Heard you broke up with Dead-Eye Dale." Chevy came up with the nickname the very first time he met Dale, and though I admonished him, it's honestly pretty apt. I find that I don't mind it at all this morning.

"How? How did you hear?"

Chevy grins. "Has someone been neglecting the app she built?"

"It's on Neighborly?!" I let out a frustrated growl and toss the book at Chevy again, hitting him in the belly.

"You're gonna get booted out of book club for mistreating novels. Maybe I'll save this conversation for post-coffee."

"Good idea."

"I made extra by the way. As in … an extra *pot*."

"I don't drink *that* much."

"Right. So, about your breakup…"

"This might be more of a post-beer conversation," I say through a yawn.

Chevy's eyes light up. "You wanna have a beer with me, Win? It's been a while."

It has. Too long, actually. I haven't carved out much time lately for Chevy. With both our parents gone, all we have is each other. We used to do a lot more together, and only in this moment, seeing the excitement in his eyes, do I realize our dinners and beers and movie nights have faded away. I make a mental note to be more intentional about planning time together.

"Are you off-duty tonight?"

"That I am. Backwoods Bar at eight? I'm meeting someone for dinner beforehand."

"Another vapid woman with false eyelashes longer than her attention span?"

Chevy clucks his tongue. "Now, Winnie, what happened to women supporting women?"

He's right—I shouldn't be so harsh. I honestly have nothing against false lashes or extensions. I might wear them myself if they didn't brush against my glasses. It's just ... Chevy dates the kind of women who have no personality, or else an ugly or irritating one. If I'm guilty of going for boring with Dead-Eye Dale, my brother goes out of his way to choose the kind of woman impossible to have a long-term relationship with short of having a lobotomy.

I climb out of bed, and Chevy scampers to the door with a girly squeal, as though my sleep shorts and tank are much more inappropriate than they are. Brothers.

"See you tonight, Chev!"

"Oh, you'll see me before that," he calls through the now-closed door. "I'll be by later to watch you and your new boss go head-to-head this afternoon."

Fantastic. I don't even want to know what my brother will say about the crackle and simmer igniting between James and me every time we enter the same room. I could pretend to be innocent and say it's sheer dislike, a personality clash. Which is at least a little bit true.

But on a level I'd rather not think about, I know at least on my end, the heat between us is not simply dislike.

———

Forget what I said. I deeply, truly dislike James Graham.

The only thing crackling between us right now is an eighty-proof irritation. The kind that will light you up and leave you with a splitting headache and light sensitivity the next day. A hate hangover, if you will.

"Should we keep this for—" I start to ask, holding up an old window.

But James barely gives it—or me—a passing glance before interrupting. "Trash."

He didn't even know what I was going to ask. I know for a fact one of the new shops going in on Main Street sells this kind of thing—designer decor right alongside old doors, windows, and antique oddities. We could spread goodwill by giving her some things we salvage or possibly even sell them.

"But—"

"Trash," James barks. "And wear these so you don't get lead poisoning or tetanus in your *delicate* hands."

He strips off his worn leather work gloves and tosses them my way. They bounce off the center of my chest. Good thing I'm wearing a practically ironclad sports bra, which in this instance doubles as a nipple shield. I bend to pick the gloves up from where they landed on the floor.

When I straighten, James has his back to me, already moving on like this conversation never happened. He strides away through the dim building, carrying a metal barrel right over his head with his now-bare hands. I don't want to look at the way his arm muscles flex from the effort, but they're kind of hard to ignore. Too bad that body is attached to the grouchy attitude.

Just think of him like Donkey Kong—that big, angry gorilla who threw barrels in the old video game.

The mental image makes me snort. A tabby cat darts by, like it had been hiding in the corner, waiting for James to leave the room. The building is FULL of cats, and I've taken a sick pleasure in watching James grow more and more irritated with every passing pussycat. He seems personally offended by their presence, which I find delightful.

I pick up his work gloves, tucking them in my waistband rather than putting them on. James is right about safety, of course, and it was thoughtful of him to give me his gloves. And yet ... the way he spoke to me makes me want to lead a mini-rebellion. I think honestly he's just mad I invited his family to help today. Along with Chevy. And maybe half a dozen other Sheeters. I thought it would be good to have more bodies and more hands, but I underestimated how much James dislikes other people meddling. Or maybe just ... dislikes other people in general.

I drag the window frame out a side door, blinking in the blinding light. I'm never going to admit it because James would give me a hard time, but I'm exhausted. Leaning against the building, I tilt my head back and stretch my pale, already sore limbs in the sun. Ah, Texas, and its unseasonably warm November temperatures.

I catch sight of Chevy pulling up to the curb. I'm along the side of a building, mostly hidden by some stacked crates, allowing me to watch James greet my brother. Chevy gets a head nod and an almost smile. I saw a flash of teeth, so it counts.

It's weird how jealous this makes me, right?

This morning, I arrived ten minutes early, bright-eyed and with a cup of coffee, thinking I'd get a redo on my terrible start yesterday. James took a sip of the coffee, muttered a clipped thanks without even looking at me, and told me to start hauling trash to the curb. Not at all what I hoped for, though I shouldn't have expected more.

Be honest—you also hated how James didn't seem to notice you.

That his eyes didn't scan over your tattoos. You wanted appreciation, maybe even interest. Approval. And you got nothing.

I hate my stupid, very correct inner voice. A part of me DID want to get a reaction out of James. Good, bad—*something*. I thought maybe he was the kind of guy who'd be into tattoos. He didn't even give me a second glance. Guess I should know better than to judge a man based on his motorcycle boots.

Sighing, I watch as Chevy and James walk away, an easy familiarity between them. My brother has that effect on people. He's like a warm chocolate chip cookie. Who can resist? Meanwhile I'm … not that. Never have been. And I'm not sure why, after years of making peace with myself, I'm feeling itchy in my own skin today.

A skinny orange cat with only one eye emerges from behind the stack of pallets and stretches. It sits a safe distance away, piercing me with its singular gaze. I remember seeing him yesterday morning too. He's so ugly he's almost cute.

"I know, I know. I should be working. Not spying on my boss."

The cat doesn't move, doesn't blink, doesn't make a sound. And yet I feel supremely judged.

I should get back inside so James can't accuse me of being lazy or not doing my job. But first, I need to save this window. It is not trash. I could see the panes painted with chalkboard paint, the window hanging in a kitchen. Or maybe next to the bar out in the warehouse with what's on tap for the day.

Ignoring the cat, who's still watching me, I pull James's work gloves from my waistband and slide them on. They're too big, of course, and no longer warm. But I still feel a little, girlish flutter knowing his big hands occupied this same space a few minutes ago.

Donkey Kong hands, I remind myself with a smile. But it does nothing to diminish the intimacy of wearing his gloves, feeling the worn inside brush against my skin.

"Winchester!" a deep voice bellows from inside. The cat is gone in an orange flash.

I hide the window behind a stack of crates for now and head inside. "Coming, *boss.* Don't get your panties in a twist," I mutter, stepping inside, where it takes my eyes a moment to adjust.

"I don't wear panties."

Well, crap.

James stands in the shadows, arms crossed in a way that shows off his impressive chest and arms.

"Did you invite anyone else today?" he demands.

"Be more specific." I don't want to tell him that a few women I know from the Ladies Literary and Libation Society are dropping by in a bit with lunch. And to pick up any morsels of gossip they can.

"Wolf Waters just showed up," James says. "I don't know if I want him here. His brother has been nothing but trouble."

"Billy is a piece of work. But Wolf is cool. Just a little … eccentric."

The Waters family is the oldest, richest, and meanest clan in Sheet Cake. They still like to think they run the town, and with about a bazillion dollars to buy people off and Billy sitting on city council, they do have sway. They had even more before the mayor, whose campaign was pretty much paid for by the Waters, up and abdicated his tiny throne. I know none of them are happy about the Grahams' plans to renovate Sheet Cake, and they've already

46

been doing what they can to block permits and stir up opposition.

James only grunts at this. "And those guys who watch all the high school football practices are here."

I try to hide my laughter. "You mean the Bobs."

"Yes, them. They can't so much as lift a board, so they're just standing around, telling people what to do."

"They're supporting."

"I'd call it heckling."

I shrug. "Potato, po-tah-to."

"So, this is all your doing?"

"If you mean, was I a good employee who found free labor for a big work project, then yes. I may have asked a few select people to come help."

"I didn't ask for help."

"Maybe that's your problem. Or, one of them, anyway."

I tilt my chin up, meeting James's gaze, which is boring into me with the precision cut of a diamond-bit drill. I am undeterred. When I put my fists on my hips, James's gaze drops to my hands. He must notice his gloves, because his expression shifts. Slight, but some flicker of life. Then it dies.

He turns on his heel and strides back across the warehouse floor, calling over his shoulder. "Like I said last night, check with me before taking it upon yourself to make decisions."

"Sir, yes, sir. No think but groupthink. Got it, boss."

I hear snickering and see Chase and Collin standing by—more like hiding behind—a few stacks of wooden pallets, clearly trying to muffle their laughter.

"You two are more entertaining than television," Collin says, wiping his eyes. "I don't remember the last time I've heard anyone talk to Jamie that way."

"Jamie?" I ask.

Chase glances around furtively. "The only one who can call him Jamie and not get punched is Harper. I wouldn't advise it."

Collin waves dismissively, then gives me a once-over. His grin is quick. "Somehow, I don't think he'll be punching Winnie."

"More working! Less chatter!" James booms from somewhere nearby.

The three of us break into laughter, but we also scurry to do what James asks, dragging pallets and junk out to the big dumpster he rented.

———

Around noon, Eula Martin and Lynn Louise show up with homemade sandwiches, sweet tea, and pie procured from Big Mo. I'm not particularly hungry, but I stop long enough to say hello and offer thanks, since I'm not sure James will.

But I'm shocked when I walk over just as he's saying thank you and offering both older women a hug. Eula Martin holds onto James a little longer than is appropriate, and I have to bite my lip to keep from laughing as she says, "My, my, my. I'm not sure why you're covering up all this with a shirt, but don't do so on our account, young man."

James mutters some kind of response, then takes one of the homemade lunches. His eyes meet mine, and I try to wipe the amusement off my face. Not soon enough, clearly, as he glares.

I can't win with him. Which means I should probably stop trying.

FROM THE NEIGHBORLY APP

Subject: ISO cat

Danielle_L

Anyone know of a good place to get one of those hairless cats? I love cats but my husband is allergic.

BagelBytes

Don't use a breeder! There are so many cats in shelters needing a good home. Buying purebred only supports the existence of kitten mills.

Vanz

Hairless cats look like wrinkly old men

Bob1

As a wrinkly old man, I take offense to that comment. Personally, I think they look like fruit bats.

WayneNGarthBrooks

I'd be happy to shave a cat for you. You provide the cat. I'll do the shaving.

Bob1

Let me know when you're planning to shave a cat. I'd love to watch.

Sall-E

Do you know the cost of hairless cats? Because you could buy a car for that price.

1BigBass

Where are you finding your cars? Also, if hairless cats are going for that, I'm in the wrong business.

BagelBytes

Again, please don't encourage buying purebred animals of any kind. Visit a shelter. They cost less and aren't subjected to terrible living and breeding conditions.

Danielle_L

As I mentioned, my husband is allergic, so we can't just adopt a random cat. Please take your anti-breeding comments elsewhere.

MaddieDVM

Your friendly neighborhood veterinarian popping in! While it's true there are many puppy and kitten mills with terrible breeding conditions, it is possible to find responsible breeders. I'm leaving a few links on how to check for the right breeder AND the right pet for your family. It's also true that we have a shelter right here with several adorable cats and kittens available for adoption! None hairless, I'm afraid.

SlimShabby

If anyone's looking for cats, downtown is overrun with them! I think they're living in that warehouse the Grahams are trying to turn into a brewery.

Vanz

If the brewery doesn't work out maybe they could open a cat sanctuary

AlisaTheCotton

Or maybe like one of those cat cafes they have in Japan? Except instead of coffee and cats, it's beer and cats?

DeltaDeltaDelta

Or maybe you could cuddle with one of the Graham brothers while drinking a beer? I'd pay for that.

The_Real_Shell-E

I second that suggestion! Beer + cuddling with a Graham brother (or their dad!!!!) = best business idea EVER

Neighborly Mod

The comments on this thread have been closed due to inappropriate content. Neighborly does not support paying for any kind of physical human contact. See our Community Guidelines if you have any questions.

Please remember to be kind and above all, Neighborly!

CHAPTER 5

James

I'M TOTALLY FEELING the phrase *too many cooks in the kitchen*. Though it's more like *too many workers in my warehouse*.

Yes, I'll concede it's been helpful to have so many hands. What I thought wouldn't take more than a few hours has turned into an almost all-day project, and we're still going. I'm glad the contractor is late because it would have been even more of a disaster if he'd gotten here two hours ago.

Despite the benefit of extra help, I'm stressed, irritated, and overwhelmed with a near-crippling frustration. All the tension has centered in my skull, giving me a headache to end all headaches. And a big cause of it all is the woman walking by precariously balancing a stack of rotten boards.

I resist the urge to scoop them out of Winnie's hands. She would fight me, first of all—I may not know her well, but I know this for certain. Plus, she's shown through the day how well she can handle heavy lifting. Now that she's wearing my gloves, I don't need to worry about her getting splinters. She should really be wearing long sleeves to protect her arms though.

Or so you won't find yourself distracted by her tattoos?

Busted. By my own internal monologue.

All day long, I've struggled. Struggled not to boil over when another person I hardly know shows up to "help." Struggled not to snap when Winnie baits me—because, oh yes, it's very clear half the things she says are to get a reaction out of me. Struggled not to stare at the tattoos covering her toned arms. Struggled not to worry about her safety—which is a thing I don't know why I'm worrying about at all.

It's not just Winnie. I also struggled not to toss Collin into the dumpster for his continued comments. Opinions about the interior setup, unwelcome suggestions about employees, and remarks about how much attention I'm paying to Winnie. Which was especially ironic considering the fact Collin spent most of the day glued to her side. Smiling, talking, even cracking jokes, apparently, based on the laughter I kept hearing from her.

"Don't forget you have a girlfriend," I muttered to him at one point.

"Oh—do you not like me flirting with yours?"

His grin was just begging to be knocked off his face. Winnie came around the corner at that point, which is the only reason the two of us didn't end up in a scuffle. When he and Chase finally drive back to Austin, I couldn't be more thrilled.

Tank left a little while ago to pick up Jo from Mari's, and the other random Sheeters have finally gone as well. I should be able to relax now that the building is quiet. My head, though, is anything but. I won't be able to really let go until the contractor shows. Plus, any minute now, Winnie will pop up with a snarky comment or some other surprise I'll hate.

She started the day by throwing me off, bringing me a coffee with a smile and not even a trace of snark. It smelled like a trap. Both the gesture and the sudden sweetness were so uncharacteristic that I threw the coffee away. I don't think Winnie is the type to put a laxative in my coffee, but I can't be too careful when it comes to her.

I hear the swish of a broom over concrete and head toward the sound. Winnie is sweeping the first and smaller room in the warehouse, the one that will become the main bar. Without electricity, the shadows pool inside the building, and I use them to hide from sight, for the first time all day allowing myself the indulgence of watching her.

Winnie is impossible to ignore, even sweaty from a day of work and dressed in baggy, athletic clothes. It's the woman herself who holds all the allure, not whatever she's wearing. My gaze falls from her messy ponytail to her full lips down to her lean but defined shoulders and arms. Winnie may be petite, but she looks like she knows her way around a weight bench. Her pale skin and lithe muscles only emphasize the dark tattoos swirling down her arms. They're something like vines or ribbons, curving and twisting over her skin with what look like words and other objects woven in. I want to trace them with my fingers, study them, ask her about each one.

Winnie suddenly pauses, looking up to meet my gaze. I jerk mine away from her tattoos. "Am I sweeping to your impossibly high standards, boss?"

That. That right there is why the muscles in my shoulders feel like they'll never unclench again. It's the teasing lilt in Winnie's voice, the slight edge of sarcasm every time she says *boss*, the glint in her eyes, more visible today without her

54

glasses. That threw me off too—the uninhibited view of her deep blue eyes. Does she wear contacts? Or are the glasses just for show?

You don't care, James. Winnie's eyesight is not your business.

"Well?" She leans on the handle of the push broom, grinning at me. Her skin glows with a light sheen of sweat. She looks tired, but the happy kind of tired, the energized kind. My work gloves still cover her hands, and I like seeing them there, touching her skin.

Something about her sets off a series of connected reactions in me, spanning the distance from anger to attraction. Turns out, those two are closer in proximity to one another than I ever thought.

"It's fine."

"I think you need to refresh your vocabulary. The word *fine* is so ... overused."

I grunt at this. No need to use words at all.

"The place looks good," she says, after a moment.

It does look good. And it wouldn't be so close to completely cleaned out if she hadn't been responsible for getting so many people here. We would probably have another day or two of work, easy. I'm working to scrounge up words to thank her when she starts to take off my work gloves with her teeth. All my thoughts die right where they are. I swear my head is about to explode.

First, because those things are filthy. She's been hauling rusty, old equipment and sweeping broken glass and picking up rotted pieces of wood for hours. My dirty gloves shouldn't be anywhere near her mouth.

But also ... watching Winnie's teeth close around the finger of my glove has me imagining her mouth biting down on my fingertip. What would a little nip from her feel like?

"James? Are you still with me?"

"Yep."

The problem is I'm a little *too* with her. I shake my head to dispel my errant thoughts. There's nothing I can do, however, to shake loose the inexplicable attraction to a woman I don't like. And the resulting frustration because Winnie's draw only seems to be growing, not diminishing.

No, now I've devolved to the point of imagining Winnie nipping me with her teeth.

This is not like me. Tank made words like consent and respect a part of our early education, saying he refused to raise a house full of men who behaved like teenage boys in a locker room. I am not a man who imagines women—much less my employee—*biting me.*

And yep—now I'm picturing it again.

She has broken my brain. Winnie plus the stress of everything I'm trying to do here, the nagging comments from Collin all day, and the dang cats infesting the building—it's all too much. That is the only explanation for my errant and inappropriate thoughts.

"When is the contractor coming? He's pretty late."

"Any minute now, temp."

Winnie's eyes light up at my words, and my stomach dips. Why did I have to go give her a nickname pulled straight from *The Office*? And yet … the nickname totally fits. She is my Ryan—the totally unqualified temp I can't get rid of.

"Hello?"

The contractor, now a full three hours late, has impeccable timing. I walk to meet him, shaking his hand as he apologizes for getting caught up at another site.

"I'm sorry I got such a late start," he says, glancing around, his eyebrows climbing his forehead as he takes in the space. "Especially since it looks like you don't have your electrical set up."

"The electrician is coming later in the week, but I'm not sure if any of the lights work anyway. We'll have to use phone flashlights."

"That should be fine, since this is just a preliminary look. Wow," he says, glancing around and running a hand through his dark red hair. "This space is massive. That's a good and bad problem to have."

That's exactly one of the issues I've been having. With a warehouse that's essentially one massive open space with a few small storage rooms and closets, I don't know how to break things up. I've been to a lot of breweries in Austin to study how things are set up. No two are alike. And none of them had a building this big and empty. I've always been more focused on the brewing side of things, and while I have the measurements and know exactly where the system of tanks will be installed, everything else is a big question mark.

"Why don't you walk me through and tell me what you're thinking?"

I balk, because what AM I thinking? Doubt is a fast-acting poison, paralyzing me where I stand. I don't know how I want to break up this massive space. I don't know how to make the leap from brewing to serving beer and having a tasting room. Recipes and flavor profiles—that I can do. But all of these details?

Not for the first time, I question the wisdom in taking on a giant project like this—upgrading from a Brewer's Permit to a Brewpub Permit and turning my Me-shed small-batch brewing into a 10,000-barrel a year operation.

I don't know how long I stand here, frozen, before Winnie steps between us, holding out one hand. She still has the push broom in the other. "Hey! I'm Winnie."

"Peter. Good to meet you. Are you his, um, partner or …?"

Peter looks between me and Winnie, and I don't know if he means partner in the romantic or business sense. I'm also not sure which of those ideas is the most preposterous.

Winnie chokes out a laugh. "No. Not in any sense of the word." She laughs again, and it shouldn't irritate me that she finds either idea as absurd as I do.

I don't say a word. I also don't stop her when she starts asking Peter questions about bathrooms and plumbing and where the brewing equipment can go.

Winnie doesn't suffer from the same visualization issues I do. Between Peter's questions and her suggestions, I start to actually get a sense of how the space will work. With the two of them doing ninety percent of the talking, I could feel like the third wheel, but Winnie makes sure to keep drawing me in. She has this way of making her ideas feel like *my* ideas. Peter doesn't seem to notice that they aren't, and if I were less observant, I might not realize it either. She's that good at sweeping people up in her world.

A good quality. Maybe a dangerous one.

"A lot of breweries now are setting up the system in sight of the bar," Winnie says. "No walls. That allows people to really see the magic. James, with the tanks along this wall, having the bar here would make sense. Is that what you were thinking?"

It wasn't, but I am now. I like the idea of people being able to see the process, to be a part of the process in a small way. This intimacy is what separates craft brewing from the giant beer manufacturers.

"I like that."

I like everything Winnie suggests. Though it would normally get my back up having someone—especially

58

someone on her second day of work as a *temp*—butting in, I'm grateful. For her ideas and for her unobtrusive way of presenting them.

It almost makes up for the fact she invited half the town today. Almost.

As we finish up, Peter gives the darkening space one more look. "This is a great start. I'll come back with some sketches and we'll get to work. I know your timeline is tight."

It absolutely is, a fact I'd rather forget. I need this part done so that when the equipment arrives in a few weeks, I can dedicate all my time to brewing. The bit of calm I located over the past hour dissipates like steam, leaving me hot and headachey again.

Peter says his goodbyes, and once again, Winnie and I are alone in the building. It's almost pitch black, and we move toward the doorway, where light comes through from the newly installed lamp posts up and down Main Street.

"That was a productive day, huh, boss?"

This is where I should thank Winnie for her help. Despite my annoyance about all the people, we did get things done faster. And her help with Peter was honestly invaluable. But the words seem permanently lodged in my throat.

"How's the website coming?" I ask instead.

"I've got the framework set up, but I have a lot of questions for you before I can do much more. We should really sit down and discuss—"

"I'm sure whatever you build will be fine."

Not even remotely true. But after today, I need a Winnie break. Being around her is doing funny things to my head. Maybe we can move our communication to text so I don't have to see her at all.

Winnie twists my work gloves in her hands. I hadn't realized she's been carrying them around for the last half-hour with Peter.

She tilts her head. "You don't seem to trust or like me, but you've got blind faith in me when it comes to your whole website?"

"I didn't say I don't trust you. Or that I don't like you."

Winnie scoffs. "Right. You just ooze distrust and disrespect and dislike and a bunch of other disses from your pores. But sure—put me in charge of something as important as your online presence. I won't screw it up or anything." Her smile has a feral quality to it.

"Thank you."

She raises one brow. "For promising not to screw it up?"

"For today." I figure it's best to keep it vague. I am grateful, yet somehow still resentful of the way Winnie jumped in with both feet. "Which reminds me—I've got another job for you."

"Why do I get the feeling I'm not going to like this job?" she asks slowly.

I grin, and Winnie drops the broom. It clatters to the ground, and we both ignore it.

"How do you feel about cats?"

Her eyes widen. "James, no."

"Your mission, should you choose to accept it—and to be clear, it isn't optional—is to rid this building of all the strays."

Her head jerks back. "What?"

I know she heard me, so I don't bother answering. In a perfectly timed display, two fighting cats screech and bolt right between us. Winnie tracks them as they disappear through a doorway. "You can't be serious."

I say nothing, just standing here, as Winnie starts to unravel. Her eyes flash. "Now, listen here, you big—"

"Hey, kids. Are we playing nice?" Chevy left a few hours ago, but he's back, ambling over to Winnie and standing shoulder to shoulder with the woman who is now glaring daggers—no, they're more like machetes—at me.

"Everything okay over here?" Chevy asks.

"Fine," I say, and Winnie must really dislike that word because the anger in her face intensifies.

"Right as a ninety-degree angle," Winnie mutters.

"Good," Chevy says. "I'd hate to think the two of you weren't getting along."

"We get along just *fine*," I say.

Winnie's eyes become slits. Chevy's phone rings, and he glances down at the screen with a grimace. "Excuse me a second."

When he walks outside, Winnie and I are left simmering in an electric tension. We stare for a few long seconds, and it feels dangerous to hold her gaze for this long. She must feel the same way, because she looks away as she steps forward, holding out my gloves.

Call me selfish, call me a total Neanderthal, but I want those blue eyes on ME. I grab the gloves but take Winnie's hand too. She jolts a little, then blinks up at me. Her confusion is evident, and well-warranted. I've been careful not to touch her today, even casually, because the attraction I feel *without* touching Winnie is bad enough.

And yet … I want her close like this. I want her *closer*.

It's a terrible one, but before I can convince my thumb of that, it traces a line up the inside of her wrist.

Winnie's lips part, and she releases a soft exhale.

Something I don't want to name hangs between us, or maybe it passes between us like a signal or current. For the moment, my headache is gone, replaced by a heady and heavy sense of want. It's deeper than just a physical connection, though it's absolutely that too. I feel like some invisible thread has wound its way through me, tethering us together.

"Sorry about that," Chevy says, walking back inside.

I immediately drop Winnie's hand, and she jumps. I feel like I've been scorched, starting with where our hands met and stretching halfway up my arm. The sensation only stops when I step back. Way back.

I need to regain some semblance of control, of dignity, of normalcy. My thoughts, my body, my everything are all out of whack where Winnie is concerned. And if there's one thing I can't stand, it's being out of control of a situation.

Even more so—out of control of my*self*.

Winnie bolts for the door without a backward glance. "See you later tonight, Chevy! Have fun on your date."

And then she's gone.

Chevy's hand lands on my shoulder and squeezes roughly. He raises his brows, a smirk on his face. "Got dinner plans? Because we need to have a word about my sister."

CHAPTER 6

James

CHEVY HASN'T SHUT up since we sat down in a booth, but none of the conversation has related to Winnie, and Mari is about to bring out dessert. I'm not sure where the pie will fit after the fried chicken I just inhaled. Knowing how good my birthday cake was, I'll find room.

So far, Chevy and I have discussed college football, which ended quickly because I'm a Longhorn and he's an Aggie; pro football, where we both lamented that we don't have a Texas team we can really get behind; and beer, which ended quickly after Chevy admitted his preferred drink is a big-name light beer.

Mari drops off two slices of pie, bourbon chocolate for me and apple for Chevy. "Was dinner bueno?" she asks, smiling.

"You couldn't tell by our empty plates?" Chevy asks.

Mari's laugh fills the room. "A woman is never going to say no to compliments."

"I thought Big Mo did all the cooking," Chevy teases, and Mari swats him.

"They're *my* recipes. Well," she amends. "They started as my recipes. The pie is all Mo. He's quite the baker."

"The food was excellent," I say, more to end the exchange than anything. I want to eat my pie, and I want to go home. I've had enough people for one day. For several days. Maybe for a week.

Mari slides the check to Chevy. I try to grab it, but he holds it out of reach and already has cash in hand. "Keep the change," he says, then winks at me. "I asked you out, so dinner's on me."

"Does this mean I'll get a second date?" I ask, taking a bite of pie, letting the flavors explode on my tongue. It is every bit as good as it sounded. No, better.

Chevy chuckles. "That depends." He grips his fork like a weapon and pins me with a surprisingly intense gaze. "What are your intentions with my sister?"

I choke on my pie. Chevy passes me a stack of napkins, a knowing smile on his face.

"What?" I ask, when I'm finally composed enough to speak.

"I said, what are your intentions with Winnie?"

"She works for me."

Chevy rolls his eyes. "Obviously. But I've seen you two together and there's this ... I don't know, *something* between you. And whether it's actual dislike or an attraction you're both pretending doesn't exist, I figured it best to discuss now, before we have a problem."

"We won't have a problem." Even as I say the words, I feel like I'm trying to convince myself as much as Chevy. I

64

already feel like Winnie is a problem. Or, at least, the complicated reactions I have to her are a problem.

"I hope not. Because I kind of like you and your family." Chevy plays with his fork, dragging it through the whipped cream melting on his plate. "Ever since our dad died, I've been waiting to ask someone what their intentions are with my sister. I'm not passing up this first opportunity."

Chevy and Winnie lost their dad? I can't stop the spread of warm empathy through my chest, a visceral ache. Losing Mom when I was thirteen changed me.

"I'm sorry for your loss," I say quietly.

Chevy shrugs. "Thanks. It sucks. My mom died when we were teenagers, so in a way, we already knew about loss. Not that it made it easier, per se. But it was less of a shock, I guess. And then again, it's like a double dose of life being unfair, you know?"

I can only nod, because a lump the size of Texas is expanding in my throat. Winnie and Chevy lost *both* parents. I wonder what my life would be like if I'd lost Dad as well as Mom. I can't picture a world without Tank in it. He's the rudder to our little family ship, steering us on a steady course, holding us together.

Or, he has been since he regained his footing after wading through grief. For a brief period, I had to be the one keeping us afloat—feeding everyone, putting the trash cans out by the curb, forcing my brothers to shower, making sure laundry got done.

I still remember the palpable relief when Dad finally emerged from his room, having showered and shaved and gotten dressed after what felt like weeks but was probably in reality, just days. Long days. Tank took back over, doing more as one man than some people get from two parents. And yet, the sense of needing to be in charge, of needing to hold things together never left me altogether, like that period of time altered my DNA permanently.

I force myself to take another bite of pie, but the taste is gone.

"I heard you lost your mama as well, and I'm sorry," Chevy says.

I nod, avoiding his eyes. Does everyone in this town always know everything? Though to be fair, my family history is readily available on any search engine.

Chevy continues. "Not that all loss is equal or hits people the same, but I'm sure you understand how loss can bond family. I look out for Winnie, even if she doesn't want or need me to."

I do understand this and wish neither of us had to know what it's like to be the older brother after the loss of a parent. Or, in their case, *parents*.

This new knowledge softens me in ways I don't want to be soft toward Winnie. It's not pity; I saw enough of that emotion directed toward me when we lost Mom, and again when I blew out my knee in college, ruining my chances at going pro. I know Winnie would hate pity just as much as I do.

No, I don't feel pity for Winnie. It's far worse.

Instead, a grudging admiration is growing along with a sense of camaraderie I definitely don't want to feel. A connection, pulling that tether of attraction between us even tighter—which is completely unacceptable. Years ago, I promised myself I wouldn't ever let myself develop deep feelings for a woman. Not after witnessing love and loss.

Tank barely dragged himself out of his grief. He recovered, but it changed him, and I swear, I always see a shadow behind his smile. He poured himself into all of us but seemed to lose a chunk of himself along with Mom.

Besides my big personal qualms about catching feelings, there are lots of other logical reasons.

Don't start going soft toward her just because you share a similar loss. She's still your employee. A meddler. And she has a boyfriend.

That last thought pulls me out of the drain I'm circling with a jolt. I haven't given a single thought to Winnie's boyfriend since I met the guy at Pat and Lindy's reception earlier in the week. It only took a minute or two in a room with him for the buttoned-up and boring Dale to rub me totally the wrong way. He seemed all wrong for Winnie. Or maybe it's just a reminder that I barely know the woman.

"You said this is the first time you've asked about a man's intentions. Haven't you had this talk with *Dale?*" I cannot help the derision with which I say the man's name.

Chevy raises both brows. "You met the guy. Do you really think he warrants this talk?"

Do I really warrant this talk? I let that thought stay in my head and simply shrug. "I don't know him. Or your sister, for that matter. But this kind of question seems much better suited to a boyfriend, not a boss."

Chevy pushes away his empty plate. "Ex-boyfriend."

I drop my fork, then silently curse myself for being so obviously shaken. Chevy doesn't miss a thing, and I swear, there's a hint of a smile on his lips.

"Since when? Last I heard, she was calling him her almost-fiancé."

Chevy rolls his eyes. "They were never gonna get married. Guys like that—if they're not giving you a ring after this long, they don't intend to. And even if he had gotten down on one knee, I know my sister. She'd have taken one look at that ring and bolted. I think she only stayed with him as long as she did because he was *safe.*"

Safe. That's such an interesting take. Winnie doesn't

seem like the kind of woman to choose anything safe. Then again, Dale didn't seem to fit her, at all. If Winnie was going for a low-risk relationship, why?

"Did you tell Winnie your thoughts on Dale?"

Chevy laughs. "You think telling my sister anything would make the right kind of difference? If I so much as said a word about Dale, she'd have been stubborn enough to dig in her heels and stay with him even longer. If I thought it was going anywhere serious, I'd have chased him off. I figured it would sort itself out in time, and it did. Which brings me back to you and Winnie."

"There is no me and Winnie. Outside of the job."

Chevy studies me for a long moment, and it reminds me of the scary way my dad could stare any of us into confessing whatever it was we were trying to hide from him. Sometimes Tank would do it even if he didn't know we were hiding something, and we'd confess things we'd have gotten away with otherwise.

It is very important I keep my face blank and my mouth shut. I'm not about to tell Chevy I don't like his sister, while I also would like to press her up against any available surface and kiss the smart words right off her lips.

Which is ... a thought that never fully formed until just this very second, at the most inopportune of times, when her brother is still giving me that look.

If I speak this aloud, I'm pretty sure I'd end up in jail or driven out of town by a mob of Sheeters with pitchforks. I try not to squirm under Chevy's scrutinizing gaze.

After several long moments, his expression slides into amusement. "You and Winnie are cut from the same cloth. I don't know which of you is more stubborn, to be honest. But if you're sure, I guess we won't have a problem."

"I'm sure."

I'm almost ready to agree and then bolt when Chevy's expression goes serious again. "If at some point, you realize you feel differently, you'll talk to me, right?"

I manage to swallow, wondering why this question seems even harder to answer than the other he asked. "I won't need to, but yeah."

"Good." Chevy stands, stretches, and then claps a hand over my shoulder in a painful grip. "Glad we understand each other."

After he leaves me alone at the table, I find myself finishing off my coffee, frustrated that the conversation ruined the rest of a perfectly delicious piece of pie.

CHAPTER 7

Winnie

"DON'T TELL me the indomitable Winchester Boyd got stood up?"

I glance up from my wobbly table as Wolf Waters sidles over to me. He tosses a bar towel across his shoulder and leans on the wall with his signature bad-boy grin, looking like he owns the place. Because he does.

"*Indomitable*, hm? That's an awfully big word for someone who lives in a bunker."

Backwoods Bar is less bar and more a glorified metal shed where Wolf slings beer out of coolers. The whole thing is rumored to be above his underground bunker. No one I know has ever seen it, and my theory is that the man lives out of his pickup.

"I learned it from *Jurassic World*," Wolf says.

"Of course you did."

His smile widens, his teeth gleaming through his trim, dark beard like the big bad fairytale creature of the same name. Wolf is a handsome man, but he's a Waters. He may have made a solid choice by burning bridges with his snobby and insufferable family, but he went a little too far in the opposite direction with the whole doomsday prepper lifestyle. Are bad-boy doomsday preppers a thing?

Personally, I prefer bad-boy bosses.

"So, who's the lucky man?" Wolf asks, and I jolt.

Surely my thoughts aren't being broadcast directly on my forehead. "What?"

Wolf gives me a look. "Whoever's running late. You keep looking at the door."

"Right." I give my head a little shake. "I'm meeting Chevy."

"Ah. Sibling hangout. What can I get you while you wait?"

"Soda water and lime if you've got it," I tell him. When he makes a face, I hold up both hands. "I'm driving, so I'm boring tonight."

"Winnie-girl, you couldn't be boring if you tried. Be right back."

I check my phone again. No texts, and it's now eight fifteen. My brother is many things—cheerfully good-natured, a neat freak to the nth degree, and smarter than he lets on. He is also punctual to a fault. I am really, really hoping this doesn't mean he hit it off with some awful woman and forgot about our plans. He hasn't brought anyone home since I've moved in with him, but there's a first time for every disaster.

I'm not concerned—YET. But I have been bored, which has given me entirely too much time to stew over the day's events. And one particular person who starred in them.

Stewing is the last thing I want to be doing when it comes to James. The man already takes up too much space in my head. Especially after our very last exchange, the one ending with him grabbing my hand. If I couldn't still feel the ghost of his thumb skating up my wrist, I might think I imagined it. His touch was so light, so tender, so UN-James-like that I almost keeled over right there in the warehouse.

It sent a thrill through me. Not simply a visceral reaction in every living cell in my body, but his touch woke something up in my mind too, the kind of curiosity I have a hard time turning off. I haven't been able to stop questioning how James really feels about me or wondering what else besides a surprising gentleness he's hiding under the surface.

There is a lot more to my grumpy boss than he wants to reveal. Which only makes me determined to slice through him layer by layer.

Bad idea, Winnie. Very, VERY bad. Layers belong in dips or winter wardrobes, not in your boss.

Chevy walks in, his hair still wet from a shower, just as Wolf returns with my drink and a can of light beer for my brother. A few other Sheeters have wandered in, so Wolf heads back to the bar with a smile and nod but no chit-chat.

I hold up my phone. "You're late."

"Well, hello to you, too, sis." Chevy makes like he's going to ruffle my hair, but, at the last minute, throws an arm around me and squeezes me in a side hug. "Sorry. I got caught up at dinner, then wanted to make sure I showered after our long workday."

I wrinkle my nose. "You didn't shower before your date?"

"My date didn't care about my smell," he says, winking.

I try to cover both my ears and eyes at the same time, which doesn't work and makes me look like I'm doing hand motions to some weird new dance. "Ew. I don't want to know!"

Chevy only grins. "I think you do this time."

"No, I really don't want any details—"

"I took your boss to dinner."

I drop my hands and stare. Then, with trembling fingers, I pick up my soda water and promptly choke. My brother grins at my reaction. I glare.

"*Why?*" I demand when I can speak properly again.

"I wanted to make sure he and I were on the same page." Chevy takes a slow sip of beer, watching my reaction. My brother has a way of putting people at ease, friendly and casual while he's actually cataloging every detail. It's why he's so good at his job, and why he should probably be a detective in a bigger city rather than a deputy here. I only hope he doesn't notice the way my pulse is fluttering in my neck. My heart has gone telltale, intent on beating its way out of my body and revealing the effect even the idea of James Graham has on me.

I attempt to keep my voice steady. "And what page is that?"

"The one where if he hurts my baby sister, he'll rue the day."

I can't tell if Chevy is kidding or not, but if he actually had some kind of fatherly shotgun-in-hand talk with James, I'm going to shrivel up and die of embarrassment.

I push my glasses up on top of my forehead and rub my eyes. I'm not used to wearing my contacts for so many hours like I did working in the warehouse today, and my eyeballs feel gritty and dry. Blinking, I put my glasses back in place. Chevy fills my view, smiling. "Tell me you didn't."

"I most certainly did."

My cheeks are burning. My heart has stopped beating altogether. Goodbye, cruel world—or maybe just cruel brother.

"Chevy," I whine, pressing my drink to my hot face.

"Why? You know James can barely stand me, right?" My eyes narrow as a thought occurs to me. "Wait—did you have this kind of talk with Dale too?"

Chevy takes a sip of beer before answering. "No."

Whatever part of my brain is still functioning shorts out at this. "But you had one with *James?*"

"Winnie, be honest with yourself. Did you really see a future with Dale?"

"No."

It's a knee-jerk no. I don't even need to consider the question. I've barely thought about my ex since we ended things. It's like our breakup and maybe even our relationship didn't happen.

Despite how well Chevy tried to hide it, I'm observant too, and I know my brother never liked Dale. Which really should have been cause to ditch him sooner. I don't want the kind of man who doesn't fold right into my family, and Chevy is the only family I have left.

Still. That doesn't give my brother the right to go talk to James Graham.

"Me not seeing a future with Dale doesn't equal you talking to my *boss.* It's not like we're dating. Or thinking about dating."

"So, you're keeping things just business?" His grin is smug and infuriating.

"Just business," I insist.

"Hm."

"You don't believe me?"

Chevy finishes his beer and waves Wolf off when he offers another. My brother and I share the same sense of responsibility when it comes to alcohol and operating motor vehicles.

"I don't know if you've noticed, but you and James are at each other's throats," Chevy says.

74

I gasp dramatically and put a hand to my chest. "Me? I'm Miss Congeniality. I get along with everyone."

Chevy chuckles. "But not with him. Don't you find that *interesting?*"

"I'll have to create a hypothesis and put my observations in a formal study. But I need a control group and some lab space …" I tap my lips, pretending to be deep in thought.

"I, for one, find it *very* interesting," Chevy says, totally ignoring my joke.

"I find you annoying."

"You seem to enjoy annoying James."

"I beg your pardon. I am a picture-perfect employee. Didn't you see how I organized help in cleaning out the warehouse today?"

"Help James didn't seem to want. Which is exactly what I'm talking about."

"I was just doing my job. Very well, thank you."

"You were doing that thing where you push and prod. It's something you do with people you care about. Something you didn't ever do with Dale."

I have no argument for this, so I take a long sip of my drink and wonder why I thought sibling bonding was a necessary thing.

Chevy continues with his way-too-astute observations. "When there's that much tension between two people, they'll end up kissing or killing each other."

I swallow hard at that statement, thinking of that game we used to play in middle and high school: marry, kiss, kill. I always argued with Lindy and Val saying when you married someone, you'd probably spend part of the time wanting to kiss them and part of the time wanting to kill them.

Now, it feels like those words have come back to haunt me.

I've thought several times today about killing James. I mean, not literally, obviously, but in the figurative sense.

As for kissing ... well, I thought about that too. NOT figuratively. Very definitely literally and also liberally.

Chevy's grin is smug, and again, I have to wonder if my brain is somehow projecting all my thoughts.

I go for humor, the great deflection. "Did you pull out your gun or badge and tell him you'd run him out of town if he hurt your baby sister?"

Chevy only shrugs. Humiliation is a hot wave creeping up my chest. I *cannot even* with my stupid brother. Groaning, I lower my forehead and bang it on the table. "You can't *do* that, Chev."

I can't even imagine how James reacted to my brother butting into the situation. I *won't* ask. Especially because a sliver of my heart is thrumming with excitement, wanting to know whether James thinks of me more on the kiss or kill side of the spectrum.

NO—wait. What if Chevy said that same thing to James about kissing or killing?

Right now, my brother just moved to the tippy-top of my figurative murder list. Which is saying something, considering the fact that James tasked me with removing all the cats from his warehouse.

"I make no apologies," Chevy says, draining the last of his beer. "I'll always have your back, Win."

"The thing is—I don't always *need* you to have my back. Like in this specific case, with James. I definitely don't."

Chevy drums his fingers on the table. "Maybe. Maybe not. But I'll take every precaution when it comes to you. Just the way Dad would have done."

The way Dad would have done.

The noise of my heartbeat in my ears is like the wings of a

giant flock of birds, taking flight. My vision goes slightly hazy, and for a brief moment, the world tilts. I'm standing before it rights itself, and I grab the wobbly table, hoping it holds me.

When sound and sight rush back in, everything is too bright, too loud. Chevy is staring at me, and I can't look at him right now. He looks too much like our dad, and I don't want to see that comparison. I throw some cash down on the table. Then I bolt. Not running but just about.

"I'm staying with Val tonight," I call over my shoulder, not slowing even a little bit.

Chevy yells after me, but it's my good fortune Wolf Waters intercepts him before he can follow.

The air is cool in my throat, and I draw in deep lungfuls, relishing the slight burn as I speed-walk to my car.

What my brother doesn't know, and what I can't ever tell him, is that he's dead-wrong about our father. We all were wrong about him. And that's the painful truth I'll carry with me to the grave, just the way Dad did.

TEXT THREAD

Winnie: *gif of cartoon clock*

James: ???

Winnie: Gasp! Have you never seen *Beauty and the Beast?*

James: Why are you sending me a gif of Cogsworth

Winnie: YOU KNOW COGSWORTH!?!!!!!!

Winnie: Are you a secret cartoon lover?

James: No

Winnie: What's your favorite Disney movie? OMG do you have a favorite princess?

James: Focus. Why did you send the gif

Winnie: It's Ariel, isn't it? Men love the seashell bra. And the singing.

James: THE GIF, WINNIE. WHY

Winnie: That was my way of telling you I'm done for the day.

Winnie: You know, clocking out? Get it???

James: Make a spreadsheet for your hours. No need to check in

Winnie: Since you seemed to be avoiding me, thought I'd make sure you knew I was working.

James: I'm your boss, not your babysitter. Spreadsheet

Winnie: You're no fun.

James: Never claimed to be

Winnie: Ugh. I bet you don't even text with gifs, considering you barely use punctuation. You're the captain of the Fun Police.

James: *gif of Rapunzel from Tangled*

Winnie: Sorry for the slow response. I passed out from shock.

James: You asked about my favorite princess

Winnie: Rapunzel, huh? Innnnteresting. VERY interesting.

James: Don't try to psychoanalyze me, temp

Winnie: You have no idea how much I've learned about you from just this conversation.

James: You've learned nothing

Winnie: I've learned EVERYTHING.

Winnie: The key question: Did you like Rapunzel before or after she cut her hair?

James: Both

James: She didn't change personalities. Just her hair

Winnie: Smooth answer. Very PC of you.

James: Are we done? I have things to do

Winnie: More important than texting me? I'm hurt.

James: How many cats did you catch today

Winnie: Oops. Gotta run!

CHAPTER 8

James

I'M JUST ABOUT to lift my hand off the rook when a small and slightly smug voice says, "Are you sure you want to move your rook there?"

My hand stills on the wooden piece, one I carved last year in between building benches and tables. I *was* sure about my next move. But one glance at Jo, who is unable to hide her smile, has me second-guessing.

You'd think mind games in chess wouldn't be something I'd need to worry about with a five-year-old. But Jo is anything but a typical five-year-old. I'm not sure if it's because she started reading at three or because she spent more time around adults than kids or just some genetic windfall, but Jo is brilliant, perceptive, and speaks like she's already got a college degree.

She's also killing me in chess, a game I taught her two months ago.

I slide the rook back and sigh, examining the board again. I'm pretty sure Jo is visualizing her *next* game, the one after she beats me in this one.

"This does not bode well for you, son," Tank says, then continues pulling chips out of his poker case. I can hear him counting under his breath.

While Jo has been schooling me in chess, Tank has been setting up for a Graham family poker night. It's the first one hosted here in Sheet Cake rather than the house in Austin. The thought has my gut churning. It shouldn't be a big deal —it's about family, after all, not the game itself or its location. Still. I don't like change. Right now, my life is pretty much ALL change.

When Tank announced he bought a whole town—a pretty dead one at that—we all fought him on it. I questioned if he still had his faculties. But he does, and this is really happening. Pat was the first to get on board, solely because Lindy is here. Well, Lindy and Jo, who I'll admit has softened me toward the idea of Sheet Cake.

I'm not sure what tipped me over the edge to decide that yes, this is where I want Dark Horse's physical location to be. I went from looking for just a brewing space in Austin to something ten times the size of what I was thinking along with a tasting room—essentially running a public bar. It's beyond the scope of what I envisioned, but now I'm all in.

Or ... I'm getting there. Even with as real as things got with the contractor earlier in the week, part of me is still in some kind of denial.

My living situation is a great example. I've been crashing here, in the guest room of Tank's newly renovated loft, and currently, I'm staying across the street at Pat's almost identical loft while he and Lindy are gone. A third loft is almost done, and Tank has offered it to me, but I've had quite enough family togetherness. No way am I living on the same street as the two of them.

I want a house. Maybe some land. A place with room for all my woodworking tools, currently taking up residence in Tank's Austin garage while my house is being leased out. I need space to move my small brewing system so I can continue recipe development in small batches.

And THAT feels like too big of a commitment. It's a period at the end of the sentence. Once I invest what little cash I have left in Sheet Cake real estate, it will be official.

For whatever reason, next to buying a house, having poker night here makes Sheet Cake feel very, very permanent.

"You're not going easy on him, are you, Jo?" Tank asks.

She giggles. "Not *too* easy."

I shake my head. Three more moves and she has me in checkmate. If that's not *too easy*, I'd hate to see her at full speed. This kid has me wrapped around her finger. I know it. She knows it. Probably the whole town of Sheet Cake knows it and is posting about it on Neighborly. Whatever.

"Good game," I tell her, shaking her tiny hand.

"Excellent match," Jo responds with a wide grin, her dimples flashing. "Now, as for my prize …"

"Close your eyes, little one." I dip my hand in my front shirt pocket, pulling out two things I hid there earlier. Like I said—wrapped around her finger. I put one in each hand, then hold out my two closed fists. "Right or left?"

Jo chews on the end of her braid, her eyes darting back and forth between my hands. "I cannot choose the cup in front of me…"

I laugh. "Have you been watching *The Princess Bride*?"

"Tank watched with me."

"And now that's *all* she wants to watch," Tank says, chuckling.

"Could be worse." I remember a time when for a week straight, my brothers and I watched *The Incredibles* twice a day. Tank finally banned it after we kept yelling, "Where is my super suit?" any time one of us couldn't find a shoe or jersey or favorite pair of jeans.

Jo taps my left hand. I turn it over, slowly opening my palm to reveal a ring pop. Her eyes light up. I tear open the package and hand it over. Only when she's got it neatly fitted on her finger do I give her what's in my other hand—a mini package of Harry Potter jellybeans. She squeals at that one.

"Thanks, Uncle James." Jo throws her arms around my neck, scattering the chess pieces. "Oops!"

"James will clean up, Jojo." Tank tugs her braid. "Why don't you grab your bags? Mari should be here any minute to pick you up."

"Are you sure you won't teach me to play poker?" Jo sticks out her lower lip, and Tank laughs.

"You'd wipe the table with us. Maybe when you're sixteen," I tell her, kneeling to pick up the pieces.

"Thirteen," she counters.

"Eighteen," Tank says firmly, raising a brow. I'm glad one of us has backbone. Even if I know he'll cave. He taught us all the year after Mom died. We played for candy, not money, but still.

One rogue knight is halfway across the living room, but I manage to find them all and put the pieces back on the board while Jo grabs her bags. I glance at the folding table Tank set up for the game, then frown.

"Did you invite extra people?"

Dad shrugs. "With Pat gone, we had space. You know our table is always open."

Maybe our table has always been open, technically speaking, but the last new player we added was Chase, Harper's husband, almost seven years ago. He was my sister's best friend for years before they finally admitted they were in love —something we could have told them long ago. Just because that turned out well doesn't mean I want to welcome a bunch of new people.

I walk to the kitchen and grab a glass of water. It does nothing to ease the tightness in my chest, the swirling in my gut, and the heat spreading over my skin.

Who else has Tank invited? The only person I can think of is Chevy, but I counted three extra stacks of chips at the table. I set down my empty glass before it cracks in my fist. Because what if he invited Winnie?

You can handle change. You're thirty now. A whole new decade. Time to chill, man. If Winnie's here, just be your normal brooding self. It will be fine.

My mental pep talks suck. I need to look into training my inner monologue to be better.

But I'm hanging by a thread here, frayed and thin. I can trace it back to my first day as Winnie's boss. Or maybe it was the workday, trying to keep my eyes from straying to her tattoos and lean muscles. It could have been dinner with Chevy, where he told me Winnie is single AND put the idea of dating her in my head.

My fingers go down to my pocket, where I'm still carrying the seed she gave me. The thing is probably going to sprout if I don't figure out what to do with it.

I have just as little idea what to do with Winnie.

I smile, remembering the high point of my day—no, my WEEK—when I walked in on Winnie facing off with a gray striped cat. With a cat carrier in hand, she crouched in front of the thing, which was bigger than her head, tail swishing and ready to attack.

"Be careful," I told her, keeping a smart distance.

"It's okay," Winnie said. "We've come to an understanding. He's going to go into the carrier like a good kitty. Aren't you, good kitty?"

The cat hissed. Winnie jumped forward, swinging the carrier like a baseball bat. And the cat used Winnie's shoulder as a springboard, leaping away into the shadows while Winnie fell back on her butt.

"It's not funny," she told me, glaring. I hadn't even realized I was laughing and did my best to stop immediately. Especially when she said, "Two words, boss: workman's comp."

Barely holding it together, I left the room, calling, "Four words: employee of the month."

Yes. I laughed, and then I made *a joke*. At this rate, I'm going to be smiling openly and hugging strangers by the end of the week. I definitely need to minimize my exposure to Winnie.

I'm still worrying about the guest list when Mari arrives to pick up Jo, followed by Big Mo, carrying a six-pack of sodas. Collin, Harper, and Chase show up moments later with their dogs in tow. The noise in the loft increases tenfold, making the pressure in my head increase too. Stormy makes a beeline straight for Jo, covering her face in slobbery kisses. Brutus, the older boxer, joins me in the kitchen. He gives me a sniff, an understanding look, and then sits right next to me like he's my emotional support dog, picking up on my stress levels.

"I know, right? It's a lot." I give him a good scratch behind the ears, observing all the hugs and greetings from a nice, safe distance. I swear, I can hear how much quieter it is without Pat.

Harper joins me in the kitchen, giving my shoulder a nudge. "Hey, biggest brother. How's life?"

"Life is life. Are you playing tonight?" I ask Harper, already knowing her answer.

She makes a face. "I brought a book. Poker doesn't interest me." She pauses. "It's weird being here rather than home."

"Thank you! It's totally weird."

"It's probably a good thing," Harper says, and this is where we'll disagree.

I'm carrying a few bottles of my beer to hand out around the table when there's a knock at the door. Despite a host of voices shouting to come in, no one opens the door. Balancing the beer precariously, I swing open the door, then immediately drop a bottle, which shatters on the hardwoods.

Because standing with Chevy is the last person I want to see, wearing a short dress with anchors all over it. *Anchors*.

"Hey, boss," Winnie says, holding up a bottle of tequila. "Looks like you could use a drink."

———

I do not let Winnie make me a drink. It's a stupid stand to take, especially since everyone raves about her jalapeno margaritas. Apparently, Winnie makes her own jalapeno-infused tequila. Good for her. I stick with one of my beers, telling myself I'm not interested in her tequila. But I can't stop thinking about testing a batch of jalapeno beer.

We're only a few hands in, and I'm already a lot of chips down. I cannot get my head in the game tonight, and the reason why has blond hair and glasses and is sitting directly across from me in a ridiculous anchor dress. I can't explain why this dress feels like such a personal affront. But each tiny, red anchor is like a smirking mouth, making me think about Winnie's lips.

"Your bet, Win." Chevy nudges her, and Winnie frowns and nudges him back, harder.

"I'm thinking," she says.

"You can call—that's when you match what's been put into the pot. You can raise, which means—"

"Will you just drink your beer and be quiet? I don't need poker mansplained to me."

But that hasn't stopped Chevy from giving her unsolicited advice every hand. They've been biting back and forth like a couple of wild dogs since they walked in, not just about poker. Is it wrong to find it highly entertaining to see Winnie so riled up? And for once, it's not because of me.

I keep my smiles hidden behind my beer as Chevy tries to explain the betting, how much each chip is worth, and what each game is. Winnie has moved from telling him to leave her alone to elbowing him. I think she stomped on his foot under the table based on the grunt I just heard.

I'll give Winnie this: she's focused, as though determined to figure out the game. It makes sense, given what I know of her. She seems to throw herself wholeheartedly into any task she's given, whether it be cleaning up a warehouse, catching cats (she's up to seven now), or learning poker. Her focus and all Chevy's tips haven't helped yet. Her stack of chips is the only one smaller than mine.

"You two remind me of another set of siblings I know. Always bickering," Chase says, rubbing his chin. From her spot on the couch, Harper snorts.

Collin presses a hand to his chest. "Who could you possibly mean?"

This earns a laugh from Winnie. Collin grins at her, making me set my bottle down a little harder than I mean to on the table. Winnie's eyes flick to me, and her smile dies immediately.

Great. Now I'm a smile murderer. Once again, Collin seems to have taken on Pat's role in absentia as the fun brother. Which is fine so long as he doesn't start hitting on Winnie. Because, if he hasn't forgotten, he has a girlfriend.

"Fold." Winnie pushes her cards to the middle. I don't miss the reassuring smile Tank gives her before he goes all in, forcing the rest of us out and claiming all the chips in the center.

Chase groans, counting his own diminishing stack of chips. Chevy shakes his head and leans toward Winnie. "That was good luck, getting out before losing any more."

"I don't believe in luck," Winnie snaps.

"How did things go with the contractor?" Collin asks. "Any update on the timeline?"

"Fine. And nope."

Harper chimes in from the couch. "When are you going to let me help with the bookkeeping?"

I crack my neck and keep my eyes on my chips. "How about no business talk at the table?"

"When do you leave for the conference, James?" Tank asks, completely ignoring me.

It's supposed to be Winnie's deal, which also means shuffling and choosing the game, but she's totally focused on me. Chevy intercepts the cards and starts shuffling for her.

"Friday. I'll stay at the hotel rather than the house just so I don't have to keep driving back and forth. You know, traffic. I just need to make a reservation."

I'm dreading the Craft Brewer's Annual Conference and Trade Show this weekend for a lot of reasons. First: people.

Lots and lots of people. I've been around enough people this week to last me a month, so the timing is poor.

The second reason is that, despite needing to connect with other people in my industry and talk to various vendors, I don't like the vibe at these things. It feels like a bearded boys' club. I attended one meeting last year and haven't felt that out of place since I was in high school.

I just want to brew the best beer I can, by myself. I don't need beer buddies or whatever. I am up for awards in the Strong Hoppy and Chocolate & Coffee categories—something I'm proud of but trying not to think about. The chances of winning are unlikely.

My plan: get in, connect with some vendors, hit a few sessions, and get out.

"What conference?" Winnie asks, as Chevy slides the fully shuffled deck in front of her.

"It's a beer thing," I say. "For work."

Winnie eyes me coolly. "When are we leaving?"

"You don't need to be there. It's boring industry stuff."

"Boring industry stuff is my middle name."

"No."

"I could be an asset. After all, it's my job, *boss*."

No. Not happening. The only thing I can imagine making the conference worse is having Winnie next to me all weekend. But I can't exactly extricate myself from this with so many eyes watching this conversation play out. I swear, even Harper's dogs have woken up and are glancing my way.

Collin clears his throat, and I don't miss the sharp glance Tank shoots my way. I know he's going to give me a lecture about manners later, one I probably deserve but will also ignore. Is the tension spiking between Winnie and me THAT obvious? When I catch Big Mo hiding a smile behind his can of soda, I have to concede that it is. I wish Tank had kept his big mouth shut about the conference.

Chevy shoots me a look, which I know is meant to remind me of his warnings. Like I could forget.

"Can we focus on the game? Your deal, temp."

Winnie sighs, giving me a look, which tells me this conversation isn't over. Turning to my dad, she taps the top of the deck. "So, I get to choose the game? Any game?"

Before Tank can answer, I jump in. "Go Fish doesn't count. Neither does Crazy Eights."

Someone—I'm betting Collin—kicks me under the table, and Tank gives me another disapproving look. I meant my comment to be teasing, but it came out of my mouth as just plain rude.

This happens to me sometimes, where my gruffness encroaches on rudeness territory. I remember in seventh grade, I started getting notes on my report cards talking about my tone of voice problem. When I stopped talking almost at all in class, the next report card said I had a tone of *face* problem.

Right now, I think I have both.

Ever so slowly, Winnie raises her brows at me. "What about Uno? Old Maid? Those okay with you?"

I lean back, crossing my arms over my chest. No need to dignify this with a verbal response. Big Mo coughs, I'm pretty sure to cover his laughter.

"What'll it be, Winnie?" Tank asks.

Though most of us prefer the classic Texas hold 'em, it's the choice of the person dealing. Every so often someone—usually Pat—chooses some stupid game like Love Your Neighbor which lasts forever, involves multiple rounds of betting, and passing cards around the table to other players.

So far tonight, we've played hold 'em and one round of five-card stud.

"Just pick something simple," Chevy suggests.

Look—I like Chevy. But despite my own comment that came out ruder than I expect, I very much dislike how he's speaking to Winnie. It's patronizing and demeaning, even if she doesn't know poker. If he weren't her brother, we'd be having words. If he were my brother, one of us would have already dragged him outside by the collar.

Winnie practically growls. "I swear—if you say one more thing to me, we're going to take this outside."

Collin whistles low.

"Wouldn't be the first time," Big Mo says. "Think you could take her now, Chevy? Because my money's on Winnie."

"Same," Harper calls from the couch. I cover my smile with my hand.

"Thank you for those votes of confidence, but I think my brother is sorry. Aren't you?" Winnie definitely kicks him under the table now.

"I'm just trying to help," Chevy says, wincing. "Stop kicking me."

"When did I ask you for help?"

"I just thought—"

"Keep thinking on your own game."

Chevy winces. "Jeez, sorry for trying to help."

She kicks him again. "That's not a real apology."

"Ow! Fine. I thought it would be nice since you've never played."

Winnie sighs, pushing her glasses on top of her head to rub her eyes, something she's done more than once tonight. She puts the glasses back in place and glances around the table, looking at each of us in turn. When her gaze collides with mine, her blue irises sear like a cattle brand on some invisible part of me.

Her focus moves on just as quickly from me as she does with everyone else at the table, and I try to tell myself I'm not bothered I didn't get an extra few seconds of her stare.

The look she gives Chevy is harder and makes him squirm in his seat. I respect the way she doesn't back down. It's actually pretty hot. Which is not good.

"Could we get back to the game?" I ask.

Winnie heaves a sigh and begins to shuffle the cards.

"I already shuffle …d." Chevy's words drop from his lips as his mouth hangs open.

Winnie's fingers fly over the deck as she expertly shuffles the cards. The room is suddenly silent, and all eyes are on her hands. Jaws have dropped around the table, and Chevy's is the lowest of all. She's not doing a standard shuffle, but something I've never seen before. It's the kind of thing reserved for Vegas dealers or movies about poker.

The *snap* and *shh* of the cards and the deft movements of her hands are hypnotizing. Why is this so sexy? It shouldn't be, but her strong yet delicate hands are fascinating to watch. Beautiful. Once again, Winchester Boyd has managed to shock me.

She clears her throat. "Omaha, high low. Low hole wild," she says, naming a game I'm only nominally familiar with, and begins to deal.

The cards fly over the table, each landing exactly where they should. Omaha isn't that uncommon of a game, but her specificity tells me two things that track with her ability to shuffle: Winnie is no poker novice, and I have even more reason to stay away from her.

When the cards have all been dealt, Winnie turns to her

brother, putting her arm around the back of Chevy's chair and leaning close.

"I never said I hadn't played poker before," she says.

"When did you learn?"

She shrugs, turning back to her cards, point made. "College."

Tank and Big Mo both begin to laugh, deep booming sounds that echo off the hardwoods. Harper has her face buried in her book, but I can see her shoulders shaking. Chase grins, and Collin looks at Winnie like she's the most beautiful creature he's ever seen. He's not wrong. But I want to smack the look off his face anyway.

"Nice," Collin says, slapping a hand on the table. "Now things are getting interesting."

He flashes a smile at Winnie, and when she smiles back, jealousy snakes its way up my throat. She winks at Collin, and I'm ready to knock out his teeth.

Chevy's eyes are still huge, and he sputters. "Were you trying to hustle us?"

Chase, ever the peacemaker, looks about ready to separate these two, but Winnie only rolls her eyes and pats Chevy on the back. She gestures to her small pile of chips.

"I'm doing a terrible job of hustling if that were the case. Which, to be clear, it isn't. I've had crap cards all night, but I think my luck's about to change. Can we play now?"

With a heavy sigh, Chevy hangs his head. "On behalf of every man who has ever made an incorrect assumption about a woman, I apologize."

"A little grandiose, but I'll take it," Winnie says. "Tank, bet's to you."

With a grin, my dad tosses a few chips to the center. "I call. Not going to miss out on this hand."

Big Mo calls, and when it comes to me, I don't hesitate.

"Raise." I've got nothing but a Jack and a great poker face.

Chase folds, and Collin and Chevy call. It's back to Winnie, and she tilts her head for a moment, appraising me. I keep my face impassive, daring her to figure me out.

With the tiniest of smiles, Winnie narrows her eyes, then tosses in a few more chips. "James Graham, I'm calling your bluff."

I swallow but otherwise do not move. It has to be a good guess, it HAS to, because if Winnie has learned to read me, I'm totally sunk—and I don't mean in the game.

CHAPTER 9

Winnie

WHEN TANK INVITED me to poker night, he warned me the guys could be pretty intense. He undersold it about as much as I downplayed my knowledge of the game. James by himself has the intensity of a front-row seat to the sun.

I totally love his intensity, for the record.

I especially loved the moment they all realized I already knew how to play poker. Considering what Chevy pulled with James this week, it was especially satisfying to shock my irritatingly overstepping brother.

We're taking a quick bathroom and drink break, and I wander into the kitchen. I open the fridge to find rows of unmarked bottles. I'd bet anything this is James's special stash. I still have yet to taste his beer, and I'm feeling a little surly about it.

"Do you prefer hoppy IPAs? Or more of a stout?" Collin

is suddenly beside me, peering into the fridge with his face so close to mine it makes my stomach do a quick twist.

I glance at Collin, then quickly away. There's nowhere for me to go because I'm trapped between the refrigerator door and Collin's body. He's not as big as James, but the Graham men are all supersized. They definitely won the gene pool lottery. All of them are attractive, more than anyone has the right to be. Other than James, they're all very nice. Definitely down-to-earth for being a fairly famous family. I'm secretly hoping Harper might want to be my friend, but she is exceptionally intimidating.

"I don't know beer as well as I should," I admit. "I'm more a fan of the hard stuff."

Again, downplaying. No need to tell him I'm a certified mixologist. It's not like I'm going to do anything with it, other than play around with recipes and make drinks for my friends.

"I loved your spicy margaritas," Collin says. "My lips are still burning."

"Then I've done my job."

Collin plucks two beers from the shelf, and we both stand. I move back a bit now that the fridge is shut. He pops them open and hands me one. The smile he flashes me is disarming, and if I weren't already struggling to tame my love/hate thing with one Graham brother, Collin would have me in a puddle on the floor. The heat of his smile practically blows back my hair like opening a hot oven door.

I smooth down my dress. It's my lucky poker dress, a flouncy black one with a sweetheart neckline and anchors. In front of Collin, it suddenly feels too short.

"This is Last Draft Pick." Collin rolls his eyes. "James has the worst names, but he won't listen to any of us about it."

I file that tidbit away for later. I don't know what's normal for naming beers and need to do some research to see what other craft breweries are using for names. One more thing to research. I have an ever-growing list.

"It's a milk stout," Collin says.

Beer and milk sounds like a disgusting combo, though from what I've learned so far from YouTube, milk stout is popular.

From the first sip, I totally get it. "Wow." It's rich, and though it has the slightly bitter beer taste I've never quite acclimated to, it's creamy with layered flavors. I'm trying to pick them out, but it's not easy. "Do I taste … cinnamon?"

"Cardamom." James's voice is so close I feel his breath ghosting over my neck. What is it with these brothers being giants but having the ability to sneak up like ninjas? They all need collars with bells.

I jump—who wouldn't?—and his hand closes around mine, keeping me from dropping my beer.

"Sorry," James says, his apology sounding less apologetic than any apology I've ever heard. Then he smiles, and if I thought Collin's smile was a lot, this is like the difference between firing a water gun and dropping an atomic bomb. It annihilates every single cell in my body, an explosive flash leaving only rubble behind.

This is the last thing I need. My feelings are already confusing enough when he's being a jerk. I don't need him suddenly handing out smiles.

Plus, I would bet anything he's only doing so because of Collin. It's simple sibling rivalry, nothing more.

"I think I've broken enough bottles for one night," James says. I'd forgotten about the one he dropped when I arrived. I couldn't decide if it was a good or bad omen.

"You two seem to have that effect on each other," Collin says drily.

"Why didn't you invite your girlfriend tonight, Collin?" James asks, without looking at his brother.

It's clear what James really means is, why are you flirting with Winnie if you have a girlfriend, Collin?

But when Collin winks at me, I think I get it. *Oh, he's bad. So, so bad.* He's just been trying to get James to act exactly like he is right now—jealous and territorial. Chevy and I have our sibling moments, but the Grahams are like watching the sibling rivalry Olympics.

James doesn't seem to have figured this out, and is standing much, much too close to me, his hand still covering mine. Collin tips his beer to me as he begins to back away. "Enjoy."

James's hand on mine feels far more intimate, probably because it's so unnecessary. The small gesture seems obscene and feels even more so. Not one time has another man's touch impacted me this way. And that is a terrifying prospect.

But my physical reactions are just that. I even got a flutter from Collin showing me attention. Except there is no comparison between how I felt when Collin smiled at me and how I feel now with James's hand curled around mine.

I jerk away from him, thankful I don't spill a drop of this beer, which might be my new favorite thing.

I focus on breathing and put on a mask of calm. "Cardamom? How'd you get that flavor profile?"

"Reminds me of Christmas. And the richness that comes from a bowl of pho." James makes a face. "The broth. Not the beef part."

Huh. I never questioned or even wondered what's in pho —just that it's delicious. Christmas and pho … like the idea of milk and beer, it sounds weird, but somehow it totally works. I wonder if James is some kind of genius, or if this is what all craft brewers are like.

If you go to the conference, you can find out.

For reasons I can't—or don't want to—fully explain, I desperately want to go to the conference Tank mentioned. I NEED to go. What's more, I think *James* needs me to go. Not that he realizes it or would admit it if he did. When the contractor started asking questions, James got this glazed look. Total donut of the face.

But when I jumped in, playing go-between, it seemed to ease James into it. He seems adamant about doing all this himself, when it's obvious to me his passion is in brewing and flavor profiles. I'd love to help with the things he doesn't want to do—aside from catching cats—if I could just get him to see how useful I am.

Knowing James doesn't want me to go to the conference only makes it more appealing. The memory of how he brushed me off earlier activates my snark.

"Did you, like, go to beer university?"

I'm aware there's no such thing. I might have googled it.

I wish I could bottle up the look James is giving me and package it for commercial sale. It would make a really great replacement for KEEP OUT and NO TRESPASSING signs. Just this look, nothing more, would be enough.

"No," he says, and it's like the word has an extra weight to it. "Did you go to liquor university to learn how to make jalapeno margaritas?"

"I'm a certified mixologist."

That shuts him up. Actually, it looks like it shut him down.

"But I learned the trick with the jalapeno infusion at a bar. They had a great drink, I asked how they made it, and the bartender talked to me about infusing. You can do it with a lot of different things. Fruit, black pepper. I tried garlic vodka once. It was as bad as it sounds."

"Garlic vodka?" James sounds intrigued rather than disgusted.

"Trust me—don't do it." I draw in a breath, realizing this might be the longest conversation outside of texting we've had. I wish I could access the text James, who seems slightly looser and more willing to engage. But so far, text James seems to exist only on the phone.

"So, how'd you get into making beer?" I smile. "If not at beer university."

Before he can answer, Tank calls out, "Five-minute warning!"

In the time I looked at Tank, James drifted away like a ghost. So much for pleasant conversation. We can just pretend I didn't try to engage James Graham in small talk.

Not that it was small—honestly, getting James to say more than single-syllable words feels huge—but I don't know him any better than I did before. I know so little about James, even things I feel like I should know. I guess there's Google, but it probably has more information than I could possibly want to know. And maybe things I don't want to know, like about past relationships.

I remember how hard it was for Lindy after she and Pat broke up to see photos online of him with other women. James probably has a pretty low profile, since he didn't get to play pro. But I don't want to see a photo of James with another woman. Let's not discuss WHY the idea makes me stabby, because I'm pretending it doesn't.

This realization does not bode well as far as my mental well-being when it comes to the brooding hulk of a man I work for.

As I head to the bathroom, I try to remind myself of

reasons I don't like James. He's rude. Seems to have even lower expectations of me than most people. Wears a dark cloud of negativity like a backpack wherever he goes. Is too hot for his own good. The shining crown on top is that James does not like me.

I'm not the kind of woman to chase after an uninterested man. For friendship or anything else. Though James did get possessive a few minutes ago when Collin baited him. I didn't imagine that. Or the way he held onto my hand much longer than he needed to if his goal was to keep me from dropping the bottle.

Whatever. He's your boss. And you don't need a man. Especially not so quickly after getting out of a spectacularly stupid relationship. You obviously are terrible at making decisions with regard to men.

I wish all of my logic was enough to keep me from peeking into the shower and lifting the bodywash up to my nose. I assume since this is the guest bathroom it belongs to James, but when I smell it, I'm certain.

There are educational programs in schools across the country warning about the dangers of drugs. But there should absolutely be a similar program about the dangers of men's body products. Aftershave, bodywash, cologne—all of them need warning labels. Maybe prescriptions or age restrictions.

May cause infatuation, wild bouts of lust, obsession, or addiction. Please use responsibly.

I set the bottle back down and catch a glimpse of my dilated pupils in the mirror.

"Gross," I whisper, pointing an accusing finger at my reflection. "You are not this person."

But I am this person—the one with a very stupid, illogical, and inconvenient crush on her very obstinate, uninterested, irritating boss.

I open the bathroom door and nearly run straight into Tank. For a second, I thought it was James. Their builds are so similar and other than the light gray at Tank's temples and the smile lines—well, and the fact he's smiling—he could almost be James's older brother.

"Sorry," I say, trying to step around him.

But Tank blocks me, shooting a furtive glance back toward the open living area where I can hear laughter, conversation, and the distinct clink of chips. "I wanted to ask you for a favor."

"Anything." My answer is automatic, an instinctive response to the power and charisma Tank exudes. I absolutely understand why he had gigs lined up on ESPN and other places after his time on the field ended. But I definitely didn't mean to say yes so quickly. Especially because I'm pretty sure this favor will have to do with his broody son.

His voice lowers. "Go with James to the conference. Make the reservations for the hotel. I'll happily cover it if I need to. I'll give you my credit card number."

This is one of those moments that feels too good to be true. Like a stranger appears, granting the secret wish you never spoke out loud.

"I can do that."

I'm not about to argue about the payment. I know Tank and the other brothers are investors, so this is a business thing. Plus, my finances are like a pair of too-small jeans right now.

Tank nods and seems ready to slip back to the poker table, but I stop him with a word.

"Why?"

Again, he glances out to the big room, I'm sure nervous James will hear this conversation. I don't need to be told he wouldn't like it.

Tank sighs. "I have some concerns. James is brilliant at brewing. But there are so many parts to what he's trying to do. More than what one person can achieve. And he won't accept help."

"Imagine that."

Tank chuckles. "He needs someone who can be a sounding board, who can help with the details he won't admit are not his forte. Someone he trusts."

"He definitely does *not* trust me."

"That will change." Tank seems sure, but that doesn't mean he's right.

"He'd hate that you asked me," I say.

Tank spins the gold band on his finger. His wedding band. The sight makes my heart shudder, a tiny movement I feel all the way to my toes.

"You already seem to understand him in ways most people don't," Tank says, and this statement gives me a little thrill of pleasure, like a gold star next to a teacher's red-scrawled *Excellent Work!* at the top of a paper. "If I didn't absolutely think he needs this, I wouldn't put you in this position. If you can't go because it's too last minute, I understand."

"Oh, I was planning to go."

When Tank smiles, a tiny, joyful explosion goes off inside me.

"I think you're going to be good for him, Winnie."

That remains to be seen. At the very least, I'm shaking the man like he's a can of soda, just waiting to pop the lid and watch the spray.

CHAPTER 10

James

IT'S NOT unusual for me to be relieved when a poker night ends. I tend to split immediately after we cash out, done with people and talking, even though it's our family.

Tonight *wasn't* just family, but I find myself wanting to linger casually, the way Harper, Chase, and Collin are with Winnie. Only … I don't really DO casual lingering. Someone —or several someones—would have to vacate the couch to make room for me. And I'm not about to ask. Or sit on the floor. Instead, I hover around Tank, helping put up the chips while trying to make out what they're talking about and what Winnie is showing them on her laptop.

"Does Mari have Jo for the rest of the week?" I ask.

"She does." Tank smiles, the way he only does when it comes to Jo. "We had a great time, but she reminds me of my age. You ended up having an okay night."

"Not terrible." I shrug. I didn't lose, but barely made more than I came with, which is fine by me. It's not a big buy-in, and for all of us, it's more about playing the game than winning some huge amount. I've never spent much more at poker than I would going to a movie and getting popcorn and a drink. Tonight, Chase shocked us all by winning. Winnie came in a close second, turning things around the last half of the night.

"I'm headed back to Austin tomorrow. Feel free to stop by when you're in town," Tank continues. He must see the protest on my lips because he holds up his hands. "If you have time. No pressure. Per the usual, we'll have Sunday brunch. And, of course, this place is all yours when Patty gets back or before."

"Thanks, Pops."

"Any more thoughts on where you want to live long-term?" He tries to hide the hope in his voice, but it shows in his eyes. "I'm happy to hold one of the lofts for you. Another one will be done next week."

"Don't hold it for me. I need something with more space. I'll look soon."

Soon is a great vague term.

Tonight is definitely not the time I want to discuss my living situation. I feel over-caffeinated and jumpy, despite drinking beer, not coffee. I also had a sip of Winnie's jalapeno tequila when no one was watching. It was smooth and spicy perfection, which I'll admit to no one.

I'm really starting to be intrigued by Winnie's skill set. She played roller derby. She makes her own jalapeno tequila. She can talk to contractors about floor plans. She plays poker like a pro. She builds websites and apps.

What *doesn't* she do?

Leave well enough alone, that's what.

106

"James," Collin calls, waving me over to the couch where he's sitting far too close to Winnie for my liking.

"Come, sit," Collin says. "Winnie was just showing us her mock-ups for the Dark Horse site."

Oh, was she, now?

I give Winnie a long look. She's showing someone else the site mock-up before me? She knows my family is involved, but *I'm* her boss. Dark Horse is *my* project. I don't like being the last to know or even the *second* to know.

"No, that's okay," Winnie says. "I'll show him tomorrow. It's late."

Winnie grabs for her laptop, but Collin does too. Now, they're wrestling over it, with Winnie almost in my idiot brother's lap as he tries to lift the computer out of her reach. He's laughing, face just inches from hers, which is enough to get my hackles up. But Winnie isn't smiling, and it's this that has me crossing the room before I can think better of it.

I snatch the laptop from both of them and then force Collin to move when I wedge myself between him and Winnie.

"Hey!" Collin protests, but he moves down as Harper relocates to the floor, sitting cross-legged and leaning on Chase's legs.

Now, I'm the one almost sitting on top of Winnie, fighting her grabby hands for the laptop. And, yeah, there is something I like a little too much about this. Good thing I stepped in and shoved Collin out of the way.

Winnie's small hands close over mine, tugging. "James— not tonight. I'll show you tomorrow."

"You showed everyone else tonight."

"Only because I begged," Harper says.

Capturing Winnie's eye, I loosen my hold on the laptop. "If I let go, do you promise not to run away?"

"Yes?"

I don't move for another few beats, and neither does she. I can smell her sweet scent, making me think of Big Mo's desserts. Her hair tickles my forearm, and my heartbeat is what I'm pretty sure medical dramas refer to as *thready*.

I release the laptop. Winnie slams it closed, but when she tries to get up, I put a big hand over her thigh. Not pushing, but with enough of a press to make her pause. And now my hand is stuck. Because it's half on her ridiculous anchor dress and half on her bare thigh.

I'm not sure which is worse.

I only know my hand will not move. Winnie is perfectly still. She's a baby gazelle hiding motionless in the high grasses, and I'm the prowling lion.

Until Winnie clears her throat, and suddenly I'm not a jungle cat but a scared kitten, jerking my hand away from her leg.

I'd all but forgotten the rest of my family and am suddenly aware of them all watching this exchange. "Show me," I demand, needing to regain control.

Winnie looks up at my gruff demand, biting her lip. "I really don't think—"

"Now."

With a huff, she opens her laptop. "Fine. But remember, I wanted to wait."

"Start with the first one you showed us," Collin says.

For a moment, I forget Winnie's body on mine as nervous energy pinballs through my body.

A website appears on the screen, and I suck in a breath. The banner along the top reads Dark Horse Brewery, but the name is the only thing familiar. My eyes dart over the page as

I try to make sense of what I'm seeing. Sweat pops up along my lower back and forehead, and I find myself clenching my jaw.

"What is this?" My voice is hardly more than a growl.

Winnie scrolls down, and it only gets worse. The whole thing is like my nightmare. Worse than a nightmare, because even my subconscious wouldn't have dreamed up a site in various shades of purple, the logo not a dark horse but an eggplant-colored unicorn with a sharp black horn and anime eyes.

Sighing, Winnie says, "You didn't give me much to work with, so I went with the dark horse vibe but pulled in the idea of a unicorn because who doesn't love unicorns?"

Me. I do not love—or like—unicorns.

Winnie hovers over the navigation bar, and a dropdown menu appears. "The interface is—"

I cut Winnie off. "Forget the interface. This is—no. It's just … no. Tell me this isn't the only thing you worked on."

"Show him the next one. It's my favorite," Collin says, and the glee in his voice tells me I might hate the next one even more.

Winnie's hand hovers over the trackpad, her chin tilted down. She glances at me out of the corner of her eye. "I don't know."

"Now, temp."

If possible, the next design Winnie pulls up is a thousand times worse. Rainbows are everywhere, with the overall design leaning heavily on pink, white, and bright turquoise. Another unicorn is on the logo, this time with a fluffy tail and mane braided with bows and a glittering horn. It looks like a tween girl's dream bedroom.

"This concept delivers the unexpected, again making use of the unicorn trend and vibrant colors which will …"

I slam the laptop shut, then get to my feet. Striding away, I drag my hands through my hair, then spin back to face Winnie. Some little alarm in my head is sounding, telling me I need to cool off before I speak. But a flood of words escapes, like all Winnie's tiny remarks finally cracked the dam.

"I took you on because my brother begged. Because Lindy begged. They both insisted you were the best, and I believed them. I trusted them. I trusted you."

I can't look at her face as I rage. Her dark blue eyes and those lips might cause me to soften what needs to be said.

"I could get better web designs off Fiverr. In fact, that's what I'll do. We gave this a try, and it's not going to work. I'm sorry, but you're fired."

My jaw clamps shut as I finish. I'm practically panting, my nostrils flaring, and my skull is pounding. If I thought saying everything on my mind would make me feel better, I was wrong. I only feel more breathless, more tense. I cross my arms over my chest, squeezing tight.

"James," Harper hisses, but Winnie waves a hand.

"It's okay."

"No," Collin says, "it's not okay. *James.* Sit down."

I don't move.

Winnie's cheeks are a mottled red as she slowly gets to her feet. Her eyes are lasers, burning straight through mine without blinking as she gathers her laptop in one hand and stuffs it in her bag. Her gaze does not stray from mine. She does not blink.

From behind me, Tank starts to say something, but again, Winnie waves a hand, shaking her head this time too.

She pauses in front of me on her way to the door. My body tenses with an urge to step closer, and I hate this reaction to the woman who has made me lose my cool. She's so much shorter than I am without her heels that it's hard to meet her gaze when she's standing so close.

"Before I go, your reservation is booked at the hotel for this weekend."

"When did you have time to do that?"

"While you were cashing out your chips. I'm very efficient," she says briskly. "I got myself a room as well—on a different floor so you could have some space. I should let you know it wasn't easy getting one room, much less two, this late. Obviously, I'll cancel my room and send you the confirmation details."

The anger I felt moments ago is beginning to sour into regret.

Hoisting her bag on her shoulder, Winnie looks at my dad. "Thank you for the invitation tonight. I hope you understand."

I'm not sure what there is to understand, but the way Tank is glaring at me feels like a betrayal. He's taking *her* side? I know I'm being rude. I could have been softer. But I'm also *right*. Her designs are the furthest thing from what I want.

Maybe you should have told her what you want, then.

"I understand," Tank says, his voice soft and eyes kind. "You tried."

Tried *what*? Am I losing my mind or is everyone just coddling her? I thought Winnie was supposed to be some app-developing, site-designing tech guru. It seems like everyone is giving her too much leeway, when she's clearly in way over her head. Meanwhile, I'm coming off as the bad guy.

Winnie turns to Harper, and my sister's anger radiates even hotter than my dad's. "You'll show him?" Winnie asks.

Harper nods, and the look she pins me with singes off a

layer of my skin. "I'm sorry," she says to Winnie. "So is Collin."

My brother crosses his arms, giving me a dark look. "I'm only sorry my brother doesn't appreciate you."

The way you've been appreciating her all night? I barely keep those words contained. I definitely don't need to go *there*.

Winnie makes a straight line for the door, passing me without a glance. Stormy follows her, whining and trying to get one last pet. She gives him a scratch behind the ears as she slips her heels on. "Have fun with the cats, *boss*," she calls, then slams the door and is gone.

The tension in the room is unbelievably thick, like the middle of July on a cloudless day, standing on hot pavement. Chevy casually makes his way over to me, though he doesn't need to pass me to get to the door.

"I thought we had an understanding about my sister," he says, before bumping my shoulder with his on the way out.

There is exactly one beat of silence before everyone starts yelling at me. I feel like I'm alone on a castle wall, flaming arrows being shot from a horde of orcs below.

Dad puts two fingers between his teeth and whistles so shrilly the dogs begin to bark. But it shuts all the humans up, and Harper quiets the dogs. Before Dad can say anything— and he definitely looks like he wants to—my sister stands and walks over until we are toe to toe.

I may have a good eighty pounds and six years on Harper, but she is *terrifying*. The key is to not *look* afraid.

"Those weren't the real designs, you big dummy."

It takes a moment. My brain is scrambled with a cocktail of emotions.

"What?"

"It was a joke. You *do* know what humor is?"

A *joke*? I don't see anything funny about it, and knowing

112

this does little to tone down my anger. It does ramp up my guilt though. Because the designs weren't a little bit off. They were the complete opposite of what I would want.

"I'll send you an email with the actual mock-up," Harper says. "Which Winnie would have shown you if you hadn't gone all anger management on her. It's gorgeous, and I bet it's exactly what you had in mind. Not that you gave her much to work with. Frankly, I'm shocked at how completely her real design has *you* stamped all over it. Especially considering the way you seem hell-bent on being an obstinate—"

Harper pauses here, and I have several guesses as to choice words she wants to say. But she looks to Tank, whose one raised brow is a reminder of how he trained us all to keep our mouths clean.

"Flaming donkey turd," she finishes. "You're a real flaming donkey turd, James. Check your email. Goodnight."

With that, she spins on her heel, Chase, Collin, and the dogs following behind. Chase only shrugs. We all know I dug this hole myself.

And what a hole I dug.

Later, after I've been thoroughly lectured and reprimanded by my dad, I head back to Pat's, the silence in his loft doing nothing to calm the nerves jumping under my skin.

I pull open my laptop first thing and find two emails. I open the one from Winnie first. It's simply a forward with the hotel confirmation, sent maybe ten minutes after I fired her. I hate the way a stone settles in my belly at the message, which has no hint of the woman who knows how to rile me like no one else.

If only she hadn't tried to prank me tonight, when my fuse was short and my patience for other people exhausted completely. Though, being completely honest with myself, I would have flipped at any time. I've always been too serious, or so I'm told. Whether this is the way I'm wired or a product of my life and my role as the oldest, I don't know.

It's not like I can change it. This is who I am.

Winnie doesn't know me well enough to understand I don't take jokes well. Then again, Collin was the one who pushed. He should have known better. He does know better. Then again, my family seems constantly interested in how they can loosen me up.

If only they understood the pressure I carry with me always. Especially now.

The weight of starting this business, of scaling up so large, so quickly and with startup capital from my family—it weighs on me constantly. The pressure is constant, unabating.

Tank, Collin, and Pat invested about equally, with Harper and Chase putting in a little as well. I stand to lose the most financially, with my personal *everything* on the line. If this fails, I'll have to sell the house in Austin. Probably my bike too. I'll end up on Tank's couch permanently, like some punk kid.

More than that—I'll have disappointed my family. And while I'm by no stretch a people pleaser, I've always taken the role of protector and caretaker in my family. Losing their investment because Dark Horse fails would be the opposite of that.

Still, this knowledge does little to assuage my shame over how I spoke to Winnie tonight.

You pushed her too, I remind myself. *You pretty much demanded Winnie show you. Between you pushing and Harper pushing, you forced her hand. You also gave her nothing to work with—that's on you.*

Hesitating for only another few minutes, I open the email

from Harper. She spends the first paragraph reminding me what a jerk and idiot I was.

Once you realize how wrong you were, grovel on your belly. If you need tips, call Pat. He clearly knows his way around winning someone back when he's behaved like an idiot.

My youngest brother lives with a perpetual foot in his mouth, so he's definitely the one to consult IF I needed help in making amends. Which I'm still not one hundred percent sure I want to, even if I should.

I use the login and link Harper sent to open up the real mock-up Winnie did. My breath catches in my throat, along with a coal-sized lump of regret.

In short, it's like the woman crawled around inside my brain and took the design I never could have put into words and breathed it into life.

I stare. Then stare some more. I scroll and click and read the sample website copy she wrote, which is, again, like it's been culled straight from inside my head. Only *better,* because we all know I don't have a way with words.

The part that really gets me though is the logo. A black horse, muscled and yet somehow delicate with fiery silver eyes atop the perfect font—strong and bold and unique.

I close the laptop and squeeze my eyes shut.

Looks like I have some groveling to do.

CHAPTER 11

James

IN THE END, I decide I don't need Pat's help. Apologizing is something I can do on my own. Because, despite the popular opinion about me, I am not an unfeeling, grouchy caveman. (At least, that's not *all* I am.) I am definitely guilty, however, of being an idiot with a short fuse and a lot of pressure stacked on my shoulders.

And maybe some slightly personal qualms with my employee. Ex-employee.

Look, I'm not dumb enough to think these qualms have to do with Winnie. Nope. This is a ME issue.

See? See how capable I am of taking responsibility when I need to? I've got this.

At least, that's what I tell myself all the way up until I knock on the front door.

Chevy opens it, takes one look at me, and steps outside,

closing the door behind him. I hear Winnie calling, "Who dares knock before coffee?"

Is it *that* early? I've been up for hours, but I guess it is barely seven.

Is Winnie not a morning person?

Who cares? I don't. I'm here for business. To hire her back, not to learn her sleeping schedule.

Chevy crosses his arms, leaning against the door in a pose that would look casual if not for the tension in his neck. "To what do I owe the honor?" His voice is laced with sarcasm.

"I screwed up. Massively. I'm here to apologize to you and to Winnie."

Good start. No hesitation, no minimizing. My tone of voice could use a little work, but since I basically have two tones—angry and not angry but still sounding slightly angry —I'd give this an eight-point-five out of ten.

Based on Chevy's unchanging expression, his ratings are much lower. "And?"

I clear my throat, sifting through my thoughts and possible additions to my concise yet arguably on point apology. Oh, wait. I said I was here to apologize. I didn't actually *make* an apology.

"I'm sorry."

Chevy stares at me for a long moment and then bursts out laughing. "Man," he says finally, through tears, "you're really bad at this. Like, terrible."

"I said *sorry*."

"Like a robot. Or a slab of granite. You know what? Forget it. I accept." Chevy is still chuckling.

"O-kay?" There is clearly a trick I am missing here.

Throwing open the door, Chevy steps aside, waving me through. "Have at it. And good luck."

He's still laughing as he walks down the front steps. I

pause on the porch for another minute before I enter his house. The place is neat as a pin, and considering I've been bouncing back and forth between Pat's barely lived in loft and Tank's rarely there place, that's saying something.

The messiest thing in the whole place is Winnie, and I stop just inside the door when I see her curled up on the couch with a blanket over her feet. Her knees are pulled to her chest, and she's clutching a mug of coffee to her face like she's Gollum and it's the ring of power.

I barely slept last night, but when I did, I apparently dreamed, because that dream suddenly floods my brain. I'm watching Winnie shuffle an endless deck of cards. The image is gauzy and soft, just her hands, her deep blue eyes, and red lips, curved up in a sardonic smile. Those *hands*. The movement of her fingers over the cards is the hottest thing I've ever dreamed.

It's as strong as a sense of deja vu, a total contrast to the ruffled, glasses-free version of Winnie in front of me. Yet somehow, they combine into a vision that has my fists clenching and my throat swallowing reflexively.

I focus, narrowing my gaze on this Winnie in front of me. She's sleep rumpled, hair mussed, no glasses. One strap of her tank top slides off her shoulder as I watch. Her eyes glitter with anger, even as she yawns so huge I can see her tonsils. It's hard to tell if she's glaring at me or squinting to see. I think a little of both.

"What?" she snaps when the yawn subsides. "Do whatever you came to do so I can tell you I don't forgive you and kick you out."

Winnie takes a sip of coffee, glaring over the mug at me. She's clearly not very awake. Her eyes are ringed with dark circles. I wonder if she slept as poorly as I did last night.

She yawns again, coffee spilling down the side of her

118

mug. When she notices, she licks right up the side of the white ceramic. My blood goes molten.

So far, this is not going according to plan.

"Stop staring," Winnie says. "You'll make a woman self-conscious."

She should feel anything but self-conscious. If she could only see inside my brain right now…

If she could see inside your brain, she'd probably slap you.

That sobering thought has me slumping in a chair across from the couch and looking at the floor, where not even a hint of a dust bunny lives.

"I saw your website mock-up," I say finally. "The real one."

"And?"

The feisty side of Winnie, or maybe the morning Winnie or barely-had-coffee Winnie, makes me want to smile. Which would be the very wrong thing to do at this moment.

"How did you do it?" I ask.

Winnie blinks, takes a sip of coffee, blinks again. "How'd I design the site? It's a simple Wordpress theme, pretty much just—"

I shake my head, and the motion alone stops her words. "No. How did you know what I wanted?"

Winnie tries to take another swallow, but I can tell that the mug is empty by how far she tilts it back and by the way she whimpers a little, staring down into the mug wistfully.

I'm on my feet, snatching the mug from her hand before I can think about it. "How do you take it?"

"Black."

She pauses as I step inside the connected kitchen and pour. This is the last of the pot, so I turn the machine off and set the glass carafe on the stove to cool.

Winnie shifts on the couch. "Um, black with a little splash of heavy whipping cream."

I manage to hold back a laugh. The carton of whipping cream is in the door of the fridge and I pour a little of it into the mug, raising an eyebrow and meeting her gaze, the carton still poised in my hand.

"A little bit bigger splash."

I pour until she nods, her coffee now the color of golden sand.

"One black coffee." I hand her the mug and somehow manage to keep a straight face.

Her hands circle around it, and she smiles before remembering she's mad at me. I sink back down in the chair.

"Are we at the part where you grovel and beg me to come back to work for you?" she asks.

"Not yet. You were going to tell me how you knew what I wanted for the site."

"Ah." She takes another sip of coffee. "It was close to what you were looking for? You didn't give me a lot to work with, so I was guessing."

"You guessed well."

"I'm observant."

"You're very good."

She smiles wide at the compliment. "Thank you. Some might even say I'm an asset to a business."

"Some would."

"They might find me indispensable."

"They might."

"I believe there would even be negotiations made in order to secure my loyalty. To the company, of course," she says.

"Of course."

Winnie waits. I also wait. Because to be honest, I'm not

sure what she'll say next, but letting her steer the conversation has worked better so far than what I planned to say.

"So?" She raises her eyebrows, but the look is less intimidating because then she squints to read my expression. "James. Come on. What are you prepared to offer to woo me back to work?"

There will absolutely be no *wooing* involved. But I am prepared to negotiate terms.

"Do you *want* to come back?"

She thinks about this. "I am perhaps … willing. But *willing* and *wanting* are two different things."

That's a good distinction. But her nonanswer also frustrates me. A strange feeling swirls in my chest, dipping into my gut. I wish she were both willing *and* wanting. And maybe not just for business purposes.

Bad idea, James. Pick one: professional or personal.

Not a hard choice. There is only one answer. Personal is off the table. I'm floundering with Dark Horse, struggling to get everything done. Even without the tight timeline, trying to open for the Sheet Cake Festival, it's almost an impossible task. Having a romantic relationship with my one employee —assuming she'll come back—is unacceptable.

And that's if I wanted a romantic relationship. Which, to be clear, I don't. I had a front row seat to real love with my parents and the pain of its loss. The idiots saying it's better to have loved and lost didn't watch their mom die of cancer and their dad fall completely and utterly apart from the grief of it.

Definitely keep things professional.

"I'm prepared to negotiate," I say. "Give me your terms."

"I want to be brought on in a more permanent capacity. Not just contract labor and hourly wages."

"So, not a temp?"

Winnie hesitates, staring down into her mug like she'll find the answer there. "A less temporary temp?" she says, finally, a question in her voice.

Pat told me her main gig is app development, and that she's poised to sell Neighborly. I assume after that, she won't have a need for this job anymore. So, still temporary.

"And a raise."

"Okay."

She eyes me carefully, like she's wondering why this is so easy. "I don't just want money. I'd like more ... *say*."

I shift in the chair, which suddenly feels too small. "You want a say in how I run *my* business?"

My words practically send icicles shooting through the room. Now it's Winnie's turn to wiggle in her spot. But she doesn't back down, and the seed of admiration I have for her grows, despite the bad soil and my resistance to watering it.

"I'm not talking like a *partner* or some official title. More like ... if I have suggestions or ideas or feedback, you'll listen."

"I listen."

She rolls her eyes. "Let me clarify. I want you not just to audibly *hear* me, but to *consider* what I'm suggesting."

I grunt, which is my version of a response.

"If you hadn't noticed, I actually feel like I can contribute —and not just with the website. I'm good with details, planning, and vision. If you let me, I could be an asset. Then you're freed up to focus on brewing, which seems to be your passion."

I swallow. Winnie has once again read me a little too well. But rather than admit that, showing my full hand, I just listen.

Winnie takes another sip of coffee, then narrows her eyes. "One more thing."

Why am I certain this is the thing I'm going to want to say no to more than anything else?

"I get to ask you one question a day." As though she can see the way I'll work around this, she continues. "And you have to answer honestly."

"A question about business?"

"Maybe. But not limited to business."

"Why?"

Winnie tucks her legs up under her, and I try to keep my eyes on her face as the thin strap of her tank top falls off her shoulder again. Absently, she pulls it back into place. It's a casual move, but its impact on me is closer to catastrophic. I force my eyes to stay on her face as she squints at me.

"Because I'm a curious person. And this whole bank vault persona you wear has me all …" She gestures with the hand holding her mug. It must be nearing empty because none sloshes over the top. "Verklempt."

"*Verklempt?*" I don't know this word. It sounds like a German sneeze.

"Frustrated. Agitated. Irritated."

Right back at you.

"I'm sorry my tendency not to voice every thought in my head *like some people do* is annoying."

"I didn't say *annoying.*"

"Is there a difference?"

"Absolutely."

We sit in a silence that's neither awkward nor companionable. It feels like a necessary pause, a retreat where we both regroup. I could run Dark Horse alone. That's always been the plan. My family knew going in they'd have little say in the business unless I asked, though Collin keeps butting in, and Tank did buy the town partially because he thought it would be a great location for the brewery.

I planned to hire contract labor as necessary, much further down the road. I'll be pulling twelve-hour-plus days once we get the brewing equipment delivered. Installation and brewing will be on me. Once we get closer to opening, I'll need more help with the serving side of things.

What I don't need is whatever role Winnie wants to fill. I don't need a voice in my ear, making me doubt, making me question, overwhelming me when I'm already walking a thin line. I don't need an assistant or adviser.

But I can still picture Winnie's site mock-up, the real one, and how intuitive it was, how it exactly aligned with my vision for Dark Horse. There were only minimal tweaks to things like the About page, where it was clear Winnie guessed and filled in some blanks. She also was incredibly helpful when the contractor arrived, pointing out some space issues and giving suggestions for seating and even bathroom setup.

Despite not giving her anything to work with, Winnie seems to have a way of sneaking past my walls and seeing straight into what I want.

She could be an asset.

She could be dangerous.

She could be *more*.

"Those are your conditions?" I ask, finally able to find my focus. "More money, opinions I'll listen to and consider, and answering a daily question?"

Winnie bites her lip, her eyes moving around the room like she's trying to find one more thing to tack on to the list. "Those are my demands," she says finally, lips quirking at the word *demands*.

I lean back in my chair, crossing my arms again. "I get a pass."

Her head tilts, and she squints at me again. "What?"

"On the questions. Some things I may not want to answer, and I can pass, but you can ask another question in its place."

"Acceptable. One pass per day. I'm not going to ask super uncomfortable questions."

What she doesn't realize is ALL questions are uncomfortable to someone like me who has barbed wire fence and KEEP OUT signs posted with guard dogs patrolling the property.

"You can ask me questions too if you'd like," she says with a shrug.

When I only stare in response, I can see her embarrassment as a flush creeps up her creamy skin. It's a good look on her, but I feel guilty for causing discomfort. I hate a lot of things, but being embarrassed is right up on top.

"Thank you."

If she realizes I'm not agreeing to ask her questions, she doesn't show it. Instead, the flush deepens in her cheeks as she smiles.

"Then it's settled. I accept your offer if you accept my terms."

I pause, somehow needing the tension to stretch between us before I answer. "I accept."

Winnie nods, but then the smile slides from her face, and she taps her mug with one fingernail. "Also," she says, and the way she won't meet my eyes makes my nerves fire up. "I wanted to say I'm sorry for messing with you."

She glances up at me, her eyes so clear, so blue in the morning light. For just a moment, I'm lost in them.

My mom used to keep a wooden puzzle box on her

bedside table. When she got sick, I would sit in bed with her, sliding the pieces in just the right way to reveal the hidden compartment. Mom placed a smooth blue stone in the hidden compartment, a prize for solving the puzzle. The stone was the exact color of Winnie's eyes. A thread of some emotion I can't name pulses once, then twice, through me.

"You're sorry for making the fake sites?"

Winnie tilts her head, a small smile playing on her lips. "No. I still think they were hilarious." She sobers, and the sincerity in her eyes makes my breath hitch. "I'm sorry for showing your family first and for showing you last night. I could tell you were tired and edgy, maybe tired of people? I knew it wasn't the right moment to joke with you. I should have waited."

Her perceptiveness, once again, slices right through me. I have to wonder if there's anything about me Winnie doesn't see. But because I don't exactly want to confirm just how right she is, I simply nod. "Collin and I practically forced you."

"Still. I could have said no. I should have waited until the next day and caught you at a different moment. Maybe then you would have found it funny."

Maybe. Not at first, but once I realized they were fake sites, which I probably would have at a different time. One where my brain didn't feel so full and my thoughts so overrun after a night with other people.

"You assume I have a sense of humor."

Winnie smirks. "I think there's one buried under there somewhere."

"Don't think you can try to excavate it. Or try to find some soft and gooey center. It doesn't exist."

"Or maybe it's buried so deep you don't even know it's still there."

"I'm not burying anything."

"Oh, James," Winnie says, her voice deceptively soft. "We're all hiding something."

What are you hiding? I almost demand. But I don't want to know. Because asking the question would be like admitting I'm hiding things too. I am—of course, I am, who isn't?—but we aren't going there. Not today. Not ever.

Winnie is my *employee*. Nothing more. Never more.

Setting down her mug, Winnie gets to her feet, holding out her hand. I don't move, and she rolls her eyes.

"We can do this the easy way or the hard way. I'm happy to call my lawyer and have her draft this in writing. You can call your lawyer and we'll be all official. Or we can just shake and trust each other."

The idea of bringing Thayden, our family lawyer and somewhat friend, into this makes me shudder. The man finds endless amusement in our family's business. From my dad buying a town to Pat entering a marriage of convenience turned real thing, he'd be all over this kind of contract. He'd zero right in on the part about the questions, and I'd never hear the end of it.

I stand. In her bare feet, Winnie is dwarfed by me. A zip of satisfaction shoots through me, likely some vestige of early man and the drive to protect, to be big and strong.

That's all it is. Biology. Survival of the fittest. Nothing more.

I clasp Winnie's hand, wishing I didn't feel her touch move through my body the way the blush crept up her neck moments ago. Only our hands touch, but I feel Winnie *everywhere*.

This is a terrible idea.

I know it, and yet I shake on it anyway. I try not to focus on the way her hand, small but strong, disappears into mine, how it feels to stand so close, to have our palms brushing. If I don't acknowledge the zip and hum of awareness buzzing through me, it does not exist.

"We have a deal," I say, telling myself it's professional, just professional, knowing as my lower back begins to sweat that my lies aren't even convincing to myself.

It's not until I'm driving home, skin still buzzing and mind a hot haze, that I realize I never actually apologized.

TEXT THREAD

James: Be ready at 7:30

Winnie: Hello to you too. How was your day?

Winnie: 7:30 as in twenty minutes from now, or 7:30 tomorrow morning?

James: Tomorrow.

Winnie: For???

James: The conference

Winnie: You decided I'm allowed to go???!!?

James: Check your email

Winnie: Wow! You got me a room and everything! Unless … are we sharing a room?

James: NO

James: You have your own room

James: We are staying in separate rooms

Winnie: Got it. You really, really don't want to share a room with me. Not surprised, given how you avoided me today.

James: Not avoiding you. Just busy

Winnie: Sure, boss. Sure. Too busy to answer my question.

You saw it, right? I wrote it on a chalkboard window, salvaged from your very warehouse.

James: I seem to remember telling you to throw it away

Winnie: That was before you fired me and rehired me. Doesn't count.

Winnie: Oh! And I caught three cats today with the help of Big Mo. I swear he's like the Pied Piper of feral cats. That's almost all of them.

Winnie: The only one I can't catch is the orange cat with only one eye. He taunts me.

James: Steak, medium rare.

Winnie: WHAT? You want to eat cats?!!?!!?

James: Don't be ridiculous

James: You asked my favorite ice cream flavor

Winnie: That was HOURS ago! And ... your favorite ice cream flavor is steak? That's about as gross as the idea of cat steaks.

James: You're disgusting

Winnie: Um, YOU'RE disgusting. You like steak ice cream.

James: I don't like ice cream. I prefer steak to ice cream.

Winnie: Blasphemy! Do you even have a soul?

James: Outlook not so good. Try again later

Winnie: Magic 8-Ball! Nice!!!

Winnie: *gif of Magic 8-Ball*

James: I like your updates on the site. I have a few tweaks we can go over on the way to Austin tomorrow.

Winnie: Yay! Also, you need to tell me about the conference. What should I be doing? Are we going to the same sessions? Divide and conquer? Any vendors we need to talk about? I looked at the list online the other day and made some notes.

James: Stop texting. Go pack

Winnie: You're no fun, Mr. Steak Ice Cream.

Winnie: I bet that's a thing somewhere. I'm going to find it. Now I know what to get you for your next birthday.

James: Please don't

James: Pack

Winnie: Should I make a road trip playlist?

James: It's a forty-minute drive

Winnie: A short playlist?

James: NO

Winnie: Ugh. Has anyone told you today that you're the worst?

James: Several people. GO PACK

CHAPTER 12

James

I'м glad I'm wearing sunglasses in the morning so Winnie doesn't see the way my eyes practically bug out of my head as she comes skipping down the sidewalk with a massive rolling bag, followed by a much less enthusiastic Chevy.

Winnie is wearing jeans. The sight hits me like a punch to the gut. All the air leaves my lungs in a sudden *whoosh*.

A woman in jeans shouldn't be any man's Kryptonite. It's just denim. A boring, basic fabric. But there is something so sexy about a woman in jeans. And because of her penchant for wearing clothes time-warped from the 1950s, this is the first time I've seen Winnie in them.

Her look is still very much her, only a little more casual, a little edgier. Her jeans hug her legs, ending at a cuff below her knee, right at the top of her clunky black boots. The boots are not unlike mine, the biggest departure from Winnie's usual heels, but they somehow really work.

Her top is a crisp white button-down, knotted at her waist with the sleeves rolled almost to her elbows. A bright turquoise tank top peeks through underneath. Her glasses are in place and her hair is in her signature high ponytail, a turquoise bandana knotted around it.

I never notice details like this about *clothes*. And yet here I am, still cataloging Winnie's outfit when she throws open the passenger door.

"Hi, boss. Where should I put my bags?"

My tongue seems unable to detach from the roof of my mouth, so I hitch a thumb over my shoulder, indicating the back seat.

What was I thinking, inviting her to the conference?

Part of it felt like a goodwill offering after firing her. I could tell Winnie wanted to go to the conference, and it seemed like a good way to get her some information on the industry without me having to hold her hand. Those are the main reasons I allowed myself to think about.

But there's more to it, more than I want to admit, even to myself.

As she disappears to throw her bags in the back, Chevy leans into the cab, eyeing me like every thought of his sister is on display. "Do we need to have another talk?"

Winnie bodily yanks him away from the truck. Not for the first time, I'm impressed with how much force she can command for her petite frame.

"You," she says, jabbing a finger into her brother's chest, "should never have had any kind of talk with *him*."

She points my way when she says *him*, and it's like she's talking about a disease. I choose not to be offended.

"There is nothing the two of you need to discuss when it comes to me. Do you understand? Nothing."

She swings her head to look at me. "James, are you interested in me?"

What a question for this early in the morning. Answering it feels like jumping rope through a minefield, but there's only one right thing to say, given the context. Mutely, I shake my head no.

Winnie turns back to Chevy. "See? And I'm not interested in him. Got it? No talks. Go arrest someone or something."

Hearing Winnie say she isn't interested leaves me feeling scraped out and hollow instead of relieved. I remind myself that I'm *not* interested in Winnie. There is attraction, yes. A grudging admiration. But she burrows under my skin like a tick, and that's not the quality I'm looking for in a woman.

You're also not looking for a woman, remember?

Chevy crosses his arms. "I wanted to do it. Dad would have."

Winnie freezes up at this, her whole body snapping tight. I know in our family, throwing Mom into any conversation is bringing in the big guns. Apparently, it's the same for Winnie and Chevy.

When the silence becomes too heavy, too painful, I locate my tongue and force it to work.

"We should go. Austin traffic is always horrible."

Winnie practically tosses herself at Chevy in a full-contact embrace. He stumbles back a step, barely able to extricate his arms from between them so he can hug her back. When he does, her feet lift off the ground so they're just standing there, holding each other. The toes of Winnie's boots drag in the dirt.

"I'd rather it be you than *him*," she says, and the distaste she uses referencing her dad has me confused.

What's that about? Did she and her dad have a bad relationship?

I file my questions away under Do Not Ask, Because You Do Not Care.

"Why would you—" Chevy starts, but Winnie shakes her head and wiggles out of his arms.

"Take care of yourself, big brother." She pats his cheek with enough force that it's almost a soft slap. "And now that you've gotten the talk out of your system, *never* do it again."

Winnie hops up into the truck and slams the door in a single motion. Almost immediately, she kicks off her boots, peels off her socks, and tucks her legs up in the seat. Her toenails are painted a bright pink.

I pull away from the curb, ignoring the way Chevy still stands there, eyeballing me even though Winnie essentially just told him to stop doing this. That's the thing about big brothers. We'll never stop being overprotective.

Having Winnie in my truck makes it feel as unfamiliar as a rental car. Her scent makes me want to stop by the diner and get a piece of pie. Or press my lips to the crook of her neck to see if she tastes as good as she smells.

NOPE. No, I do NOT want to do that.

I crack my window, but it doesn't help. And even though I've got my eyes firmly fixed on the road before me, I'm aware of every move Winnie makes. I'm like a workhorse in need of a good pair of blinders.

She fishes out a notebook and a pen from her purse. She uncaps it with her teeth and opens the notebook to a blank page and writes the date at the top. Her pen raps out a staccato rhythm that matches my heart, which has picked up speed.

Is she … going to take notes on our road trip? I shift in

my seat. The very comfortable, worn-in jeans I chose for the trip suddenly feel a size too small.

"I know we're on a schedule, but do we possibly have time to stop for coffee?" she asks.

"You seem fairly well-caffeinated."

"I've been up all night, so I'm kind of wired. But I didn't get coffee before I left."

"Everything okay?"

"Just couldn't sleep."

She doesn't say she was too excited, but she doesn't have to. I could see it in the way she skipped down the sidewalk, and I can see it now in the way she's smiling slightly, twitching in her seat. But I can also see signs of her exhaustion under the excitement. The dark circles under her eyes are slightly hidden behind her glasses, but definitely there. Her shoulders have started to slump, and while I'm trying to keep my eyes on the road, she yawns.

I hesitate, then gesture to the second stainless steel mug in the console. "For you."

Her response is dead silence. For two whole minutes—I check the clock—Winnie says nothing and does not move. Even the pen stops tapping on the paper.

"You brought me coffee," she says finally. A statement, not a question.

I wish I hadn't.

This morning, I was making a pot, so I thought why not double it? Why not offer an olive branch to hopefully maintain the peace?

The thing is, Winnie is acting like this mug of coffee is some amazing gift, like I showed up with a herd of giraffes or something.

Hesitantly, slowly, methodically, Winnie reaches out for the travel mug.

"It's just coffee."

She takes off the lid, looking inside. A flush rises in my chest. Because I didn't just make extra coffee, which was bad enough.

"You used heavy whipping cream." She sounds shocked. "Do you even have heavy whipping cream?"

I'm not about to admit I stopped at a convenience store, bought a carton just to add a big splash to her mug, then threw the rest away. I raise my eyebrows and glance over. "How do you know it's cream?"

"The color is different from just milk. I can tell. Wow. Thank you. This is surprisingly thoughtful."

"Surprisingly? You don't think I can be thoughtful?"

Winnie glances over. "I guess it's not that. It's surprising you'd do something thoughtful for *me*."

Now, that just makes me feel bad. But also, I don't want Winnie reading into the gesture. There's nothing to read.

"You're a valued employee."

"I'm your *only* employee."

"Exactly."

Winnie takes a long sip of coffee, then puts it back in the cup holder and picks up her pen. "You said you wanted to discuss tweaks to the website."

"Right."

"But before that, I wanted to ask some questions about the conference. Like, what sessions are we going to attend?"

"You can look." I nod to the console between us, where I've printed up the schedule, marking the sessions I plan to attend. I feel strangely self-conscious as Winnie glances through my choices.

"Looks like you're sticking closely to the brewing track. Don't you already know a lot of this stuff? Wouldn't it make sense for you to alternate with some of the business sessions or the ones focused on running a brewpub and taproom?"

Winnie has a point. But I can't muster up any interest for sessions about things like brand-building, community outreach, or taxes and legal issues. "You're welcome to attend whatever sessions you want."

"Thanks, boss," she says, sarcasm layered heavily. But she pulls out her own program and a highlighter, glancing from mine to hers as she highlights sessions. "We can divide and conquer. I'll take one for the team and hit up some of the boring business things and then the social media and promotion. I actually enjoy that."

Winnie's talking more to herself than me. Or, at least, she starts that way. Then she turns in her seat, facing me as she lobs way too many questions at me, rapid-fire style.

"What are your goals for this weekend? What do you want to walk away with? Are there any particular vendors you want to check out at the exhibition hall? Other breweries or people you want to connect with? Are you going to any of the networking events?"

She continues with the questions, but I don't hear the individual words anymore. My head fills with white noise, Winnie's voice like a high-pitched whine cutting through it. My thoughts are racing by with a bright neon buzz, like those marquees in the stock exchange.

"James?"

I shake my head, trying to clear it. Cars have stopped at a red light in front of us, and I have to tap my brakes a little harder than necessary to stop in time. Winnie grabs the handle above the window to steady herself.

"Sorry," I mutter.

She chews on the end of her pen for a moment before asking. "Too much?"

"Yes."

"Sorry. I can be a bit … enthusiastic."

That's one word for it. Her barrage of questions, at least, before they became too much for me to track, sent me into a mental spiral of all the things I have left to do for Dark Horse, things way outside my wheelhouse. All the things it will take to turn my very small single-person-brewing operation into a full-fledged ten-thousand-plus barrel business.

I'd hoped to walk away from the conference feeling more secure, but I'm going to walk into it overwhelmed. Someone honks, and I realize the light turned green with me still sitting here. I pull forward, lifting a hand to wave an apology. The driver behind me waves back, but then passes me, zooming by. I realize I'm clenching my teeth and try to relax.

"Let me dial it back," Winnie says.

"I'd appreciate that." My voice sounds sharper than I mean to, but my skin feels tight and hot.

Winnie reaches into her bag and pulls out a few sheets of printed paper. I can feel sweat starting to bead on my forehead. I roll my window down a bit more and a gust of wind fills the car, blowing Winnie's papers around. She grabs for them, and I roll the window back up a little and turn up the air conditioning, directing the vents toward my face.

"Let's start with the schedule and go from there," Winnie says, straightening the papers. "Today there's a welcome reception in the exhibition hall after check-in. Then the welcome keynote from the head of the Craft Brewers Association, followed by …"

It was a mistake to bring Winnie here. Maybe to re-hire her. And not just because she's tempting in ways I don't want to consider. It's this—the go-getter attitude and the overachieving. I know she's trying to be helpful, but it's too much. Way too much. None of this is in her job description. I don't need someone planning out my conference schedule, telling me what I should or should not attend, which is what she's doing now.

"You may want to talk to someone about insurance if you haven't already. And the session on expanding production is probably—"

"Winnie."

"Yes?"

"Stop."

I don't look, but I can sense her frustration without seeing it in her face. "You don't want to talk about the different sessions so we can figure out which ones we should attend?"

"No."

"So, which ones should I go to?" she asks.

"Whatever you want."

"And you're going to go to—"

"Whatever I want."

"I see." She pauses, shuffling the papers into a neat stack before putting them back in her bag. Then, she seems to change her mind and pulls one of them back out. I can see it's been highlighted in different colors with notes scrawled in the margins. "As far as vendors to talk with, do you think—"

"Winnie." My head is pounding now, and I try to remember if I packed any ibuprofen. "Enough."

"I'm just trying to help." Her voice is soft, and the vulnerability there should soften me toward her.

Instead, it makes me snap. Because she's not just helping, she's micromanaging. She's sticking her fingers in all the areas of my business, making me question myself, question what I need to do. I'm already stressed about all of those things. It's too much talking. Too many ideas. Stepping too far over the bounds of her job parameters.

"Your help isn't helping."

Winnie doesn't respond but closes her notebook and folds her hands in her lap.

"Just do what you want," I say.

There's that tone-of-voice problem, rearing its head again. I meant this as my way of freeing her up to enjoy the conference, to attend the sessions that interest her—while also not worrying about me. Instead, it sounds dismissive and rude.

I could say something. I probably should say something. At the same time, I don't want to give Winnie any illusion that I'm really going to let her into the inner workings of my business. I did agree to listen and consider her suggestions, but she doesn't need to know that consideration isn't really going to happen.

She's still a temp. Until she gets a new job or sells her app or whatever. It wouldn't be right to make her feel like she's actually a part of things, or that I need her help. I don't want or need her fluttering around with her notebook and her highlighted papers and her questions and her sexy jeans.

For a few minutes, the car is silent, the air filled with an unspoken argument, as though if either of us did speak, we'd be shouting.

I switch on the radio. "Do you like country?"

Winnie shrugs, and it drives me nuts that I can't tell if it's a shrug that means she does like it, she doesn't like it, or she hates country music and also my guts.

Probably option number three. And as Luke Bryan croons about women and whiskey and Winnie sits stiffly beside me, we make our way toward Austin, every mile seeming like a bigger and bigger mistake.

CHAPTER 13

Winnie

WHY IS it that when James acts like he doesn't need my help, it only fuels my desire to show him EXACTLY how much he does?

At some point, I need to cut my losses and give up. But this is not that point. Right now, standing in the lobby of the hotel and conference center, I'm doubling down on making him see how much help I can be.

I got mad in the truck, or maybe hurt is more like it. I'm sure some of my delicate emotional state was due to Chevy bringing Dad up just before we left. I hate talking about Dad or thinking about Dad or being forced to hear someone else talk about Dad. I'd like to enact a permanent Dad-ban on my life. Especially when I then have to sit in the cab of a truck and listen to James Graham dismiss me like I'm nothing.

This morning kind of sucks. The excitement I had about

this trip has deflated like a discarded party balloon. I'm trying to recover, trying to focus on my new goal of becoming indispensable to the man who seems like he wishes he'd left me by the side of the road. Or maybe back in Sheet Cake. I'm honestly not even sure at this point why he brought me along.

The stuff with my Dad is always going to linger. It's fine. I can shove it into a dark corner where it belongs. As for James, I don't need to take anything personally. He is frequently short and snappish with people, and I don't always think it means he's mad or thinks they're dumb. He's just … like this. So, I'm not going to be offended or put off by what he said on the drive. I'll simply prove my worth.

Val, who is obsessed with the enneagram, would say this is because I'm an eight—the challenger. That's her unofficial assessment of my number, anyway, since I won't take the test. (Which she says also affirms my eightness.) Whatever the reason, I'm determined to learn everything I can at the conference, make a connection with as many essential vendors as possible, and walk out of this weekend with a whole arsenal of things to make Dark Horse succeed.

Not just because I love a challenge. I actually found myself excited about the sessions and the conference as a whole. I thought of this job as something to keep me afloat until I find something else or sell Neighborly, but I'm honestly more interested than I have been about anything in a long time.

The hotel in downtown Austin is teeming with people, not unlike the ant farm I tried and failed to keep alive when I was a kid. Apparently, in addition to the Craft Beer Conference, there's some kind of multilevel-marketing convention peddling leggings—at least, that's my guess based on the sea of blinding colors and dizzying patterns on legs of all shapes and sizes.

Then there's the Junior Clowning Coalition. If you thought adult clowns were creepy, you just haven't seen a child in full sad-clown makeup miming being trapped in a box. Or a teenager with white makeup pancaked over acne.

If the creepy kid clowns are known by their face paint and the MLM boss women by their leggings, I'm guessing the craft brewers are the big group sporting flannel and beards. There are a few fancy mustaches mixed in, the kind where the ends are delicately curled, probably with some high-priced product called Stache Wax. But so far, James is the only man I've seen with stubble-free cheeks.

"What's the holdup?" I ask James, as he's turning a snarling face away from the reception desk.

"Room mix-up," he grumbles.

With a teasing smile on my lips, I lean close—ONLY so he can hear me, NOT because I love the way he smells. "Worried we'll be stuck in a room with one bed?"

James jerks back like I've just pressed a cattle prod to his skin. "What?"

I realize my mistake the instant he moves away. James Graham doesn't read romance novels. He probably can't even spell romance. For sure, the man doesn't know why the only-one-bed thing is, well … a THING. By the shocked and somewhat horrified look on his face, he gets the gist of what I meant, and he does not like the idea. At all. I remember his texts insisting we weren't sharing a room, and it's hard not to laugh.

Clearly punctuating every word, he says, "We are not sharing a room. Or a bed."

The word *ever* isn't spoken, but I hear it as clearly as though James shouted it. I want the bowels of the earth to open like a giant mouth and swallow me whole. Does he have to be SO horrified?

James turns his snarly face back to the woman behind the desk, and I shrink away, letting myself get distracted by pint-sized clowns juggling white plastic eggs. One of them drops an egg, which splatters all over the modern hotel carpeting.

Okay, so NOT plastic eggs, then. They shrug, step back away from the yolk, and continue juggling, leaving the mess for someone else to handle.

"Let's go." James brushes past me, key cards in hand.

His long legs eat up the stretch of ugly carpeting, heading for the two-story escalator at one end of the lobby. I scurry after him, trying to avoid a teenage clown tying balloons. One of them almost hits me in the face, and I duck out of the way. They're probably supposed to look like swords, but they all look like penises instead. And I'm not usually one to crack jokes about stuff like that. They really, really do NOT look like swords.

When I catch up to James, I'm snickering.

"What?" He raises one dark brow at me, and my laughter dies.

I consider telling James, but the man's sense of humor is severely underdeveloped. Plus, if he freaked out about me mentioning one bed, his brain might legitimately explode if I mention phallic balloons. "Nothing."

Glancing back down to the lobby, I watch the teen hand two of the balloons to an elderly couple. Is he just bad at this? Or does he know what they look like? As the elderly couple walks away, the boy gives a high five to another teenage clown.

Oh, yeah. He knows.

And that, ladies and gentlemen, is why you don't let teenagers make balloon art.

I choke on a laugh. James looks more than a little horrified now. "You like clowns?"

"They're not my favorite. But I guess they can be funny."

His gaze flicks down to the lobby and I take the opportunity to admire his clenched jaw, shaven clean just this morning, I'd wager. Is it bad I plan on keeping a mental tally on how fast his scruff fills in? A lock of his dark hair falls over one eye as James turns his attention back to me. Every time his hair falls across his face, I have to curl my fingernails into my palms to keep from brushing it back.

"Clowns are *not* funny," he says, looking horrified. "They're evil nightmare creatures."

Now I'm really laughing, clutching the rubbery moving rail of the escalator to keep from falling over. We reach the top before I can speak, and James practically has to drag me and my bag off.

"Those are just kids, James!"

"Even worse." He shakes his head. "I'm not sure I'll be able to sleep knowing they're in the hotel."

He visibly shudders under his leather jacket, and I bite the inside of my cheek, reminding myself how unpleasant this man is. How frustrating. Not funny. Not the kind of man I share smiles or jokes with.

He leads us to a bank of elevators, and my snickers return when just before the doors close on our car, a clown child and his mother rush in, followed by a large group of legging ladies.

James and I are squished into the back of the elevator. He reaches around one of the women to jab the number ten. When one of the ladies brushes against James, definitely on purpose, I do my best not to tell her to back off. The look James gives her does just that, and I have to look down at my boots to hide my grin.

"That's our floor!" the clown mom says, as though this is the most interesting coincidence ever. She's wearing a shirt that literally says, Proud Clown Mom. Her daughter, probably around Jo's age, looks right at James and squeezes her red nose. When it makes a honking sound, James jumps. I bite the inside of my cheek to keep from laughing.

As the legging ladies begin loudly gossiping about their upline, I lean toward James, whispering, "I've heard if you make eye contact with a clown while they honk their nose, they can steal your soul."

His immediate expression is horror, but it slips into an angry mask when he realizes I'm barely holding it together. He gives me a nudge with his shoulder, and I nudge him right back, a little harder.

"Don't worry. I'll keep you safe, Jamie."

He glares, a rumbling growl coming out of his chest. I didn't think growling was a real thing guys did. But it most definitely is something James does. It's stupidly unfair how much I like it. It totally makes me understand the appeal of all those wolf shifter novels I see selling online. Maybe I need to pick one up…

The clown in front of us bursts into tears, clutching at her proud clown mom, who gives James a dirty look. I can feel the tension vibrating from his body like a motorcycle engine. Tears squeeze out of my eyes, and I know I'm shaking with laughter.

I half expect James to shove the few remaining people out of the way when we get off on the tenth floor, but he manages to control himself. Thankfully, the still-sniffling clown and her mom turn in the opposite direction. James moves like an Olympic speed walker down the hall. I don't bother chasing him. I'm sure he'll give me my room key at some point. Probably.

In my original reservation, I requested rooms on different floors. And no, I don't want to talk about why I thought that separation was a good idea.

Our new rooms are directly across the hall from each other. At least we're not sharing a wall and won't have one of those shared doors connecting the rooms. Based on his response in the lobby, James probably would have put a chair under the knob or dragged the dresser in front of it to keep me out.

I wave the card in front of my keypad and it flashes green. I wrangle the door open and shove my bags inside before turning back to James. "Should we meet up and go down together, or …"

He isn't listening, because he's fighting with the door and the key card. Based on the rising tension in his shoulders, the man is about to lose it. The angrier he gets, the faster he swipes his card and yanks on the door handle, always too soon, which resets the locking mechanism. The handle is about to break off in his hand.

I flip the deadbolt lock on my door to keep it from shutting all the way and stride over, snatching the card from James's hand, giving him a nudge out of the way with my hips.

"You're too impatient," I tell him, waving the card over the sensor. I wait until the little light flashes green and then turn the handle. "Ta-da! You just have to wait until—what is that *smell*?"

I drop the keycard to cover my mouth and nose, jumping back and away from the wave of putrescence wafting from his room. The door slams closed again.

"That's disgusting." James covers his mouth too, looking about ready to throw up.

I move away. If he barfs, I'm going to barf. My stomach is

as weak as a baby kitten. The smell alone has me halfway gagging. I keep my hand over my mouth until the feeling—and the smell—dissipates.

"This kid in my elementary school used to keep rabbits. That's what it smells like. A rabbit hutch. With one hundred rabbits making baby rabbits and some of them dying and no one cleaning it, ever." My own words make my stomach roll again.

"Did you see anything?" James asks.

I shake my head. "No. Should we go back down to the front desk?"

James clenches his jaw, then seems to decide something. "I'm going in."

"I don't think you should. What if someone died in there?"

"It didn't smell like death."

"It smelled *worse* than death. Don't go in there," I say, as James swipes the card over the door, this time doing it perfectly. "James!"

He glances back at me once like he's saying goodbye before he charges into the room. I step way back as the smell again permeates the hallway. What if the smell *is* death? What if someone was murdered in there? What if James never comes back out?

I barely have time to worry, because James comes barreling back into the hallway, his shirt pulled up over his mouth and nose. It's a shame the smell is so terribly awful, because I barely get to examine the abs on display. James bends over, definitely dry heaving now. My own stomach clenches and rolls. I turn my back on James, giving myself a very strong pep talk.

Stay strong, tummy. Everything is fine. Think of flowers and the smell of the ocean and James's cologne.

Okay, maybe not that last one.

"It's so bad," James says, clearly done with gagging. "So. Bad."

"But what *is* it?"

He only shakes his head. "I can't even—no. Just, you don't want to know." His gaze darts back to the door, and he rubs his eyes, like he's trying to scrub whatever image is now in his brain.

I'm dying to know. But then I look at his face again. Maybe I DON'T want to know.

While James is down in the lobby, I check the closet for murderers (duh) and unpack my clothes and portable steamer, wishing I'd brought a hanging bag to keep things from getting wrinkled. But I didn't want to appear too high maintenance. Even if I kind of am.

I'm lying on the king-size bed, checking email, when James knocks. The moment I open the door and see his face, I know what he's going to say. I let him in and he paces for a minute before turning back to me.

"There are no more available rooms," he says. "They're going to clean it but …" He makes a face, then shoves his hands in the pockets of his jeans, staring down at the carpet.

Guess I'll be getting that one-bed trope after all.

Gulp.

CHAPTER 14

Winnie

"AND WHAT PRODUCTION level are you looking at?"

I don't even know what measurement a brewery uses for production? Bottles? Fluid ounces? Barrels? Mississippis?

The man with the strong Minnesota—Minnesotan?—accent waits patiently as I fumble for an answer, silently cursing James for not supplying me with the most basic of information about his business.

After destroying any fears—or hopes—of the whole one-bed thing by insisting he'd leave later and stay with Tank tonight, James told me to head down to the conference while he made a few phone calls from the room. It's now been over an hour with no sign of the man. He missed the welcome reception and the opening keynote. Or—he's here somewhere, hiding from me.

Then again, it might be that the man hates crowds so much he's hiding from *everyone*.

I've been killing time in the exhibition hall before the morning breakout sessions, trying to make connections with some of the vendors.

"I'm not actually sure about production levels or even what equipment we'll be using," I answer. "I just started working here."

"Want me to talk through the equipment we have for various levels?" His voice is kind, even though it's totally and completely idiotic for him to be spending time talking to someone who doesn't know the most basic thing like how much beer James plans to brew.

"If it's not too much trouble, I'd love to hear about the different options."

With a nod, the rep begins talking me through brewhouse systems, which are more complicated than I'd imagine. All the stainless steel tanks look alike to me, but I furiously scribble notes in my notebook, asking questions when I have them, all the while wishing my boss had at least let me know basic stuff. Just little things like how much he plans to brew per year and what specific kinds of tanks we'll need. Because it would be too simple for them all to be alike. No, if James makes lagers, there are horizontal tanks to speed up the process. There's even a fruit crusher if he brews fruit or sour beers. I don't even have a list of all the beer James brews.

He's probably already ordered equipment. Right? I try to remember what James said when the contractor came. He had a general area where the brewing equipment would go, because he mentioned needing to add floor drains. But I can't recall what he said specifically about the brewing tanks.

My lack of knowledge about the industry in general and our brewery specifically is embarrassing. I feel this even more keenly because I'm one of only a few dozen or so women in the exhibition hall. It's a bro fest as much as it's a beer fest, and I know there's an automatic assumption I don't know much. In this case, it's true.

Still, I press on. Because I want to prove James wrong. Even if I'm feeling angrier with the man by the second.

First, for what he said in the truck. I got over it. Then I decided I'm not over it.

Second, for making me feel unimportant and also kind of disgusting because he can't handle sharing a room that, yes, only has one bed, but also has a perfectly acceptable pullout couch. There's no need for him to stay with Tank tonight. Austin traffic is the worst, and it doesn't stick to the normal rush-hour times. The highways are always backed up, and the downtown streets are just as bad, with cars everywhere, cyclists, and now idiot tourists on electric scooters.

The most obvious and practical thing would be for the two of us to share a room. But nooooo. James can't handle being trapped in a room with me.

Finally, I'm furious with him for giving me exactly zero relevant information about his business, making me look and feel stupid.

The thing is, I'm actually enjoying this. The more vendors I talk to, the more I find myself wanting to know. I'm taking notes for James, sure, but for myself as well. I've caught the excitement in this place. I pick up snatches of conversation with lingo I don't know, making notes about unfamiliar words I'll google in the privacy of my room tonight.

It's not just about James and the push-pull I feel with him. Being here has leveled up my excitement about Dark Horse.

Too bad James doesn't care if I'm excited or not.

After thanking the man for explaining the varieties of

brewing tanks (of which there are apparently *many*), I grab his card, then head to one of the tables serving beer samples. These are much more popular than the vendor tables, which has worked well for me, since I'm trying to get as much information as I possibly can. I've already scrawled five pages of notes.

I finally make my way through the line and grab a beer in a plastic cup. I forget the name as soon as the man says it but remember the descriptions as light and hoppy. I take a sip and try not to make a face. I'm not sure I like light and hoppy.

I drop the cup in the trash and move on to another vendor, scanning for James like I've been doing the whole time. Where is he? I did give him a room key since his bags are up there. Maybe he's hiding out in the room. Or maybe he's here somewhere, totally avoiding me, ducking behind booths to stay out of sight. That seems more likely.

I visit the table of the largest US supplier of hops and yeast, then an insurance company's booth. There are way too many worst-case scenarios to list, but I scrawl down as many as I can, all the while hoping James has insurance.

I'm drawn to the booth of a company who prints labels for cans and bottles, checking out vibrant designs from their current clients. There are examples in metallic, glossy, matte, and embossed for the cans and varying kinds of paper for bottles.

"Do you do the designs in-house?" I ask, running my hand over one of the glossy metallic labels.

"Usually, people come to us with their own," the woman behind the table says. She looks a little older than me, but her hair is almost pure white and hangs down to her waist. It's stunning. "We have a few people on staff to work with simple things like resizing, but no actual designers. Are you looking for cans or bottles?"

Great question. *So, James—are we using cans or bottles?*

"Cans now, but we might expand to bottles." I'm taking a wild guess here. Cans seem like they'd be cheaper to start with, right? The woman nods, so maybe I guessed correctly.

Does James already have designs in mind? Has he hired someone? Design isn't my top skill, but I like to dabble the same way I dabble in so many things. He seemed to like what I did for the site, but he didn't specifically tell me if he liked the logo mock-up. If he does, I might be able to save him from hiring a graphic designer. First, I'd need to know the kinds of beers, the names, and what style of design James is looking for. All of this will require talking for more than two minutes and in more than two syllables, which at this point, seems unlikely.

"This one is ours." A woman with short, dark hair steps up next to me, handing me one of the labels. It's metallic and trippy. Honestly, it makes me feel dizzy, like the room is spinning around me.

She leans closer and whispers, "So terrible, right?" A laugh bursts out of me, and she grins. "I'm Kyoko."

I shake her hand. "Winnie."

"I think we should be friends. Because we don't have beards, for one. And you have killer boots. We can stick together and fight the beertriarchy—that's patriarchy plus beer—together."

"Sounds perfect."

Looping her arm through mine, she starts to pull me away. The woman at the table holds out the label. "You can keep this, if you'd like."

"Sure. Thank you." Kyoko smiles and takes the label. "That company is great to work with for labels. My bosses, on the other hand, are horrible. They don't listen to anything I say, yet sent me here alone."

"Sounds familiar. Bosses suck."

"One more thing we agree on." Kyoko tosses the label in the nearest trash can. "I want to grab some coffee before the breakout. Any more beer and I'll fall asleep. Can I snag you some?"

"Please." I pause by a high-top table. "I'm going to be right here, taking notes."

Kyoko pats my head. "A little nerdling. Love it. Be right back."

She disappears behind a wall of mustachioed flannel, and I pull out my notebook. I'm grateful to have a buddy. Already, the tension in my chest has eased somewhat. Who needs James? I've got Kyoko. Which means I've got a person who may not mind answering my millions of questions.

"Are you a reporter?"

I glance up from my notebook, adjusting my glasses with my free hand. The guy grins, leaning on the table a little closer to me than I'd like. He has golden-brown eyes, olive skin, and dirty blond waves. I guess he'd technically be classified as attractive.

But he's wearing the kind of amused, patronizing look I truly hate. It's the *Aw—Isn't that cute, a woman trying to figure out man stuff!* look. It's the same look I get when I take my car to a mechanic that isn't someone I personally know. I also got it during college when I decided to play guitar. Any time I went to the guitar store, I had to deal with this kind of look.

"Nope." I close my notebook and shove it back into my bag, looking for Kyoko. "Not a reporter."

He snaps his fingers like he's having an *aha* moment. "An influencer?"

"Also incorrect."

"You sure?"

"I think I know who I am."

Though I have zero idea what my title is. I guess I can always say I work for Dark Horse. That about covers it. I don't even have a job title. But I don't need to tell this guy anything. He smells like beer and drugstore cologne and keeps giving me that I-want-to-be-punched look.

"Okay, then. I'm Carl. And you are …?" He tries to peer at my lanyard, but it's turned backward. He reaches for it, which means he's essentially reaching for my chest.

I react instinctively and am about to smack his hand when a much larger hand grasps Carl's wrist, yanking it away. I recognize the rumbling growl before I recognize the hand.

James. I shouldn't feel so giddy at his sudden and unexpected protective side. It's not like I *need* a rescue. I'm used to handling myself. But after getting the complete cold shoulder today, I'm not going to complain about James swooping in. Especially not if it means Carl goes away.

James drops Carl's hand. "No."

Just *no*, like the guy now rubbing his wrist is a dog who tried to steal a hamburger off the counter. It takes no small effort not to beam at James. I'm pretty sure he'd disappear in a puff of smoke if I did.

"We were just talking," Carl says. "She doesn't need a guard dog."

James assesses me with a brief glance, and I cannot for the life of me read the expression in his dark eyes.

"I'm sure she could handle you on her own. But that doesn't mean she should *have* to. Leave."

If I liked the way James stepped in to physically protect me, I love his verbal defense even more. I have a theory. It's that every woman has two fantasies—one where she's

157

rescued by a dashing hero, and one where she doesn't need a hero at all and rescues herself.

James just delivered both these fantasies to me on a silver platter.

The impact this has on my heart is devastating. All the anger and frustration I've built up dissipates and turns to dust.

James crosses his arms and looms over Carl. I try not to look wildly enamored, but I feel like I'm turning into a real-life heart-eye emoji.

Holding up both hands, Carl backs away, shooting us both narrow looks. His attention dips to James's name tag and recognition crosses his features.

"James Graham," he scoffs. "The failed football player who thinks he can brew beer."

"Hey!" I lunge toward Carl, not even sure what my plan is, only that I never stand by when someone goes after one of my friends.

James gets a fistful of my shirt and yanks me back against his hard chest. As much as I'd still like to chase down Carl and make him regret his words and bad taste in cologne, I really do NOT mind being hauled up against James.

James says nothing, and I close my eyes for half a second, feeling his breath on my hair. I could stay here all day. Who needs a hotel room? I've got James Graham's broad chest. It's better than a penthouse suite.

Almost immediately, he takes a big step back. I pretend I'm not internally weeping. Instead, I watch as Carl is absorbed into a crowd of guys who all have handlebar mustaches. Every single one. I'd like to make them line up according to length, but they probably wouldn't appreciate it.

James and I are now left standing together in the crowded room, just outside the rows of vendor tables. Though there is a dull roar in the room, our little bubble of silence feels loud. And maybe a little awkward after the whole full-body contact incident.

I consider various responses and decide not thanking James is the best option. Eyeballing his black button-down shirt, worn jeans, and motorcycle boots, I say, "I'm surprised they allowed you in here without the proper uniform. No flannel, no beard, no service."

James makes a sound that I almost think might be a chuckle. I try not to show my delight in getting any kind of reaction out of him.

"You're not in flannel either," he points out.

"Yeah. And I'm missing that darn Y chromosome. Still. It's been a productive morning already."

I watch as James's dark eyes sweep over the room, taking in the tables and the clusters of people with plastic beer cups in hand. His eyes are wary, and I don't miss the way his body shrinks away from the crowds.

He says nothing else, so I go on. "Though I've realized how much I don't know about Dark Horse's operations."

When James offers up nothing, I pull out the conference schedule. "You're hitting up the session about hops, right? Or are you going to stay here and network?"

He still says nothing. I don't know why I expected a little more from him after he stepped in with Carl. Guess we're back to him playing our respective roles of boss ignoring his sole employee and sole employee seething with resentment while trying to prove her usefulness.

It only makes his determination to shut me out more frustrating. I remember when I first met James months ago, I told Val and Lindy he would be trouble. I stand by that assessment.

"I'm going to Brand Awareness and Building a Social Media Presence," I tell him.

Still nothing. My anger mounts.

"Then I'm probably headed to the one on successful customer service and atmosphere. I think that will be helpful for when we open."

I said *we* on purpose, expecting James to bristle. One thing I've noticed for sure—James is not about the we. Dark Horse is an *I* kind of business. But even this doesn't elicit a response. I guess James only cares when the Carls of the world are encroaching.

As if to prove my point, James starts to back away. "See you."

I watch him duck out of the room just as Kyoko appears with two coffees. "Who was that hunk of man?"

"My boss."

Recognition passes over her face. "That's James Graham. James Graham is your *boss*?"

"Unfortunately."

"I hate to tell you, but you're not looking at him like you think it's unfortunate."

"Ugh. Can we talk beer and not bosses?"

Kyoko sighs. "If you insist. But I'm putting a pin in this conversation. What session are you going to now?"

"The brand and social media one."

"Me too! Fancy that. Let's go."

Kyoko hands me my coffee and we head for the doors. I spot James standing by the wall outside the exhibition area, looking at his phone. He glances up and I swear he sees me, but his gaze slides right by like I'm nothing.

And this is the same guy who just practically tore some guy's hand off for getting near me? As I follow Kyoko toward the conference room, I tell myself I really need to stop caring.

CHAPTER 15

James

I REALLY NEED to stop caring. No, that's not accurate. I never started caring. This isn't *care*. It's … *concern*. If I saw a guy trying to put unwanted hands on Harper—or any woman, for that matter—I'd step in if needed.

Okay, and maybe the guy was going for Winnie's lanyard, not grabbing her. But Winnie didn't look happy about him getting handsy.

Most guys would do something—wouldn't they? It means *nothing*.

Yet I can't stop replaying the moment over and over during my morning sessions. Some guy from some company is talking about supply chains, which apparently, I should be paying attention to. If I thought I knew all the things that could go wrong with Dark Horse, I was wrong. Shipping and sourcing on a bigger scale is a challenge.

My head gives a mild pulse of pain, right up top behind my hairline. The dull headache has only worsened through the day, despite buying ibuprofen at the tiny, overpriced store in the lobby. I swallowed them down with a warm beer sample, which was less than pleasant. So far, the pounding just keeps growing, matching the worries I have about expanding my business and the other worries about the woman who seems to have taken up residence inside my brain.

What session is she in now? Has that guy left her alone? If he has, is someone else bothering her?

Or maybe is someone else *not* bothering her? My ribs feel like they're constricting at the thought of seeing Winnie enjoying another man's company.

I'm startled by clapping and the sound of shuffling bodies. The session is over, and there's a mass exodus toward the double doors at the back of the room for lunch. People are mostly clustered in groups of three to five, many sporting T-shirts (under their flannel, of course) with their brewery logo. As I follow the herd alone, I feel an odd pang of … something I can't identify or maybe just don't want to.

The smell of Tex-Mex has my stomach rumbling. But I can already see the line snaking out the door of one of the larger conference rooms. The noise out here becomes like a living thing, and the crush of bodies bumping into each other, bumping into me, is too much. I move away from the big room hosting the lunch included with our conference ticket. I'm too hungry, too surly, and too over-peopled.

Winnie's probably in there, cozying up to strangers, making friends and taking notes in her little notebook like some sexy nerd librarian. Nerdbrarian—can that be a thing?

Absolutely not.

Forcibly shoving thoughts of Winnie out of my head, I

make my way downstairs to find more chaos, more people. You know what? Flannel isn't so bad compared to eye-blinding leggings and child clowns. This whole trip so far—from the way I hurt Winnie's feelings on the drive to the smell of my room (not to mention the whole one-room issue) to the guy hitting on her—it's all adding to the pain in my head. Whatever help I thought it might be to have Winnie here, the real estate she takes up in my head cancels it out.

I push through the lobby doors, taking in deep lungfuls of cold air. Better. Much better. The weight of worry eases a little now that I'm not in the midst of crowds. Hopefully, I can find a place within walking distance to eat. Almost directly across the street is what looks like a small pub. Even though it's lunchtime in the center of Austin, this side of the hotel is on a less busy street, one of many under construction, and I don't see a single person heading in or out. Perfect.

This illusion shatters the moment I walk inside to see Winnie. She's seated at a long table with three guys and one other woman, all wearing the same black shirts with Straight Shooter emblazoned on them. I pause, midstride, wondering if I can get back out the door before it swings shut behind me, before she sees me.

Too late.

Winnie's eyes have already found me, as though I've got some kind of homing beacon. After a sliver of hesitation, she lifts a hand to me. "James," she calls. "Join us?"

Maybe it's the tiny waver in her voice, the one I'm sure no one but me hears, which has me nodding. She sounds like she expects me to say no or simply walk away. There's that dagger in my chest again, the one telling me I'm a first-rate jerk.

I order a beer and a sandwich, all the while feeling the table watching me. I can hear them speaking in lowered voices. Winnie's probably telling them I'm ... what? How exactly will Winnie describe me to them?

Probably something like her grumpy boss who brought her to a conference only to abandon her while everyone else has a team.

I don't need a team, I remind myself. *And if I did, Winnie wouldn't be part of it. She's temporary.*

I don't need togetherness and matching shirts.

So, why do I feel so uncomfortable on the outside looking in?

As I reach the long table with my beer, Winnie scoots over on the bench seat, leaving me no choice but to sit next to her. I hang my jacket on a hook next to the table and sit down. A guy with a long ponytail is on Winnie's other side, and I feel a stupid surge of pleasure that she scoots a little away from him as I sit down. Of course, that means our thighs are touching. Our shoulders brush when either of us takes a breath. This will not be distracting at all.

Because I don't care.

"I see you also had the urge to duck and cover," Winnie says. When she turns to smile at me, our faces are much too close together.

"Yup."

"Great minds," she says, clinking her beer glass against mine. I don't clink back.

"James Graham." My name rolls a little too easily off the tongue of the woman across from me. It's practically a purr, and it makes my spine straighten.

I don't like it, because I immediately recognize it for what it is. I may not have ever had the fame or notoriety my dad and brothers did, but I'm known. And too many people, this woman apparently included, seem more than happy to grab what they can get.

"Everyone, this is James." Winnie jumps in with introductions, leaning forward on the table, forming a shield between me and the rest of the table.

I immediately forget all the names. Hopefully I can count on Winnie to carry the conversation. She does not disappoint.

"James," Winnie says, giving me a small smile that makes something shift in my chest, "is the owner and mastermind of Dark Horse Brewery."

The minute Winnie sits back, the woman across the table leans closer to me. She's punk-rock pretty with dark eyeliner, an eyebrow ring, and long platinum hair. Her name was something aggressively strange. Pleather, maybe? That can't be right, but that's the name stuck in my mind. She sends a flirty smile my way, which I do not return.

"I've heard good things about you. Where's your brewery, James?"

I tense. How did I not think of this moment? The one where I'd have to admit my brewery will be opening in a town with a name as ridiculous as Sheet Cake?

Winnie jumps in before I can speak, leaning forward again like a tiny little lineman protecting her quarterback. "He's based right here in Austin."

Not completely true, but not a lie either since my setup is still here in town. Winnie shifts closer to me, giving my arm a squeeze. She leaves her hand curled against my biceps. I'm not sure if it's because she senses my discomfort or because she's staking some kind of claim. Both seem unlikely, but I can't think of another explanation for her touch.

Either way, I don't hate it. Even though I want to. I feel

strangely grounded by her hand on me, warm even through my shirt.

"Nice," Pleather says. "We're in San Antonio. Not too far. Just a few minutes up the road. An easy drive."

I can hear the suggestion in her voice, the offer implicit in her words. Winnie's fingers tighten on my arm.

"We're aware of Texas geography," Winnie mutters.

Winnie is definitely staking a claim, then. Interesting.

"And you two ... work together?" the woman asks, her eyes flicking to Winnie's hand on my arm.

"Very closely," Winnie says, and I barely keep myself from breaking into a grin. Jealousy is a look I like a little too much on her. Especially when it's jealousy involving *me.* I stay quiet, happy to watch this play out.

"And what do you do?" the woman asks, taking a sip of her beer. She's very clearly undeterred and rather seems to be taking Winnie's actions as a challenge. I feel a little like a steak that's been thrown between two lions, and I'm not sure how I got here.

"A little of everything," Winnie hedges, and again I hear the uncertain note in her voice.

I think of how I told her on the way here I essentially didn't want her around. How I ditched her after check-in, heading downstairs almost as soon as she went inside her room. How I kept her in my sights in the expo hall, just so I could stay out of her line of vision.

Not just so you could stay out of her line of vision.

Fine. If I'm being completely honest, I enjoyed observing Winnie without her knowing. Total creeper behavior, I know. But despite myself, I find her fascinating.

And attractive.

Dude. How about we ease up on the honesty, subconscious?

166

Yes, it's no hardship to look at Winnie. But I found a sense of admiration growing as she approached tables, asking questions, putting people at ease, scribbling notes and cramming her bag full of promotional materials and business cards.

To be honest, she's probably done more than I have for Dark Horse at the conference so far. I spaced out in the two sessions I attended, either thinking about Winnie or stressing out about all the things I still have to do, things I don't know how to do.

"Ah," the woman says, her smile sly. "Kind of an assistant, then? Daniel, we should really think about hiring a secretary too."

Winnie's nails dig into me, and I'm thankful I've got on long sleeves.

The guy on Winnie's other side, who must be Daniel, says, "I think technically, that all falls under my task list. Are you saying I'm slacking at my job?"

The other guys laugh, but Winnie and Pleather or whatever her name is kind of just bare their teeth in poor attempts at smiles. The server arrives with our sandwiches and I miss the opportunity to say something—*anything*—to defend Winnie, to say how necessary she is to Dark Horse.

What would I say? Because she isn't necessary. I don't need her. A glorified assistant is pretty much what she is. Taking notes doesn't really fall too far outside the role of an assistant, after all.

When her hand falls away from my arm, I tell myself it's because Winnie needs to eat, not because she's upset I didn't stand up for her. I also tell myself I don't miss her touch on my arm.

But the same stupid part of my subconscious that keeps calling me out whispers that I'm bluffing.

As we eat, I settle into a silence just broody enough to keep people from shooting questions my way. Pleather finally gives up. I half listen as the conversation hovers around the morning sessions, different kinds of beer (which has Winnie looking like she wants to pull out her notebook), and the rooftop party tonight, which I totally forgot about, since I wasn't planning on attending.

That's my general stance on parties: NO.

"Are you going tonight?" I realize Daniel has asked this question of Winnie. And *only* to Winnie.

My back stiffens. I ball up the napkin in my lap, waiting for her answer. Winnie's eyes dart my way, then back to Daniel. "Oh, I don't know."

"Come on—it'll be fun."

He bumps his shoulder into hers, and she shifts closer to me. Without giving myself time to think about how stupid this is, I stretch my arm over the back of the bench, my fingertips resting lightly on Winnie's upper arm. She tenses under my touch, and I curl my hand more firmly around her shoulder, massaging gently. She releases a breath and relaxes against my arm.

"We'll be there," I find myself saying.

Because I *really* want to attend a party ... with Winnie, of all people.

Now I'm the one acting jealous, staking a claim. And because I tend to go all in whether I'm playing a game or making a mistake, I don't remove my arm.

Daniel scoots a little farther away from Winnie. "Cool. Yeah, we'll probably see you guys there."

When our table mates get up to leave a few minutes later, my arm is still behind Winnie's back, my fingers still cupping her shoulder. My fingertips are tingling, because my hand fell asleep a few minutes ago. The moment Daniel and his ponytail are out the door, I remove my arm, shaking out my hand.

Winnie scoots down the bench and crosses her arms. "Is this how it's going to be?"

"How what's going to be?"

"This whole possessive thing?"

"You started it with Pleather."

Winnie blinks at me for a second, then laughs, muttering, "Pleather." She digs in her pocket, pulling out a balled-up napkin and tries to hand it to me. I just shake my head. With a roll of her eyes, she opens it to reveal a scrawled name and number.

"I intercepted this, but it's none of my business. Heatherette, aka *Pleather*, tried to slip you her number."

Heatherette. I was sort of close.

"Take it," Winnie says.

"No."

"James."

"No."

"Fine." Winnie balls up the napkin and drops it in her empty beer glass. "You want to know why I was acting possessive? Before you got here, *Pleather* was already asking tons of questions about you and the famous Graham family. Apparently, she saw me with you earlier and was trying to make an inroad. I thought I'd save you from someone just interested in your name. Seems like the kind of thing you'd hate."

I do hate that. I really, really do. Still, I can't seem to find it in me to thank Winnie.

"So, what's your excuse? What were you protecting me from just now?"

I have no idea what possessed me to scare Daniel off … or

don't want to admit it. I shrug. "A man who doesn't know when to get a haircut."

Winnie stares for a moment, then laughs, sliding down in her seat, wiping her eyes underneath her glasses. "Classic. Are you going to tell me next to stay away from guys with beards? Because that would be half the conference."

"Guys with mustaches too."

"Good thing I came here to work, not meet some musta-chioed man to sweep me off my feet," Winnie says, and even the idea of her meeting a man has the back of my neck getting hot.

She slumps even farther down in the booth. "Too many fries," she says, groaning. "Why didn't you help me eat them?"

"You didn't ask." And I probably wouldn't have anyway, just out of principle. I'm uncomfortably full, and Winnie ate at least as much as I did.

I almost jump out of my seat when Winnie's hands deftly click open the button of her jeans. Immediately I avert my gaze. "What are you doing?" I hiss.

From my periphery, I see Winnie untuck her tank, covering the top of her unbuttoned jeans. "Relax. This is a common practice among women, James. Eat too much, unbutton your pants after a meal."

"No."

She laughs. "No, it's not a common practice, or no, I can't do it?"

"The second one."

"You may be my boss, but you're not the man in charge of my buttons."

The man in charge of her buttons. I'm on my feet instantly. My brain is filled with images of buttons, followed by zippers and—I need to instantly bleach this idea from my brain—being the one in charge of them all.

Just to note: Her shirt is all buttons, all the way down.

"No," I say again, thankful I've spent years working on my poker face. "Just … no."

As Winnie slides out of the booth, I manage to corral my thoughts into a place where buttons do not exist. I keep my eyes averted still as I grab my jacket.

"Sheesh, sorry. I figured with a sister, this kind of thing would be old news. I didn't mean to scandalize your poor, innocent brain."

"Harper is very particular about her clothing choices," I say. We head outside and start on the quick walk to the hotel.

Winnie groans again, patting her stomach. "I may go upstairs and change. Though I think the only thing I have more comfortable than jeans is pajamas. And I'm not wearing those."

"You're in luck," I tell her, holding open the lobby door, the same way I would for anyone else. "I think there are leggings for sale on the third floor."

Winnie turns around, walking backward and barely missing a young clown passing by on a hoverboard. "Why, James," she says, grinning and fluttering her lashes in an exaggerated way. "Did you just make a joke?"

I did, and like so many other things I've done today, it disturbs me. Because I don't make jokes. I also don't get jealous and act the way I've been acting. I most especially shouldn't be doing it with Winnie.

"I'll catch up with you later," I say, hopping on the escalator just before a group of women in matching purple zebra-striped leggings.

I don't see Winnie for the rest of the afternoon, but that doesn't stop me from constantly looking for her.

FROM THE NEIGHBORLY APP

Subject: Is it cancer or ebola?

SlimShabby
I have this spot that's red and inflamed. I thought maybe cancer but when I googled, it looks more like Ebola. Now I'm scared to see a doctor in case I spread the virus.
Does this look like Ebola?

Chels
Ew! It's not Ebola but definitely an infection. See a doctor. As soon as possible.

1BigBass
How do you know it's not Ebola? Are you a doctor?

BobToo
Looks like an ingrown hair.

Cal_45

Looks like my ex-wife

Vanz

Looks like a hairless cat

Danielle_L

Posting a photo of Possum Boots, our hairless cat, for comparison. That looks like a staph infection, not a hairless cat.

Cal_45

Also looks like my ex-wife

SweetPea43

Cal, I swear, I'm gonna key your car if you keep talking about me on here.

Cal_45

I said what I said

BagelBytes

Has Winnie stopped moderating Neighborly? I've reported this post several times for a NUMBER of reasons but no response.

SlimShabby

THIS IS A SERIOUS MEDICAL QUESTION. PLEASE TELL ME IF IT'S EBOLA. HERE'S ANOTHER PICTURE FROM A DIFFERENT ANGLE.

FanGirl12

I can't even tell what body part I'm looking at.

Vanz

You don't want to know what body part that is

FanGirl12

EWWWWWWWW!

Neighborly Mod

The comments on this thread have been closed and photos removed due to inappropriate content. Please remember to be kind and above all, Neighborly!

CHAPTER 16

Winnie

I'VE SETTLED on a perfect nickname for James: Houdini.

It's wild how a man easily a head taller and a whole lot broader than most everyone at this conference can manage to disappear. And I know he's here somewhere. Every so often I do catch a glimpse of his dark head, usually ducking away like he knows I've spotted him and he's trying to remain hidden.

Whatever, man. Give me whiplash with your back-and-forth. I care not.

I check my phone again for the time. And maybe to see if James has texted me. His bags are still by the door, but so far as I can tell, he hasn't been back up to the room. I'm not sure when he's going to Tank's house or if he's having dinner first.

More importantly, I don't know if he meant it about going

to the party with me. Based on what I know about his aversion to people, my guess is he has no plans of going.

And I'm not waiting for him.

When it's almost seven and the party has already started on the roof, I decide I don't care about James. James, who? I'm definitely not dressing for him in my tight black pants, sky-high heels, and favorite pink blouse. I put my hair in a signature high ponytail, curl the ends, and ride the elevator up to the roof. Alone.

Without mini clowns or legging ladies to distract me, my nerves build. I should have gotten Kyoko's number earlier. I lost track of her after the afternoon sessions and hope she'll be up there.

When the elevator doors slide open, I step off and spot Kyoko almost immediately. She waves like a maniac, her smile easing the tension in my chest.

"Winnie!" Kyoko grabs my arm and hauls me toward one of several bars set up around the patio. "Thank the stars you're here. It's a total bro fest. I was about to leave."

I snort and let her pull me over to one of the bars. "I almost went right back down to my room, so good thing you were standing there."

"What do you want to drink?"

What I WANT is something like a Tom Collins or vodka tonic, but because this is a craft beer conference, my choices are beer. Or other beer.

"Order for me? I don't know what I like, except less hoppy, please. Maybe a stout?"

Kyoko steps up to the bar. While she's ordering, I glance around. The rooftop has a heated pool in the center, the steam rising lightly off the surface. There are topiaries and larger potted plants giving it a garden party feel. Space heaters placed sporadically keep it from being too chilly, even with the light breeze. Some kind of indie rock plays through speakers I don't see, and the mood is raucous. If possible, there are even fewer women here than there were at the conference today.

I feel eyes on me and understand why Kyoko was about to leave before I got here. I won't last long, even with her. I'd rather risk a horde of legging ladies and go down to the lobby bar.

Of course, in my quick scan, I don't see James, not that I was looking. (I was totally looking.) He'd probably rather hang with the child clowns than attend a party. My guess is that he left his bags in the room in order to avoid me and just went back to Tank's house as planned.

"Here you go. I got you a coffee stout." Kyoko hands me a plastic cup with a wry grin. "Clearly, they spared no expense on the glasses. But I won't complain about an open bar."

I stuff a ten in the tip jar because very few other people seem to be tipping. My wallet cries out in protest, but I make it a silent promise that we'll get back on our feet soon.

We manage to snag a cabana area being vacated by a group of men who could be lumberjacks, claiming two cushioned lounge chairs. We kick off our shoes, laughing. Kyoko taps her glass to mine and we drink, the beer cool and rich on my tongue. Okay, I could get used to this. Before we start talking, I make sure to get her phone number. I'm sticking to her like superglue's stickier cousin for the rest of the conference.

"So, you want to give me a crash course in craft beer?" I ask, taking another sip. Yep—I'm a fan of coffee stout. "This is perfect, by the way."

She grins. "I saw how many cups of coffee you went through in the afternoon sessions. And you seem to have a thing for rich and dark." She winks, and I groan.

"Are you making a reference to my boss? Who is, might I remind you, my *boss*."

"Yeah, yeah. Where is he, by the way? I'm shocked he's not here since you are."

"I think you're confused. James is not here *because* this is where I am. The man has found a way to be everywhere I'm not all day."

I spot Daniel at that moment, and he lifts a hand, smiling in greeting, then starts to move our way, followed by a few other guys. *Oh, great.*

Kyoko, meanwhile, is laughing.

"What?" I ask.

"Honey, you may not have seen him, but James Graham had his eye on you all day. He was like some kind of ghoul, hanging in the shadows, always with you in his sights."

This thought, absurd as it sounds, makes my skin prickle with a strange awareness. "No way."

"Very much way. I noticed, even before I met you. Because the man is hard to ignore. Every time I saw him, he was totally focused on something across the room. You were that something, Winnie."

Daniel reaches us then so I don't have a chance to argue anymore with Kyoko, who is definitely wrong. She must have confused James with some other tall, dark, and broody male, not bearded or in flannel.

"Hey, Winnie," Daniel says, smiling as he runs his hand over his ponytail. It seems to be his nervous habit, one I noticed at lunch. It's kind of cute, just as Daniel, with hazel eyes and crooked smile, is kind of cute.

And I realize suddenly that James with his hot sulkiness has reduced perfectly attractive men to *kind of cute*. I am ruined.

"Daniel, this is Kyoko."

He says hello and introduces the other guys he's with. Without being asked, they descend, not unlike locusts. Or bed bugs. A few grab other chairs, dragging them over. Daniel sits down right on my chair, forcing me to move my legs over, and one of his friends does the same to Kyoko.

She and I exchange a glance, and I wish we had taken the elevator down when I arrived.

"Where's your, uh, date?" Daniel asks. "Or boss? I wasn't sure which he was."

You and me both, Daniel. You and me BOTH.

I shrug. "He has a way of disappearing."

When Daniel smiles, it warms his hazel eyes. I try to elbow James out of my head and see Daniel through untainted eyes. I'm not wild about the long hair, but he seems like a genuinely okay guy.

Do you want another okay guy?

Or a difficult, broody one who definitely doesn't like you?

I don't want a guy at all.

And that's the crux of it. I need to remember that simple fact. No men.

"His loss," Daniel says, then rubs a hand over his jaw. "I would say that I'd never let you out of my sight, but that would be cheesy, huh?"

"Cheesy, but not *terrible*," I offer, trying to find the fine line between friendly but nowhere near flirty.

Daniel laughs. "Is not terrible considered good?"

I'm grateful when Kyoko jumps in, steering the conversation to beer, which this group is happy to talk about. Loudly. I pick up what I can, making mental notes. The guys refill their beers once or twice as the evening wears on, but I sip mine, slow and steady.

"You're awfully quiet," Daniel says, leaning a little closer.

His hand drops to my bare ankle. As his face moves a little closer than I'd like, I realize how red-rimmed his eyes are and how strong the scent of beer is. His smile has definitely moved out of *kind of cute* territory.

"I'm not really interested in talking," I say.

"Me neither."

Daniel's hand slides farther up my leg, and I am officially *done*. I sit up, dislodging his hand and kicking my feet over the side of the lounge chair. I slip on my shoes and grab my bag. Kyoko gives me a little nod, and then her gaze flies to something behind me, going wide.

"I told you," she says, a smile breaking over her face.

I don't have time to see what she means because Daniel grabs my arm. I'm too distracted to shake him off, and whatever he's saying becomes like a gnat's one-note whine in my ears.

Because my heart is thudding like one of those giant orchestra drums, drowning out all other sound. James Graham has just stepped off the elevator, looking like some quintessential vengeful bad boy in his leather jacket and motorcycle boots. His hair falls over his eye, and I'm delighted to see that his clean-shaven jaw from this morning has disappeared under a layer of dark stubble.

James scans the crowd until his gaze lands and sticks right on me. I swear, the intensity in his dark eyes reaches all the way through my chest and grabs hold of my spine. When his gaze drops to where Daniel grips my elbow, the darkness becomes lethal.

I can't take my eyes off him as James stalks through the crowd, which parts for him. It should be terrifying, but it's dead sexy.

Daniel is the only one in our group who fails to notice

James, and by the time he reaches us, the other guys are gone.

"... okay, baby."

Daniel's voice comes into focus at those last two words. I have no idea what else he said or why he thinks he can call me baby, but it doesn't matter.

"Go." James says only one word, but it's a single syllable ranking at least a nine on the Richter scale. It causes a tremble in me, starting in my toes and working its way up to my heart.

Daniel, unfortunately, is a little slower to react. He turns, startling at the sight of James looming over us. Daniel's hand loosens but does not let go of my arm, and it's this point of contact James fixates on, not Daniel's face as he answers.

"Oh, hey, man. I asked about you earlier but—"

In a move that will forever be etched into my fantasies, James grabs Daniel, and like he's no heavier than a throw pillow, tosses him into the pool.

James turns away, totally dismissive, and holds out a hand to me. When I don't immediately respond, a low, rumbling sound comes out of him, rattling my chest like a tiny echo.

I'm a lot of things—awed, angry, confused, irritated, and absolutely turned on. But I slide my hand into James's larger one, and he pulls me to my feet with a gentle strength totally unlike what he just used to throw Daniel into the pool.

On the way to the elevator, as I scramble to keep up with James's long stride, he pauses long enough to direct a bearded man's attention to the pool. "Don't let him drown." The man nods quickly, eyes wide, and James continues tugging me along.

The elevator doors slide open, and though a whole group is waiting to get on, one look from James has them stepping back and away.

As the doors close, I settle on a single emotion—anger—and yank my hand out of his. Whirling on James, I give his impressive chest a shove, which moves him exactly nowhere. Because he's a Marvel superhero, not a mortal man.

"That was—this is—completely out of line!"

He crosses his arms, his eyes never leaving my face. A single muscle tics in his jaw.

"Half the time you ignore me. The other half, you're actively dismissing me. And then the rest of the time—and ignore my bad math because I know I'm over 100%—you're acting like some possessive beast who thinks he has some right to claim me!"

I'm breathing heavily when I finish shouting, and still, James stands there, expression infuriatingly blank.

"Well? Aren't you going to say anything?"

"I'm sorry."

"The least you could do is—wait, what?" I think my emotions must have shorted out my brain, because did James just apologize?

"I'm sorry."

Nope, there it is again. An apology.

"You're right," he continues, "and I'm sorry. For all of it."

As I try to dissect his soft words, for once devoid of all growling and grumping, and attempt to make sense of the sudden heat flaring in his eyes, James steps forward, crowding me against the elevator wall. His big, rough hands cup my cheeks with a tenderness that knocks the breath straight out of me.

"I'm sorry, Winnie," he says again, and I could listen to him say my name with that sweetness all day, every day, for the rest of my life.

His eyes drop to my mouth, and all the air leaves my lungs. "May I—" he starts to ask.

"Please."

And then my eyes flutter closed as James drags one hand into my hair and fuses his lips to mine.

CHAPTER 17

Winnie

Bliss. The kiss is sheer, complete perfection. A fifty or maybe hundred-and-fifty out of a possible high score of ten. No, make that a thousand out of ten. *Infinity.*

James's lips are softer than I would have expected, yet firm enough to completely direct mine, to urge them into compliance.

Not that I'm fighting him. Nope.

The kiss feels inevitable, like this is where we were always headed, despite my shock that it's actually happening.

James Graham is kissing me.

After *apologizing.*

But—more importantly, HE'S KISSING ME.

At first, his mouth is as tender as his hand is on my cheek, each brush of his lips sweet and gentle. It's as much a caress as a kiss, a gentle exploration, an extension of his apology, a request for forgiveness.

I'm not sure how long we're kissing before the elevator stops and the doors slide open. I start to pull away, but James says, "We're full," in that deep growly voice of his, and there's a rushed apology before the doors close again.

I yank him by the shirt back to my mouth, where he belongs. Where it feels like he was made to be.

The sweetness gives way to something a whole lot stronger. We're both more aware of the time limit. At some point, we'll have to get off this elevator and deal with what happened inside of it. But I'm in no way ready for that, so I focus all my attention on James.

The kiss becomes more of an argument, one made with lips and teeth and tongue rather than words. We're battling now, the push and pull we've had since the start of our relationship exploding into motion. James gives my hair a soft tug, and I scrape my nails over the back of his neck. He presses closer to me, and I press right back.

My glasses keep bumping his face and I rip them off, tossing them in the corner. Who needs eyesight? Not this girl.

James drops his hands to my waist, squeezing gently, and I drag my hands roughly through his hair. He growls against my mouth. I grab his shirt more tightly, yanking him around so he's the one with his back against the wall. He doesn't put up an ounce of fight, letting me control the speed and intensity of the kiss.

I slow things down. Wayyy down.

I want to savor the heat of his body, the bite of his stubble on my cheeks, the heavy press of his hands as they slide up my back. This is the most loose, the most unfettered and unguarded James has been since I've met him.

Except maybe when he was firing me.

And it's this thought that makes me want to enjoy every millisecond of this kiss, which I feel certain has an expiration date. James will flip the switch on me again, which will not be easy to take now that I've had his mouth on mine.

I give James everything I can in this kiss. There's no conscious thought as to why, only that this matters, *he* matters, and I don't want to hold back the way I always have with everything else in my life, with every*one*. I have never given anyone as much as I give James in this kiss.

It's risky. It's reckless. And I really don't care.

He pulls back just slightly, his pupils dilated, lips brushing mine as he says, "I can't tell you how many times I've thought about kissing your smart mouth."

Well, then.

"You say the sweetest things," I say before fusing my smart mouth to his again.

There's a jolt as the elevator reaches the lobby, and when the doors open this time, it's to an unignorable amount of noise. James and I jerk apart. We end up on separate sides of the small elevator car, both of us breathless. His eyes are practically black, but now, it's not with desire.

No—he looks panicked. My stomach bottoms out as the panic shifts into something more like regret. Which shouldn't surprise me. It's exactly what I should expect from James. But that doesn't ease the sting of it.

My eyes narrow. *Oh, no. Don't you DARE to take back what just happened. We are going to discuss it like adults and finish our conversation and maybe even do that again and—*

A whole crowd of women pile into the elevator, oblivious to the tension between us. As they get on, James manages to slip out into the lobby. I'm trapped against the back wall in a crowd of perfume and leggings and hands holding cocktails in plastic cups.

I'm still glaring at James—well, half glaring and half squinting since I can't see—as the doors start to close, torn between letting him go and chasing after him to tell him what a coward he is. Just before the doors slide shut, he mouths, *I'm sorry* one more time.

Yeah, well. I'm not sure I forgive him this time.

"Are these yours, hon?" One of the women bends to retrieve my glasses, holding them out.

I almost wish they were broken. Then they'd match how I feel.

"Thanks." I slide them back into place, blinking as things become clear.

"Girl," another woman says, looking me up and down with heavily lined eyes and smiling ruby lips, "you look like you were just thoroughly kissed."

My fingertips brush over my lips, which can't possibly be swollen but certainly feel that way. My cheeks are tender from the rough graze of James's stubble.

"It was nothing," I find myself saying, and it feels like the biggest lie I've ever told.

CHAPTER 18

James

I OPEN the back door of the house to find something no man wants to ever see: my dad, standing in the middle of the dark kitchen in nothing but his briefs.

And as far as briefs go, they are *brief*.

"Dad! Where are your pants?"

Tank doesn't seem nearly as startled by my presence as I am by his. He smirks, then takes a sip of water before answering. "It's my party. I can wear pants if I want to."

I groan at his twisted-up song reference. "No. That's … no."

"Fine. I'll grab something so I don't offend your delicate sensibilities."

Chuckling, he disappears into the master bedroom. If possible, from the back, his briefs are even briefer. Is this what I have to look forward to? Growing older and my choice of underwear growing proportionally smaller?

I grab my own glass of water and drink like I've been running a marathon. Not just ... running away, which is absolutely what I am doing. I squeeze my eyes closed and set the empty glass down, gripping the counter.

"I thought you were staying at the hotel," Tank calls.

And I thought you'd be asleep. Thought, hoped, maybe even wished as I pulled in the driveway of the home where I grew up. The house was dark, so it seemed like I had a good chance of sneaking in and going to bed. The plan was to get up before Tank woke, heading back to the hotel like I'd never been here at all.

"Everything okay?" Tank calls, sounding closer.

Not even remotely.

I'm not the kind of guy who kisses and tells, and I most definitely do NOT want to tell my dad about what just happened with Winnie. He would, of course, be thrilled. Winnie seems to have won him over, and I know Dad has been ecstatic seeing Harper and now Pat getting married.

Even if I wanted to share, I don't know what to say. There is zero processing happening in my scrambled egg of a brain. Only the memory of those few minutes in the elevator where the world, including all my worries, disappeared.

When my mouth met Winnie's, when I had her in my arms, the connection was more than any kiss, more than anything physical I've had with a woman.

I loved formulas in chemistry, the same way I love finding the right combination when developing flavor profiles. Words aren't always my thing, but to put it in terms I understand, our kiss was like beer that's been barrel-aged and complexly developed. Not something new. Not a *first*. It was like working for months or years refining a recipe, letting it age and develop to perfection.

With Winnie it was instant, immediate, unquestionably amazing. We were perfectly melded flavors, an unexpected pairing.

We had something no one has from the start. It was … undeniably amazing.

Until I bolted like a big baby.

Tank returns in a worn shirt and joggers. "So, what happened?"

"There was an issue with the room. I'm going to crash here, if the offer is still open."

"The offer will always be open." Tank assesses me. He may be getting older, but his insight is still keen. "So, an issue with the *room*. I see."

I nod.

He nods.

We both stand here. Nodding.

I'd like to play it cool, to be Mr. Casual, just popping in because I need a place to stay. But my palms are sweating, my head is pounding, and I'm still nodding like I'm trying to break a record. Weirdness or hesitation when it comes to a nosy family member is a drop of blood in the water near a bunch of hungry sharks.

And Tank's grin is very sharklike when he finally stops nodding and smiles. "Bull."

I could run. I could fight Tank and maybe even win. We're evenly matched in terms of size and both have bum knees. I've got him in age, but he has me in experience.

But there is little fight left in me.

So, I let Tank steer me by the shoulder out to the back patio. He doesn't turn on any lights, but ignites the gas fireplace, dragging two chairs closer to it.

"Do you need a sweatshirt?" he asks, but I shake my head. "Sit, son."

I sit. But I can't get comfortable in any position. Not when I'm leaning back, sprawled with my legs out in front of me, not when I'm tensed and leaning forward, my hands falling between my spread knees. I shift again, crossing one leg over the other, but my foot won't be still, tapping out a fast rhythm in the air.

"You finally realized you like her."

I freeze. "What?"

"Winnie. You finally caught up to the rest of us and realized you like her."

I turn slowly to my father, who's trying and failing to contain his smile. "*Finally?*"

"Since you met, the two of you've been pushing and pulling like a couple of magnets that can't decide which way to point."

I sneer, but his grin only widens. Then he laughs. *Laughs.*

I almost leave. I do. But when it comes to my family and especially with my father, there's not really an escape. If I leave now, I'll be dealing with him tomorrow. And the next day. He's not going to let this go, so might as well get it over with now.

I regret this decision as he starts to speak.

"You should have seen me with your mother at the start. I was a fool for her."

I become a statue. Maybe more of a gargoyle—completely made of stone, frozen where I'm hunched over with my elbows on my knees, head in my hands.

Bringing up Mom is like invoking some kind of special vow, a promise of total truth, of vulnerability. And when Tank does so now, when I'm already feeling shattered and exposed and all messed-up, I am powerless to move, even though what I want to do is hop on my bike and roar off.

I don't remember Dad ever talking about dating Mom. It's always been about the shared memories, the period of time after they were married and dove right into having a bunch of boys like ducks in a row, followed a little later by Harper.

I can't even move my mouth to ask the thousand questions Tank's statement invokes, so I simply wait. It hurts to talk about Mom, to hear about her, to acutely feel the loss every time she comes up. But I'm also desperate for a new story, something I don't know about her.

Dad stares into the fire, the smile from moments ago paired with a look in his eyes that's both happy and sad. "My career was everything. I made a promise to myself playing college ball that I wouldn't be derailed from my goals. Not by partying. Not by lifestyle or money. Not by a woman." He chuckles. "Especially not by a jersey chaser."

I almost fall out of my chair. "Mom was a jersey chaser?"

I can't imagine my mother as the kind of woman all pro athletes are warned about. There are different names—jersey chaser, cleat chaser, puck bunnies—same idea. These are the women who show up near the private exits, in the restaurants and clubs players frequent, who manage to find the teams' hotels while they're traveling. Hoping for a hookup or more with a player, any player.

For some, it's the money. Some, the fame. Some hope for a baby so they'll have a steady paycheck for years to come and a more permanent position, even if it doesn't end up being marriage.

That's not all women. But it is absolutely *some* women. My brothers and I have all had our run-ins, starting in college. Thankfully, because of Tank's strong cautions, we've wisely avoided them.

But—MOM was one of these women? No.

"She definitely was not." Tank shakes his head, and I can feel my shoulders relax. "But I thought she was. One of her friends got some kind of fake press pass and got them past security and close to the locker room. Which wasn't as hard to do back then. Things were more lax, especially with college ball. Bianca only came because she thought her friend had too much to drink at the game."

"Now, *that* sounds like Mom."

Tank smiles as he continues. "She wanted to keep her friend from doing anything stupid. Like falling for a football player. Which is exactly what your mother did."

I close my eyes, falling back into my chair, an image of Mom's face before her sickness flashing before me. She was beautiful, so full of life.

And snark, I think suddenly, remembering her through new, adult eyes. I can hear her laughter and a sassy remark that has my dad chasing her through the house, tickling her until she couldn't breathe.

For years, I've kept my memories of her tucked away, only pulling them out here and there, and only a little at a time. Keeping them, keeping her, keeping myself safe. Now, a flood of images and emotions wash over me. I'm seeing more than just the few easy stories I always keep near the surface.

I hear Mom and Dad arguing heatedly, then embracing with just as much passion. Mom could be sarcastic, though it was in a teasing way, never mean. Not cutting or cruel. She teased and needled and pushed Dad, but always in the best way.

Not unlike Winnie.

I swallow, and Dad continues, "The attraction between us was instant, but I refused to acknowledge it. I refused to give up my focus. To risk what I'd been working toward. Plus, I

194

had the wrong impression from that first meeting. It took a while for her to wear me down."

"She chased after you?"

"Not exactly." Dad scoots his chair closer to the fire, rubbing his hands together. "She was a smart woman. She didn't chase me so much as just became ubiquitous."

"Use the word in a sentence, please."

Dad grins. "As in, your mother became *ubiquitous*, appearing somehow everywhere I was, all the time. Not chasing me. Not flirting. Just … present. Always there, impossible to ignore, yet not showing interest either. There was eye contact, acknowledgement of my existence—but no smiling or flirting. It drove me wild. First, I was irritated. Then I was intrigued, and finally, I was irrationally desperate. I didn't ask her out so much as I picked a fight."

"I can't picture any of this."

Reaching out, Dad grasps my hand. He's all about touch—something he and my brothers both share more than Harper and me. But I can't remember the last time Dad held my hand. Maybe when I was a kid? It's both strange and comforting, and I want to pull away and squeeze him tighter. I choose the second.

"I think I've done a disservice to you, to all of you, by not talking about your mother enough." His voice has a gruff edge, the kind that comes from holding back tears. I can hear it in his voice. "I've realized this even more, watching my children struggle as you fall in love."

I stiffen, and Tank squeezes my hand tighter. My mouth is dry, my scalp tingly.

"I'm not … I don't …"

The words won't come. I'm not even sure what words are *trying* to form.

He's talking about Harper. About Pat. Not about me.

Definitely not me.

"It's okay, son."

It is … and it isn't.

The unspoken things hang between us like the chill in the air.

I am two different men underneath my skin, and they are at great odds. One is calm and steady, telling me to settle into what Tank has shared, to let the memories and the emotions work their way through me, bringing things up to the surface where they can breathe, where they can stop being scary, being hidden.

The other man is in a panicked state of fight or flight. He wants to do both, simultaneously. Fighting while flighting. He's having none of this. Not even a little. No memories. No emotions. No processing.

Run! Punch! Go! Flail! Fight!

Tank holds my hand hostage, and only this keeps me in my chair. I focus on just my breaths. Steady, steady. Slow. The gas fire flickers, casting a shifting glow over us. I keep my eyes on the flames, letting the light sear my eyes until I'm seeing nothing but black.

Tank clears his throat, and I startle. He gives my hand a last squeeze before reclining back in his chair. I can tell he wants to say more. I also can tell the moment he thinks better of it and stands, stretching.

"This old man needs sleep. Will you bring Winnie to family brunch Sunday morning?"

I nod before I can think better of it, before I can think about whether Winnie will even be speaking to me then.

Tank slaps me on the back before turning off the fire. "Good. Can you get yourself settled?"

I stand, shoving my hands into my pockets. My fingers

brush against the seed Winnie gave me. It's still there, despite my jeans going through the wash yesterday.

"I think I might actually go for a ride, clear my head."

He frowns. "At this hour? I don't like to think about you out there in the dark."

Dad habits never fade, I guess, even when I'm no longer a kid. I pat his shoulder as I pass, heading for the garage where I've got my motorcycle stored along with an extra set of keys. "So, don't think about it."

Which is exactly what I plan to do while riding my favorite hills and curves and long stretches of road: not think at all.

But Tank's voice makes me pause halfway through the garage. He stands in the doorway, and even in the dim light, I don't miss the intensity on his face.

"Son, I know you may think you're too old for advice—"

"Dad, I'll wear a helmet. I'll be safe."

He shakes his head. "No. I mean, yes. Do that." Tank pauses, and I realize before he speaks again that he's going to go deep, maybe with something I'm really not ready to hear. "But I was going to say you can't control everything. You have to take the risk. You have to try. Even if sometimes you lose."

As my bike eats up mile after mile in the dark, his words play on repeat in my head: *Try, risk, lose.*

But are the first two worth the possibility of the third?

CHAPTER 19

James

THE QUESTION IS STILL BANGING around in my head when Winnie opens the hotel room door the next morning. "James," she says. Her tone is very much, *Look what the cat dragged in.* "Did you lose your keycard? And, perhaps, your way?"

Actually, yes. I did lose the keycard she gave me. Maybe my way too. For the first time, I realize she might have worried when I didn't come back to the room. I should have at least texted her. The gravity of all my failures hits me with crippling intensity.

I understand Winnie's flat gaze, and the way she doesn't immediately move to let me in. It's early—*very* early. I smell like gasoline and exhaust. I'm freezing, more than a little filthy, and my body still feels like it's vibrating from the bike.

More importantly, I kissed her, then ran away last night, like our kiss wasn't life-altering.

I wouldn't let me in the room either.

I also have no idea what I'm going to say. No plan. Which is why I just stand here stupidly. More stupidly even than usual.

Winnie leans on the doorframe. Her hair is loose around her shoulders, and she has a brush in one hand, as though I've caught her in the midst of getting ready. She's dressed in a classic white blouse paired with jeans so tight I can't give them more than a passing glance or my gaze will get stuck there. She has on no makeup, and her full lips are a natural, pretty pink.

The memory of our kiss floods me, and I rock back on my heels.

My voice seems to have disappeared somewhere on my ride, and when I open my mouth to speak, my teeth chatter instead. The temperature dropped during the night, but I hardly noticed. Only now do I realize how the cold has seeped through my jacket and clothes. My bones are brittle ice.

Winnie's guarded look disappears, swallowed up by concern. "Where have you been?" She tosses the brush behind her and puts her hands to my cheeks, frowning. "You're freezing!"

"Y-y-yeah." The word stutters out between my chattering teeth. I resist the urge to nuzzle into her palms like a big dog. I don't deserve her kindness.

"Get in here, you big idiot."

Or … her Winniefied version of kindness.

Winnie grabs me by the arm and drags me inside the room. My bags still sit by the door, and I wonder if she snooped through them.

Why do I hope she did?

Winnie disappears into the bathroom, and I hear the shower start. Her voice echoes off the tile. "I thought you went home."

"I did. Couldn't sleep. Went for a ride." I've found my voice but haven't managed to locate more than two-syllable words.

I stand next to the door, unable to make myself walk any farther into the room, which is filled with Winnie's sweet scent. The bed is rumpled, her pajamas in a pile next to the dresser like she got undressed right there, not long ago. I turn away, facing the ugly wallpaper like I'm a kid who's been put in timeout.

Winnie emerges from the bathroom, followed by a cloud of steam. She leans on the doorframe for a moment, arms crossed as she studies me.

I kissed those lips, I think. *The best kiss of my life.* And then, stubbornly, *But it was just a kiss. I'm not falling for her.*

Two truths and a lie.

Try, Tank told me. *Risk.* I want to do both, but the how is the hard part. It's like turning off all my default settings, rebooting a very slow system. Right now, my brain is just a blank screen with a blinking cursor.

"There may not be a lot of hot water left," Winnie says. "I took a long shower this morning. But it should be enough to thaw you out."

I swallow, attempting not to think of Winnie taking a long shower. "Thanks."

Winnie blinks, then brushes right by me, grabbing her messenger bag. "There are a few clean towels hanging up. I'm headed down to get breakfast before the first session. The room is yours."

When she walks by me again, not even looking my way, I

almost reach out, almost grab her hand to—what? What would I say or do, exactly? I let her pass, though I make no move to enter the bathroom.

I don't know how to do this, to be honest and vulnerable with a woman. I've never done it. There has never been anyone who gave me reason to think about opening up. Not even close.

Winnie's going to walk right out before I can find my tongue or my courage. But she opens the door, then closes it again, leaning against it. She keeps one hand on the handle like she's poised for escape. I don't look away under her intense gaze.

"Question of the day," she says.

The questions. I had forgotten all about them, and though the last thing I want now is to answer anything, I'm desperate for anything she'll give me right now.

"Okay."

"Do you regret it?" Her voice is barely above a whisper.

She doesn't need to say what the *it* is. The kiss hangs between us, right along with my idiotic response. The memory of it is more palpable than the steam billowing out of the bathroom. The sad look in her eyes makes me hate myself.

Winnie is not a regret. She could *never* be.

I capture her gaze, unwavering. "No."

Winnie studies me, her eyes tracing a path I can almost feel over my cheeks on down my shoulders, pausing around my collarbones. "Are you *sure*?" she asks. "And before you argue, this doesn't count as a question. It's a clarification." Her voice breaks a little, and it kills me. "Because you really looked like you regretted it."

I shake my head. For once, I envy Pat for his way with words. Or, at least, his ability to just let them fly so easily from his mouth, even when they're dumb. He'd know what to say right now. And it might be stupid, but his mind wouldn't be blank, his tongue wouldn't be stuck to the roof of his mouth.

"I don't regret it. I just ... don't know what to do about it."

Winnie doesn't smile, but something seems to loosen in her countenance. "I don't regret it either. Though I probably should."

Hope springs up inside me, just a sliver of it, but enough. "Good."

"Good."

Steam fills the air between us, and it shouldn't make me think about pressing Winnie's back up against the door and kissing her again, but it does.

Before I have time to think about acting on what would surely be another impulsive decision, Winnie sniffs, her nose wrinkling. "You should shower. You smell like a truck stop."

The door slams, and she's gone.

CHAPTER 20

Winnie

"NOPE," I say a little too forcefully to Kyoko. "Hard pass." A guy about to sit down in the empty seat next to me gives me a startled look and backs up. I wince. "Sorry. I didn't mean you ..."

But he's already walking away. Next to me Kyoko covers her mouth as she laughs.

"Way to scare away the nice boy," she says, then waves a hand. "Anyway, back to James. I'm not saying give me intimate details about the kiss, but I need *something* to get me through this session. I mean, tracking distribution and inventory?" Kyoko closes her eyes and makes loud snoring sounds.

I'm actually excited about the session, even though I'm distracted by thoughts of James. But at the moment, I'm too derailed by the first part of what Kyoko said.

"Who says I kissed him?" I demand, perhaps a little too forcefully, based on Kyoko's smug grin.

"I think you just did."

I try to press my lips closed. Instead, I blurt, "What happens in the elevator stays in the elevator."

Kyoko's eyes go wide and she grabs my hand with bone-crushing strength. "You kissed him on the elevator!"

"Shhh!"

Way too many heads are turning. I open my notebook, then use it to hide my face.

"Oh, no. You don't get to retreat like that. Even if you did just make a cringeworthy and cliched reference to Vegas. Which I'm never going to let you live down, by the way."

Despite the hard time she's currently giving me, I love that Kyoko casually said *never*, like we've got a long future friendship ahead of us. Which I honestly hope is true. Nothing forms the foundation of friendship quite like being the two people with boobs in a room filled with beards.

The emcee steps up to the front and starts introducing the speaker, saving me. Kyoko leans close and whispers, "Later. I'll drag it out of you."

Not gonna happen.

I won't talk about it. Instead, I just replay the moment over and over again.

It was the kind of kiss that starts wars or ends them. The sort that sonnets are written about. Country songs too—the happy ones that you line dance to, not the sad ones or the vengeful ones. (Though I do love some vengeful Miranda Lambert.) As much as the thought should terrify me, it's the kind of kiss that becomes your last first kiss. Because I can't imagine any other kiss will ever come close.

So, yeah—I'm not admitting that.

Kyoko makes a valiant effort to drag more out of me

though, paying for a rideshare and treating me to lunch at a Mexican place with queso so good it's almost drinkable. I don't crack, even with the drugging effects of melted cheese and perfectly seasoned fajitas. Every time she asks about James, I counter with a question about operations at the brewery where she works. And because she's nice and I'm stubborn, she keeps answering even when I don't.

"You're really not going to give me *anything*?" Kyoko pouts as we finish off a post-meal basket of chips. Because if you're not eating chips as the bookend to your meal, you're doing it wrong.

"No."

"What if I ask a series of yes-or-no questions?"

This makes me smile, thinking of James and our questions. I catch myself smiling when Kyoko grins wickedly at me. I clear my throat and my expression.

"Nope."

"I've got it!" Kyoko waves a chip for emphasis. "I'll ask questions that aren't about James. And if you happen to read into them and spill some vague but juicy details, who will be the wiser?"

I bite into another chip while I consider. Normally, I'd talk to Lindy and Val about James. I did consider calling them last night after James ghosted me, but I didn't really feel like talking. More like yelling or breaking things.

Plus, Lindy is somewhere in Europe, and phone calls are supposed to be for emergency purposes only if something happens with Jo. It's also a little weird since she's married to James's brother. I don't know how she wouldn't be biased in favor of the Grahams. I mean, being Lindy's sister-in-law? Come on! That's maybe the best argument in favor of James.

NOT that I'm thinking about marriage. Just, you know,

205

for argument's sake. Lindy's mind would definitely follow that path to its logical conclusion.

Val would be way too enthusiastic. She's always been the romantic out of the three of us. Plus, the minute she laid eyes on the Graham brothers, she was trying to get us to call dibs. There would have been zero chill if I told her James kissed me. She would have squealed on the phone for half an hour and told me to get off the phone and go kiss him some more.

"Fine," I say, leaning back in the booth. "Two questions."

"Squeee!" Kyoko laughs, then shakes her head. "I just said squee. Like it's a real word, not a sound."

I hold up both hands. "Hey. No judgment."

"First question. You're renovating your bathroom and have to choose wallpaper."

"This is already the worst question I've ever been asked."

"Shh! As you're deciding on the wallpaper, you're torn between a dark velvet with gold leaf or a light and bright romantic floral print. Which do you choose?"

I stare at Kyoko. "I'm sorry, but why, of all the rooms in the house, am I putting sexy wallpaper in the bathroom?"

Kyoko shoves the basket of chips out of the way and leans across the table, her eyes bright. "So, the kiss *was* sexy?"

I bite my lip but find myself smiling and answering anyway. "Yes."

"Squee!" Kyoko says again, and this time I laugh with her. "Will you do it again?"

That question is one I can't answer, because I have no idea. James is harder to read than a technical manual on building car engines written entirely in a foreign language. He said he didn't regret the kiss but also that he doesn't know what to do about it.

And that's where we're for sure on the same page. I have no idea what to do about it either.

I've never been casual. I don't have enough chill for casual. I've mostly had long single periods, punctuated here and there by boring monogamous relationships. Like the one I just got out of, though Dale already feels like some distant memory. Compared to the rush of emotion I have for James, what I felt for Dale at *most* is like watered-down, lukewarm tea.

"I hope so, but I don't know."

Kyoko nods. "Given the way he looked at you last night before he threw Daniel in the pool, I'd say chances are high."

Given the way he disappeared after and how wrecked he looked this morning, it's not a hand I'd bet on. He said he didn't regret it. But there's a lot of room between not regretting something and wanting to repeat it.

We head back to the hotel, Kyoko cradling a to-go pint of queso like it's a baby. "Hey, promise me something."

The suddenly serious look on her face makes me wary. "Okay …"

"When Dark Horse is ready, convince James to hire me."

Not what I was expecting. It takes my brain a second to switch gears. "You want to work for James? It's no picnic, I'll tell you. And I even … sort of like the man."

"I think we've established you more than *sort of* like him. No matter how hard he is to work with, I'd prefer James over my current situation. I'm overworked and undervalued. I'd be an asset to Dark Horse. And he'd listen if you told him."

"You'd want to move to Sheet Cake?"

"I mean, sure. Sounds like the town is starting to come alive. And you're there. We're already half-besties. So, yeah."

"That actually sounds … great. But I don't know when

he'll be hiring. He doesn't tell me details. And he's not the best at working with others."

"He'll have to learn," Kyoko says, like this is some kind of easy task, not a massive leap. "Running a brewery isn't a one-person job."

"I'll see what I can do."

"Thank you. And no matter what, you've got me. I'm harder to shake than a leech."

"Ew."

"Speaking of shaking me," she says, "there are only two more sessions and then the big award show."

"We should go out to dinner or something instead," I suggest. "The award show sounds boring."

Her eyes go big. "You can't skip it. James is up for two awards! Did you not know?"

"Nope."

This knowledge shouldn't shock me. It's not like the man fills me in on much. And even if he weren't so closed off, James is totally the type to not tell anyone about something like an award, something that puts the spotlight on him. I bet not even his family knows.

Though the man is as stubborn as a whole pack of mules and set on doing everything himself, like Kyoko said, he *needs* other people, and on some level, I think he knows it.

The man may act like he wants to be an island, but underneath his poker face—and he really does have a good one—I've caught glimpses of something else. Like the other day at lunch when his gaze kept falling to the logos on their matching brewery T-shirts. Maybe anyone else would have missed it, but I didn't. There's a longing somewhere underneath that big grumpy exterior, a longing for others.

His exterior is like one big bluff.

And I'm going to call him on it. Starting with the awards

show tonight. An idea takes shape—a risky but really good idea—and I'm itching to start making phone calls.

As we walk inside the hotel, I give Kyoko an apologetic look. "I'm going to skip the next session or two. Can I borrow your notes later?"

Her expression is sly. "Of course. Does this have something to do with James?"

"Duh. I'll need your help too, so keep your phone handy."

We part ways in the lobby, and I'm already firing off texts, setting plans in motion. Whether I can pull this off in the next few hours is the big question. But I'm nothing if not up for a challenge. Especially where James Graham is concerned.

The realization scares me, but I decide, like with so many other things, to worry about it later.

TEXT THREAD

James: Where are you
Winnie: Wouldn't you like to know
James: Yes. That's why I texted
James: ????
Winnie: I'm around.
James: Define around
Winnie: Aw, you miss me that much?
James: Where are you
Winnie: Taking care of some things. Can we meet up and go to the awards show together?
James: I was planning to skip
Winnie: No way! I want the whole conference experience.
James: Have fun
Winnie: You're really not going to come with me?
James: No
Winnie: Fine. I'll sit with Daniel.
James: What time should I meet you

CHAPTER 21

James

IF I THOUGHT I was miserable the first day of the conference, today is worse. Much, much worse. I'm not sure if it's the fact I'm dealing with the aftershocks of kissing Winnie or the fact that I'm walking around smelling like her bodywash. Probably a combination of both. Add in the lack of sleep and I'm on edge.

Her body wash, for the record, is called Caramel Perfection. The scent of it is driving me mad. Every time I turn my head, it's like Winnie is right there with me. Except she isn't right there. She isn't anywhere.

Not in our room, not in the exhibition hall, not in any of the sessions—and yes, I walked into every room during the middle of presentations—and not in the hotel bar. I even checked across the street at the little place where we ate lunch. No sharp-tongued blond looking like a pin-up dream. She is a ghost.

Yesterday, I managed to deal with the crowds, the noise, and the overwhelm by focusing on her. Just seeing a flash of her blond hair across the room, a sliver of her smile, the nervous way she pushes up her glasses. It amused me more than I care to admit watching her take notes in a little notebook. Even though Winnie didn't know I was watching, she anchored me. Seeing her calmed the buzz in my head always caused by crowded events.

So, after today, the last place I want to be right now is waiting outside the big room for the award show. But when Winnie mentioned Daniel, I didn't have a choice. I almost crushed the phone to dust in my hand when I read her text.

Someone bumps me, and I snarl. I feel like a train barreling its way off the track at full speed. The voices in the hall build to a fever pitch, and I'm rubbing my head when a singular voice cuts through it all, the only voice I care about hearing.

"There you are!"

Winnie. Her hand lands on my arm and all the air whooshes out of me.

She smiles up at me, causing all my muscles to loosen up and relax. Except the big meaty one in the center of my chest, which is beating double-time. My right hand slides into my pocket, touching the seed. It's become like a weird talisman, though I'm not sure if it's bringing me good or bad fortune.

A guy wearing sunglasses passes much too close to Winnie, and it's all I can do not to drag her out of here. To somewhere quiet and private. Another elevator. Or a closet. Or our shared room, which we need to discuss before tonight.

"Hey." I rub my eyes, suddenly feeling every bit of the exhaustion that's been clinging to me.

Winnie studies me. "Did you get a nap today?"

I frown. "I'm not a toddler."

She rolls her eyes, but she's smiling. "Adults take naps too, James. It's a whole thing. You should try it sometime. Maybe it would help with this disposition."

She pokes at my frown, and I push her hand away before I can act on the impulse to kiss her fingertip.

The urge startles me. Have I ever wanted to kiss a woman's finger? Not that I can recall. But when I look at Winnie, there's a whole laundry list of places I'd like to press my lips. There's the inside of her wrist and each corner of her eyebrows. The tip of her nose. The freckle I've just now noticed on her forearm.

And, of course, her lips. Especially now that I know how they feel under mine and how she tastes.

"Come on, boss. Let's get seats."

Winnie begins dragging me and I let her, though the last place I want to go right now is this awards show. Winnie hasn't mentioned it, so I'm guessing she doesn't know I'm a finalist in two categories. She's definitely the type to say—or *do*—something with that kind of information.

We're in the middle of a crush of people, and I lean even closer to Winnie, letting our shoulders brush. I'm not sure if it's more for her protection against the crowd or mine.

The feel of soft fabric against my forearm grabs my attention, and I realize that she's changed clothes since I saw her this morning. "You're wearing flannel?"

Winnie stretches out one arm, examining the soft red and black plaid shirt. It's too big on her—the sleeves are rolled up and the shirt is knotted at the waist, a black tee barely showing underneath.

214

She tugs at the collar. "I know, right? It's growing on me. Must be something in the water. Or in the beer. Over there— Kyoko saved us seats. I'll introduce you. She's brilliant."

Winnie directs us to a row near the center of the room. I'd prefer the back, but at least I get the aisle seat. I can easily escape if needed. Winnie introduces me to her friend, and I do my best to be polite, though I'm honestly running on fumes and done with small talk and, most especially, people who aren't Winnie.

"Nice job last night with Daniel," Kyoko says.

I shrug. "It happens."

Kyoko laughs and hands Winnie two coffees. Winnie tries to press one of them into my hands. "For you," she says. "To get some pep back in that step, boss."

I bite back a retort about not being a peppy kind of guy and instead take the proffered coffee. I admit, after a few sips, it helps. Marginally, anyway. The emcee is just beginning when I lean close to Winnie.

"Thank you."

Her eyes glint up at me as the lights dim a little. "It's nothing."

It doesn't feel like nothing, but I don't argue with her as the emcee announces the first category. I submitted beer in five categories and was picked as a finalist in two. Though the taste tests were done blind, I can't help but think my reputation will factor in somehow.

No one in this room thinks I deserve to be here. To them, I'm just a dumb jock clinging to his family's fame. That's what more than one article has written about me. A few others gave Dark Horse a positive spin, but the bad reviews always hit harder and stick longer.

I try to quell the stupid hope in my chest as my first category approaches. Maybe I care more than I wanted to admit

215

about the validation this award would provide. It also doesn't escape my notice how no one goes up to accept awards alone. Even the smaller breweries have three to five people going up to the stage, most wearing T-shirts with matching logos. A team.

Which you've been saying all along you don't want and you don't need.

What's more, every time a winner is announced, other groups stand up to offer the winners bro-y back slaps and hugs. I've only spoken to a handful of people at the conference, one of whom I threw in a pool last night. I shift in my seat, which suddenly feels too small.

When the Chocolate & Coffee category is up, Winnie leans forward slightly, wrapping her hand around my arm. It's obvious she found out somehow. I shouldn't be surprised. She's too smart for her own good.

They announce the bronze and silver winners. Not me.

That's it, then. I relax slightly in my seat. If I didn't win those—

"James," Winnie hisses.

I grunt, and she says my name again, louder, punctuated with a little shove. "Get up there! You won!"

"What?"

Realization dawns slowly. Too slowly. The room is poised, waiting. Winnie's eyes urge me to the front, and I see the name Dark Horse projected on the screen. I won.

I won?

I stumble a little as I get to my feet. Winnie whoops, and I debate about whether I should grab her hand and drag her with me, but she gives me a shove and says, "Go on!"

I glance back once more as I leave the row, just as she and Kyoko hop up on their chairs, clapping and cheering. Some guy down the row tells them to sit down, and I hear Winnie snap, "Cram it, you hipster wannabe lumberjack."

I make what feels like an endless walk to the front with a huge grin on my face, ignoring the people who are clapping politely, maybe even somewhat begrudgingly.

I can't bring myself to care. Because I WON.

I manage to climb the steps to the stage without tripping over my boots. One of the emcees gives me a genuine smile as he hands me a small gold medallion on a strip of leather. They're meant to be worn like a bolo, but I simply hold it in my palm, loving the weight of it.

Honestly, after letting go of my football dreams, I never thought I'd have something like *this* again, this feeling of pride. Of winning. Of doing something significant on this scale. Maybe few people outside this room would care.

But I do. No matter what I tried to tell myself beforehand —I DO care about this win.

"Congratulations," he says, ushering me on even as they begin to announce the next category.

I almost walk right by the photo op at the end of the stage, a big backdrop with all the sponsors' logos and the conference name up top.

"Smile," the photographer orders.

"No." But I do pause, holding up the award.

It's then I hear familiar voices cheering and shouting, making entirely too much noise. There's a whole row in back standing on chairs, clapping wildly and making an inappropriate amount of noise. I do a double take when I realize who they are.

It's my family: Tank, Collin, Harper, and Chase. I squint as I come down the stairs. They're all wearing matching black shirts with the Dark Horse logo Winnie designed for the site mock-up. The *real* logo. Not the unicorns.

My chest tightens as I walk down the steps. I don't need anyone to tell me Winnie is responsible. She did this. She got my family here. She made T-shirts. I realize when I catch her eye that she's ditched the flannel, and she's wearing one of the Dark Horse shirts too.

How? How did she do this so fast? And when?

The bigger question I don't want to consider is *why*. I don't deserve this. Not after the way I've treated her. The clipped responses. Firing her. Ditching her at the conference. I definitely don't deserve this after the way I responded to the kiss.

And I absolutely should have dragged her up there on the stage with me. The regret is as instant as my resolve to do better. To be better.

I am intensely focused as I make my way back to her. Determined.

Try, Tank said. *Risk*.

My gaze captures hers, and I don't let go. I'm lucky not to trip over anything. But I suspect any and all things would have moved out of my way, not daring to get between me and Winnie.

When I reach her, I do not hesitate or second-guess. I don't worry about being the caveman my family accuses me of being. I simply grab Winnie around the waist and lift her straight off the chair she's standing on. She squeals, then laughs. I lower her down so we're face-to-face, but her feet still don't touch the ground. Like it's the most natural thing in the world, her hands wrap around my neck.

"I don't deserve you," I mutter.

"Few men do," she says lightly. "Now put me down, you Neanderthal."

"No."

"Sit down," some guy mutters from behind us, and I send him a look that makes him cower.

"Come on, boss," Winnie says, patting me twice on the shoulder like this is a cage match and she's tapping out. "Let me go."

"Not a chance."

Instead, giving my amused family members a nod, knowing they'll follow, I march Winnie up the aisle and right out of the room, ignoring everything but the weight of her in my arms.

CHAPTER 22

Winnie

"WHO KNEW you were a secret party animal," I say, squeezing James's hand. Then, because I'm taking full advantage of the fact I'M HOLDING JAMES GRAHAM'S HAND, I give his fingers another squeeze.

We're walking back to the hotel—*strolling* is a more apt word—and I'm trying to avoid feeling like Cinderella at the end of the ball. Instead of a nonexistent carriage turning into a pumpkin, I'm fully expecting the James who has been touching me nonstop since he carried me out of the awards show to turn back into the James who runs away after giving me the best kiss of my life.

He gives me a playful side-eye. "I hate parties."

"Let's not forget people," I add.

He grunts and nudges me. "Not *all* people. Some of them I actually like being around."

Though it's a roundabout compliment, I can't fight the goofy grin on my face.

I bump him right back. "Still, you seemed to mildly enjoy socializing back there."

"*Mild* being the operative word."

After he won his award and carried me off like a less hairy King Kong, Tank suggested we all catch a late dinner. And wouldn't you know it? The pub we walked to was hosting the conference afterparty. More like a *during*party, since it was already in full swing with conference-goers like us who had skipped out early.

James looked for a moment like he was going to bolt, until a few guys walked over to offer congratulations. I watched his face move from suspicious to a little more open and maybe even pleasant. His family bowed out pretty quickly, as the Grahams all together can't help but make a scene. They tower over normal humans and carry a sort of unignorable gravity with their presence.

Even I felt inexplicably starstruck. Harper must have noticed because she smiled and said, "You should see how it is when Pat's here too."

I could only imagine. Of all the Graham men, Pat has the biggest personality. Not to mention the size of his mouth. I could picture him pausing at various tables to autograph napkins without being asked, posing for photographs, kissing babies. Not that there are babies in the bar, but the point stands.

After they left, I thought I'd fade into the background, watching James. But his gaze sought me out, landing on where I stood against the wall. He held out a hand to me, I took it, and he hasn't let go since.

His possessiveness turns to awkwardness when we arrive back at the hotel. For the first time in hours, James takes his hands off me, putting them in his pockets, giving me distance I don't want. And there goes my pumpkin carriage.

"I should probably see if there's an available room," he says.

James looks unsure. I feel unsure.

I consider telling him to forget it, just to stay in the room with me. But I don't. I'm not that brave or sure of what I want. I'm torn between wanting to follow this wherever it takes us or running for the hills.

"Okay."

We'll let fate decide. If there are extra rooms, that's that. And if not … we can be adults. Adults who kissed the night before, don't regret it but also may or may not do it again. No problems or complications there.

I realize I'm staring at his mouth (not for the first time today) and jerk my gaze away. "I'll just be in the room, watching your bag." *Well, that sounds weird.* "Not that it needs watching. It's not a dog. Or a child." *Even weirder, Winnie. Well done.* "I'll be upstairs."

A more normal thing to say, but my tone sounds more like someone who will be waiting upstairs to ax-murder you.

James looks mildly alarmed. Rather than risk saying more embarrassing and nonsensical things, I wave and start to walk away.

That's when I step into a sci-fi movie. Or, at least, a sci-fi movie is the best explanation I can think of for what I see just across the lobby. It's Dale … except *not* Dale. This is where the sci-fi part comes in, because the first leap my brain makes is that I'm looking at an alien in some kind of body-snatching scenario.

First of all, alien Dale is wearing tight jeans and a Henley —a HENLEY—with all the buttons open, revealing a sickly pale swath of his upper chest. When we were dating, Dale

222

had exactly two looks. Work Dale, which meant a suit, complete with jacket and tie, and Casual Dale, which meant a polo tucked into jeans or khakis with a belt that matched his shoes. I didn't think the man *owned* jeans or a Henley, a kind of shirt that acts like catnip to women—when worn correctly. I take a tiny bit of pleasure in the fact the shirt looks terrible on Dale.

Then there's the woman with him, who must be the other woman he mentioned in our breakup conversation. She has waist-length chestnut hair and a dress that someone's going to have to cut her out of at the end of the night. Based on the room keys in Dale's hand, it's going to be him.

I swallow, waiting to feel some kind of hurt or jealousy. Instead, I'm just perplexed. Dale doesn't look like himself—or who he was with me—and this woman is certainly nothing like me on the surface.

She inspires so many questions. Like: is it hard for her to sit down without actually sitting ON her hair? And if she does accidentally sit on it, does it strain her neck? Also: is she part of a religious sect where hair-cutting isn't a thing? Or is this a stylistic choice?

While I'm watching—because I couldn't stop watching if I tried, just like with every *Real Housewives* franchise—she hitches her leg up over his hip in a way that does *not* scream religious sect and *does* scream yoga practice five times a week for flexibility.

Alien body snatchers aren't really a thing. What about doppelgängers, like in *The Vampire Diaries*? Because, just like Dale never wore anything like what he's got on now, he definitely *never* kissed me with that kind of passion or intensity. Or slobber. There some serious wetness involved. Ew, ew, ew!

As though he feels me watching, Dale's eyes fly open, his

gaze landing directly on me. I swear I can hear the sound of their mouths pulling apart with a wet smack. Dale blinks, his mouth opening and closing like a caught fish.

There's no need for this to be uncomfortable. Awkward, sure. But seeing him with another woman solidifies exactly how little of my heart he ever held.

I draw in a breath and start toward them. With every step closer, Dale looks slightly more ill. But I'm determined. *Be mature. Be the bigger person. Get in, get out, then walk away.*

They're standing next to a potted plant which an alarming number of people have used as a place to deposit their chewed gum. It's a perfect way to set the scene for this conversation.

"Winnie, hey," Dale says, looking sheepish and apologetic and ridiculous in his Henley.

The woman with him, on the other hand, looks strangely ecstatic. Which I quickly realize is due to James, who is standing right behind me.

I tilt my head up, surprised he followed me over. His eyes, which I'm coming to realize are capable of expressing much more than grumpiness, are asking if I'm okay. I give a slight nod, and he steps forward, placing a hand on my lower back.

I could have done this alone. But it's so much better feeling his warm palm through my shirt.

"I'm Celia," the woman says, looking right through me as she holds out her hand to James.

He simply stares down at it like he's never seen a hand before, then nods. Just *nods*. I love him for it.

Celia wilts a little, then wraps an arm around Dale's waist, like she wasn't just turning flirty doe-eyes on another man. I give her an awkward wave.

"I'm Winnie."

Celia holds out her hand again, much less enthusiastically

224

than she did to James. Unlike James, I shake her hand, which feels wilted and slightly damp, like a lukewarm cafeteria-style fish filet.

"I'm Dale's ex. Not like a creepy stalker or still obsessed ex. A very peaceful, no-drama ex."

I attempt to appear and sound nonthreatening. I'm not sure I succeeded based on Dale's stricken expression and Celia's narrowed eyes.

"I'm happy for you both," I add, wiping off her fish filet handshake on my jeans.

This brightens Celia's expression, and she beams at Dale, who seems to find the carpet especially fascinating. "Thank you," Celia squeals, again holding out her hand.

Another handshake? What is her deal with hand-shaking?

But then I notice the very large, very sparkly ring on her finger. Her *left ring* finger. The diamond's size falls somewhere between one carat and better-do-some-arm-exercises-to-hold-that-thing-up.

My entire body goes taut. James's chest rumbles behind me. His hand slides from my back to my waist, gripping me like he thinks I'm going to launch an attack or maybe drop into a faint. I don't particularly feel like doing either thing, but I settle back against him, needing the stable feel of his chest.

"Oh," I say, fighting for normalcy. Why is my mouth suddenly the Sahara? "Congrats on the engagement."

Celia laughs brightly, adjusting her hand so maximum sparkle levels are achieved by the angle. I swear a beam of light coming off it just pierced my retina.

"Well, the engagement is old news, but we've finally chosen a date and a venue."

Words link together to help my slow, slow brain understand: finally, old news, date, *chosen.*

225

I pin my eyes on silent, Henley-wearing Dale. "How long?" My voice sounds small yet deadly, like one of those tiny species of octopus who live in Australia and could kill you within minutes of their venom hitting your bloodstream.

"Winnie," Dale says. It's a placating voice. A coward's voice. A guilty man's voice. He looks at me, but his gaze slides right off and back to the floor.

Celia steps in again, looking between us like she's just starting to get the picture. I hope, for her sake, she does. "We've been engaged for six months. Together for ... well, it seems like forever. In a good way. Right, babe?"

Zero math is needed for this equation. I barely register the way James presses even closer, his hand banding tighter around my waist until there is no space left between us. He becomes a human splint, the only thing keeping me together.

It's not the revelation of the cheating, at least not solely that. There's the reality of being the unwilling other woman in this situation, which makes me want to hurl all over Dale's shoes. Or hurl my shoes at Dale's face.

But there is an even deeper betrayal to this, one Dale of all people would understand.

My own pulse creates a deafening whoosh in my ears. "You knew," I say. "You were the *only one* who knew, and you still did this?"

Dale looks miserable, but not miserable enough. "I didn't mean to—"

"No," James says, repositioning us so he's between me and Dale. "You do not get to speak to her."

Though his protectiveness makes something swoop in my belly, the humiliation of James witnessing this moment is intensely, keenly painful. I remove his hand from my waist, and without looking back, I bolt for the escalator.

CHAPTER 23

Winnie

I'M SO frazzled I can't get the keycard to work. I know it's because I'm swiping it too fast, the way James did with his biohazardous room when we first checked in. I *know* this, yet I keep doing it again and again until the keypad itself is a blur in front of me.

A big, warm hand closes around mine. "A wise woman once told me you need to go slowly."

I watch our joined hands, fascinated by the simple movement as James swipes the card, pauses the exact right length of time, then turns the handle when the little light blinks green. He doesn't let go of my hand right away. Sliding the key card out of my palm, he links his fingers with mine and leads me into the room.

When we reach the bed, James takes my shoulders and pushes gently until I'm seated on the edge of the mattress.

"So bossy," I whisper, watching his boots instead of meeting his gaze.

He huffs a soft breath, almost a laugh. "Yeah. I am."

I nod. "I like how you are."

Kneeling before me, James lifts my right foot and begins unlacing my shoe. They're black Converse high tops. He could easily loosen them just a little and slip them right off. But he takes his time, untying and then unlacing with a gentle, careful precision that feels ridiculously intimate.

I watch his hands and also his bowed head, the dark sweep of hair hanging over his forehead. His focus is intense, his fingers steady. He slides the shoe from my foot and places it next to the bed. Instead of moving to the next, he cups my heel in one hand and begins to massage my foot with the other. I want to watch, suddenly fascinated with his hands, but my eyelids flutter closed as his thumb presses into the arch.

"I don't know you well enough yet to know how you process." James's thumbs move in time with his voice, punctuating different words and dragging a soft groan out of me.

What I hear the loudest is *I don't know you well enough YET.* It's a sneaky promise. Maybe an unintentional one? Either way, the idea makes my stomach flutter, and I tuck it away somewhere secret inside me to revisit.

"If you need to talk it out or you need silence or to go hit baseballs, just tell me what you need."

His words make me ache. I don't particularly want to process at all. I'd rather block out the whole exchange from the lobby and block out the other, even uglier memories it stirred to the surface like silt kicked up from the bottom of a stream.

I fall back onto the bed with a sigh as James deepens the massage. "I don't know what I need."

"Then let me take care of you," he says.

Well, I'm not going to argue with THAT.

James continues to massage my foot until I'm drugged into a hazy half-sleep state, then jolts me awake with a touch too light to be anything other than a tickle.

"Hey," I protest through giggles.

"Wanted to make sure you're still alive."

I kick at him, lightly, and he chuckles, giving my foot a final squeeze before moving to the next one, repeating the slow untying of laces and gentle massage.

When James finishes, I'm mush.

"Stay," he says, like I could move even if I wanted to.

To be clear, I don't want to move. And not just because my bones are liquid. I wasn't lying when I said I like James bossy. Sometimes, his stubborn vehemence makes me want to argue even if I agree with him. Right now, I only want to comply with this protective tender bossiness.

I hear him rummaging through his bag and then the water start to run in the bathroom. James returns a moment later, towering over me, his legs touching mine where they hang off the bed. I crack open one eye. James has the tiniest hint of a smile on his lips, and his eyes are fixed on me.

"What?" I ask.

"I've just never seen you so ... relaxed. I didn't know you had this setting."

I speak before I think better of it. "Emotional overwhelm and a good foot massage will do that to me."

A frown replaces the tiny smile. "He's a jerk who never deserved you."

"Agreed." I cover my eyes with one arm.

There's a long pause. "I'm sorry he hurt you, temp."

A little thrill moves through me at the nickname, one I

229

shouldn't love so much. "He ... didn't. At least, not in the way you might think."

And that's all I'm going to say about THAT. No sense dredging up the even older wounds Dale uncovered tonight.

James seems to sense this, because he takes my hands and, with no small effort since I've turned into a lumpy sack of potatoes, tugs me to my feet. I groan the whole way but secretly enjoy James fussing over me. He practically carries me into the bathroom, and is it bad that I wish he would sweep me up into his arms, bridal style? Probably. At least I have the self-control not to request it.

The tub is filled, steam rising slowly off the bubbly surface. He's turned off the main light, so only a single dim light remains. And the room smells like ...

"It's my bodywash," James supplies. Apparently, my sniffing wasn't so discreet. He lets go of my hands and backs up, leaning on the doorframe.

"You didn't have to do that. Mine is right there." I point to the bottle, sitting on the edge of the tub.

"I know. I used it this morning."

A flush of shame rises, I'm sure bringing a blush with it. The room suddenly feels too small, too hot, too ... *something*. "You could have just gotten yours out of your bag this morning."

"But I didn't." He crosses his arms, his face unreadable. "And I had to spend the whole day smelling like you."

"You don't like the way I smell?" I scuff my bare toe along the tile, making plans to throw my Caramel Perfection body wash in the nearest dumpster. Then, set it on fire.

"That's not it."

James leans forward, just enough to touch my chin with a finger. The slightest pressure has me tilting my head up, lifting my gaze to his. Deep brown eyes burn into mine.

"It was torture," he says. "And now it's your turn to suffer."

With that, James gives me the tiniest, most devilish smile.

"Thank you," I whisper.

He starts to leave, but I tug him to a stop. "Wait—what about tonight? Did you get another room?"

His smile fades, but his eyes blaze. "There are no more rooms."

And with that, James leaves the bathroom.

CHAPTER 24

Winnie

LATER, while James is showering, I make a mental survival guide. It would be perfect for one of Lindy's Buzzfeed articles. Mine would be called: How to Share a Room with James Graham. Or, for better mass appeal: How to Share a Room with a Man You're Attracted to But Trying Not to Fall Head Over Heels For.

- Schedule bathroom times so as not to have awkward run-ins while in a towel *(so far, check)*
- Take clothes into the bathroom with you when showering so you don't need to leave the bathroom in a towel *(check, only because James was kind enough to push my bag into the bathroom while swearing his eyes were closed)*

- You must wear full coverage pajamas and for the record, boxers do not count as pajama bottoms *(so far, check)*
- Do not use each other's bodywash because it's very, very distracting *(total fail here as I can smell James on my skin, and he's right—it's torture)*
- Do not, in any circumstances upon penalty of death, share a bed *(pullout couch at the ready, so, CHECK!)*
- If there is only one bed, someone should sleep on the couch *(check)*
- If there is no couch, someone should sleep on the floor *(n/a)*
- Keep air-conditioning at a reasonable level to avoid visible nipplage *(check, but is nipplage a word?)*

The last one has me grinning in a way that apparently James finds disturbing, because he gives me a look as he exits the bathroom. I'm glad to see he's following the rules (even if he doesn't know there ARE rules) and is fully dressed.

Though, as I try not to stare at his fitted T-shirt and sweatpants, I think I need to add another rule.

- No sweatpants! *(because MUSCULAR THIGHS IN SWEATPANTS ARE TOO MUCH)*

"What?" he asks, toweling off his damp hair. This only emphasizes his massive biceps.

"Nothing." I shift on the pullout couch, trying to avoid the weird bar that seems to come standard with every sleeper sofa ever made.

"Hey—I told you I'd sleep on the couch." His frown deepens, and it makes me want to laugh.

"And I made the executive decision while you were in the shower that you're too big for the couch. Sorry—you snooze, you lose, boss."

James heads back to the bathroom with his towel. When he walks away, I do my very, VERY best not to track the way his butt stretches the fabric of his sweatpants.

Seriously—sweatpants shouldn't make a man look hot. They're a 1980s relic, bringing to mind out-of-fashion dads and the whole giving-up-on-life vibe. On James, though, they only accentuate his narrow hips and his thighs—which look powerful enough to crush cars. I never thought of myself as a thigh woman, but here we are.

GIVE ME ALL THE THIGHS! Or, at least, two very specific thighs attached to one very specific man.

James stretches out on the bed, which is across and a little to the side of my couch bed. I can feel him watching me as I do my best not to meet his gaze. My emotional state is much improved—a foot rub, hot bath, and hotter man taking care of me will do that. But these things also make my emotional state with regards to James more complicated.

And I don't need *complicated.*

I tick off the reasons why this is a terrible idea in my mind. First, he's still my boss. That's reason enough. But since that doesn't seem to be enough to stop all my feels, I keep going.

Second, maybe he didn't *regret* the kiss, but he also said he didn't know what to do about it. And he hasn't tried kissing me again. Which, to be clear, he *could.* And despite points one and two, I would not stop him.

I'm going to toss out the third point, which is that I just got out of a relationship and shouldn't be thinking about another so soon. Seeing Dale with Celia—at least before I realized the whole situation—made me realize just how little

234

of my heart he ever held. Even so, I shouldn't jump into anything. Even if James's thighs in sweatpants make me consider otherwise.

"What are you watching?" James asks.

Honestly, I'd forgotten I was watching anything. I was busy making lists in my head and trying not to drool over James's legs. I glance at my phone.

"Just TikTok." His lip curls, and I can't help but laugh. "You're such an old man. Hating TikTok. Wearing sweatpants."

He glances down at his legs. "What's wrong with my sweatpants?"

It takes me a moment to swallow, because my throat has closed up. "Nothing." Absolutely nothing.

James makes a growl that sounds like disagreement, and I keep my eyes glued to my phone. But when he climbs out of bed, I can't ignore him. He's wearing a smoldery expression —another thing to expressly forbid on my survival guide—as he crosses the room to me.

He possesses all the languid, powerful grace of some kind of large jungle cat. A large jungle cat in low-riding sweat-pants that are going to be the death of me. I stare up at him as he reaches me, unsure if I should run or stretch out my neck in submission. Isn't that what animals do to show loyalty or submission? It would also give him easy access. You know—if he decides to kiss my neck.

In a move that surprises me so much I gasp, James stretches out on my couch bed with an easy grace. That is, until his butt hits the metal bar.

"Ouch! What is *that*?" he grumbles, wiggling.

The mattress is thin, with little support. James's weight —and all the wiggling—sends me rolling almost into his lap. I grab the arm of the couch and manage to right myself, sitting up cross-legged. And if my knee is touching his thigh, it's because there's no room in this tiny couch bed, not because I'll take any contact with his thighs I can get.

I DO find myself wishing the human kneecap possessed more nerve endings.

James is definitely breaking at least several of the survival guide rules. Okay, so maybe I haven't *told* James any of the rules, but still. Shouldn't he *know* he can't just climb into my sofa bed with me? It simply isn't *done*.

My thoughts are now apparently channeling some proper English Lady abiding by the rules of manners. All I need is a corset, an embroidered handkerchief, and a dance card tied to my wrist.

Annnnnnd now I'm picturing James as Mr. Darcy. *Great.*

"It feels like you're on some kind of torture device," he grumbles, still adjusting. His feet practically hang off the end of the mattress.

"That's the bar for the fold-out thingy. Just part of the luxurious sofa bed experience." His blank look has me reeling. "Wait—have you never slept on a pullout couch before?"

James simply stares, blinking and expressionless. What I hear him saying is, *I'm too fancy for pull-out couches. And I've been too tall to fit on something like this since I was fourteen.*

That's what I imagine his expression means, anyway.

I cluck my tongue. "Oh, you poor, privileged boy."

"I thought you said I was an old man. Pick a lane." He squirms some more, and his brows knit together. "This is impossible. I told you I'd let you have the bed," he growls.

I don't know if it's the growl or all the talk of beds, but my cheeks feel too warm. I cannot talk about beds with James Graham. Especially not while IN a bed with him. Even a sofa bed. Though the bar is acting as a chaperone, keeping things from being TOO comfortable. My cheeks grow even hotter.

"No. It's fine. But why are you over here?"

"Because you accused me of being an old man. I'm here to watch TikToks." He glances at my phone's screen and frowns. "What is *that*?"

I laugh. "A contouring tutorial."

"Is that, like, a makeup thing?"

Oh, sweet, innocent James. He may have a sister but Harper is a fresh-faced beauty. I'd wager she wears little more than lip gloss and maybe mascara here and there. I love makeup, and I don't even do contouring. I happen to find it fascinating (and also relaxing) to watch the videos.

"Just wait." I angle my body and the phone toward him, still trying to maintain distance. Not an easy feat when James is so big he could take up this whole bed himself. I try not to giggle at his sour expression.

"Why is she putting those dark lines on her face?"

"Sh! Just watch."

He grumbles but does as I ask. I can practically see his head exploding as the time-lapse tutorial shows a woman going from a paint-by-numbers face to looking flawless and cover-model ready. James watches the video, and I watch James, which is much more entertaining. He looks shocked, horrified, and unreasonably angry.

"No," he says at the end, shaking his head vehemently, which jostles me toward him. "No."

I manage to keep myself from falling into his lap, but just barely. "Okay, so no makeuptok. We could do beertok?"

"Beertok?"

A crease forms between his brows, and without thinking about it, I smooth it away with my finger. James goes still at the touch, and when I glance at his eyes, they're dark, and on my lips. I drop my hand to my lap and clear my throat, feeling my heart thudding like a battering ram in my chest.

"So, um, on Tiktok, you can follow certain hashtags or communities around topics. Makeuptok is all about makeup. Booktok is about books. I haven't really looked, but beertok is probably a thing."

"No more beer."

A thought comes to mind, and I bite back a smile, then type something into the search, navigating until I find a video I've watched before.

"Alligators?" James asks.

"Just watch."

James's frown returns, but this time I don't dare reach up to smooth away the crease between his brows. "What's it doing?"

I didn't quite think through the awkwardness of explaining this to him. "It's, um, something the males—bulls—do during mating season. They bellow to attract females, and the sound frequency is so low it vibrates the water above their backs. This reminds me of you. Except you're growling to scare people off."

James raises one dark brow, then does his best impression of an alligator bellow … which sounds just like his normal growl. Only a little more playful.

"How's that?" he asks.

I grin. "You didn't scare me off."

"I wasn't trying to scare you off."

Whatever maturity I've earned in my twenty-eight years flees at his words. I suddenly, desperately need to not think about James, growling NOT to scare me off. James, in thigh-hugging sweatpants, next to me in this horribly uncomfortable couch bed. James, who stepped in between me and Dale,

238

who took off my shoes, massaged my feet, and drew me a bath.

"What should we watch next?" I zero all my attention in on the tiny screen. "Bloopers? Dance videos? True crime? What are you into?"

For a moment, James freezes, and I feel like I've unintentionally hit a nerve asking about the most mundane of things. I can see the thoughts flying behind his eyes as he tries to come up with an answer.

I lightly touch his arm. Before my fingertips get any ideas about exploring, I pull them back. "It's okay if you don't have one thing you're into. Or if you're unsure."

He crosses his arms, his face taking on the stubborn bent of a two-year-old fighting bedtime. "I like brewing beer. And making furniture."

"Okay."

"Okay."

It feels like we're fighting, but I'm not sure about what. But I file this whole conversation away for later. James plucks the phone out of my hand and clicks it off before setting it down on the table out of my reach.

"No more Tiktok."

"Okay, *boss*. Can I have my phone back?"

"No."

I laugh. "I need to make you a T-shirt with your favorite word."

"What's my favorite word?"

I blink at him. "Really? You don't know?" When he only shrugs, I have to laugh. "It's *no*. And I swear, it accounts for at least ninety percent of your daily word count. Maybe ninety-five."

James pauses for a beat, then, with the smallest sliver of a smile, says, "No."

I totally lose it then, and though James doesn't laugh, I swear, his small smile grows a tiny fraction before he turns away, hiding it from view.

"So, that's what you do to unwind—watch mindless videos on TikTok?" he asks when I've finally stopped laughing and can breathe again.

"Don't judge, old man."

"I'm not."

"You're not judging? Or old?"

He glares. "Either."

"Hm."

"I'm not," he insists. His brown eyes look almost golden this close. There are tiny flecks of an olive green I hadn't noticed before. James at rest has a perpetually hard expression. But right now, his eyes are softer.

I realize I'm staring and pull myself back to the conversation. "If I'm trying to unwind, it's Tiktok or novels." I lift my chin. "Romance novels."

He makes a humming sound in the back of his throat that makes the tiny hairs stand up on my arms.

"What about you? Or do you ever unwind?"

He ignores my dig. "Woodworking. Or I ride my bike."

"Bike as in bicycle or bike as in motorcycle?"

"Motorcycle." He gives me a look like my question is the most ridiculous thing ever.

"Don't act like it's a dumb question." I toss a pillow at him, and he looks startled as it bounces off his face and onto the floor. I wonder if anyone is ever playful with James, or if they're too scared of his gruff exterior.

"Can you see me riding a bicycle?"

And now I'm imagining James in bike shorts. Those thighs in Spandex would be lethal. LETHAL.

I know I'm probably blushing. I can feel the creep of heat

moving over my skin. "I guess the leather jacket and boots should have clued me in. Your style is much more MC than Tour de France."

James is quiet for a moment, then says, "You have an interesting style."

"I can't tell if that means you like it or hate it."

"I don't hate it."

I roll my eyes, but I'm still smiling. "Thanks. Best compliment I've had all day." James grunts, and before he feels obligated to say something nicer, I add, "I got into the pin-up, rockabilly thing when I was thirteen. I guess you could say I zagged when everyone else zigged into fringed vests, liquid leggings, and babydoll shirts."

"Any reason?"

I pick at the edge of the sheet, drawing it up a little higher over my lap. "My mom loved the 40s and 50s. She didn't dress like this, but she loved the style and music and pretty much anything from that era. She collected vintage posters, calendars, that kind of thing." I pause, drawing in a slow breath and letting it out just as slowly. "Then, she died. This felt like a way to connect with her. It also felt a little bit like my own personal armor."

I think I've gone too deep, bringing up my mom, but after a moment, James says, "It suits you."

Our eyes meet and hold. As the moment stretches to two … three … four … it's hard not to let my gaze fall to his lips. I've spent way too much time today thinking about James's mouth. It is lush and luscious and I'd like to pay the first and last months' deposit and move in.

Complications, I remind myself, dropping my gaze.

I find myself leaning into humor, just like I did with Tank at dinner. I press a hand to my chest dramatically and channel my best Southern belle. "Why, James Graham—I do believe you paid me half a compliment."

He grunts, and like that, he's up and out of the bed. The thin mattress can't handle the sudden change of weight and I faceplant into the space he left with an *oof*. I manage to dig my face out of the James-shaped dip in the bed just as he stops halfway into the bathroom.

I worried I offended him, but that tiny grin is back, even maybe a few millimeters bigger. *Oh, the things that smile does to my heart!*

With the kind of half-smile marketing teams use to sell absolutely anything at all, James says, "It was three-fourths of a compliment, temp."

CHAPTER 25

James

I WAKE IN THE DARKNESS, instantly on alert, but unsure where I am or why. My whole body is tense, my fists clenched in the sheets. It's the unfamiliar fabric that makes me remember the hotel room and Winnie.

There's a whimper and another sharp cry from across the room.

Winnie.

I'm out of bed and next to her in an instant, heart thrumming in my chest.

Harper used to have nightmares, right after Mom died. Maybe not so frequently, but in my memory, there were a lot of them. Tank wouldn't hear her because the master bedroom is across the house, and both Pat and Collin could have slept through a truck driving into the side of our house.

I remember those nights now as I stand over Winnie,

who's thrashing in her sheets. It's dark, but from the dim light coming through the curtains, I can see her shaking her head, brow furrowed, eyes squeezed closed.

"No," she moans, twisting her whole body. "Don't."

Licking my lips, I hesitate with one hand outstretched, stopping just short of Winnie's shoulder. With Harper, I had to be gentle with waking her or she'd react violently, getting even more upset. It became like instinct after a while, hearing Harper's cries, jogging across the hall to her room, curling up beside her and gently stroking her hair until her breathing evened out. Most of the time, she wouldn't even wake up.

Can I—should I—climb in bed with Winnie like that?

As I stand here, debating whether or not this falls outside the line of consent or if she'd want me to get in bed with her or how bad of an idea it would be for me, a broken sob escapes her throat. Decision made.

I lean forward, cupping my hands around her shoulders, smoothing gently down. "I've got you. Shh—Winnie. I'm here."

The words sound stupid to my own ears. Why should she care that I'm here? Why would my presence offer any comfort when I've done so much to confuse her, when I've pushed her away?

But Winnie shudders under my hands, leaning toward me, seeking my touch. Her eyes fly open, her breath coming in gasping pants as her gaze skates over my face.

"Scoot over," I whisper, already climbing into the bed. I can tell she's trying, but her legs and torso are tangled in the sheet. I'm so caught up in watching her I forget about the metal bar. It was only annoying earlier, but as my bad knee bangs into it, I curse under my breath.

How is she even sleeping on this? No wonder she's

having bad dreams. I want to rip the bed apart and toss the metal bar straight through the window. Without meaning to, I've tightened my grip on Winnie's shoulders. Shaking my head, I shift so one hand is under her back and the other cups the backs of her thighs.

"Forget this." I lift Winnie from the bed, stumbling back a little as I adjust.

Her hands slide up my bare chest and around my neck. I barely contain a shiver at the feel of her fingertips toying with my hair. When she rests her cheek against my chest with a shuddering sigh, something warm moves through my chest. It's a physical reaction to having her softness pressed so close, but even more, it's a flare of protectiveness, something far deeper than attraction.

I don't allow myself to think about it, instead focusing on getting Winnie into the big bed without more touching or limbs tangling than necessary.

Kneeling on the edge of the bed, I deposit her as gently as I can in the center of the mattress. Her hands fall away from my neck, tugging the sheets up over her body. Reluctantly, I start to slide my hand away, backing toward the edge of the bed, still on my knees. But her hand shoots out, grabbing mine, tugging me toward her.

"*Please.*"

The word sounds like it's been ripped out of her. I freeze for an instant, too tired to debate with myself, too eager to stay close to argue myself out of it.

She needs you. Winnie needs you.

It's this thought that has me disregarding any shred of self-preservation as I climb fully into bed, letting her direct me with the one hand still stubbornly holding mine. She turns on her side, and I bite my lip when she positions my hand over the shirt covering her stomach. It's all I can do not to let my fingertips explore, to lift the edge of her shirt enough to feel her soft skin—

Get yourself under control. She just had a nightmare bad enough to wake you up.

I'm glad for the sobering reminder, and I curl protectively around Winnie, the oversized spoon to her tiny spoon. She sighs with contentment, pulling my hand tighter and wiggling until her back is flush with my chest. For a few long beats, we both still, the only movement our breathing, and the rapid pounding of my chest, which I hope she can't feel.

"You lost your shirt," Winnie says.

A chuckle rumbles its way through my chest, and Winnie arches back, as though trying to chase the sensation. "I can't sleep with a shirt on." I pause. "Does it make you uncomfortable?"

Winnie's answer takes a few seconds. "Not uncomfortable, no."

She doesn't say what it *does* make her, and I can hear the way she's holding back, the restraint in her voice. I bite the inside of my cheek to keep from pushing. I'm far too desperate for her compliments.

For a few minutes we stay this way, my breathing syncing up with hers until we're moving in tandem, slow breaths in and out. My heart, however, can't seem to slow or find a steady pace.

"Is this normal—the nightmare?" I ask.

When she nods, the warm surge of protectiveness rises again. I remember nights spent soothing Harper, the feeling of wanting to be her safe place. This is that, but very much without the brotherly vibe. I'm feeling anything but familiar right now. It's the same urge that had me stepping in when the guy reached for her lanyard. And when I threw Daniel in the pool. I want to protect Winnie from the things outside this room as much as from her own dreams.

"Do you want to talk about it?"

Something about being this close, having Winnie in my arms allows me to sense more of what she's feeling even without words. Unless I'm imagining the connection, but I don't think I am. She wants to tell me, but she needs a push.

"Tell me." My tone is demanding, but Winnie responds almost immediately.

"The dreams don't matter. Not really. They're all variations of the same theme." She draws in a ragged breath.

I tighten my arm around her waist, her shirt bunching a little as her fingers tangle with mine, squeezing.

"You can talk to me, temp." What I mean is that she can trust me.

Her other hand moves, sliding up my forearm, then back down. She lightly circles my wrist, and I love that her fingertips can't touch. Her body seems to relax even more against me, tension I didn't realize she still carried dissipating.

"My dad had an affair."

Her words are such a stark contrast to the tenderness, the intimacy of the moment that I jerk a little, sucking in a breath. Rage, hot and thick swirls through me as she continues.

"One that lasted years and years. My nightmares always revolve in some way around that, or just around him. They bring up the feelings I had when I found out."

"How did you find out?" My words are clipped. It's hard to keep the edge of anger from my voice. She must feel it, because Winnie tenses slightly. I brush my lips over her hair, softening my tone. "I'm here."

That promise must be enough.

"I didn't find out until after he died. Chevy handled most

247

of the big details—I was a wreck—but my one task was his phone and email. A woman contacted me, trying to reach him. Only after the money stopped coming."

"What was the money for?"

"He was helping to support her. She said she didn't know he was married—it started way before my mom died. He told her he traveled a lot for work, the same thing he told my mom. Which he did, but …" She trails off.

"I'm so sorry."

I'm sorry, but I'm also furious. Cheating is … an unacceptable thing. And though my dad still has my utmost respect, I have seen him at his lowest. I still remember the way it felt to lose some sense of trust in him, realizing he was human and could make mistakes.

He didn't make any like this. Not even close. And anyway, an affair spanning years—it's enough to make me flush with rage. I can only imagine the complexity of finding this out after his death.

"The thing is, she wanted money. And there was barely any. Even for us. I mean, we'd been financially struggling for years, and here he was helping put some other woman's kid through college."

She scoffs, and I vaguely remember Lindy and Pat mentioning student loans when they were begging me to hire Winnie.

"What did you do?"

"I had to pay her off. I didn't want Chevy to ever know, and I was afraid she might keep contacting me and somehow end up reaching him. So, I gave her the little I inherited and told her not to contact either of us again."

My brothers sometimes tease me about being unfeeling. And it's true, at times I'm more stoic than emotional. But when it comes to other people's suffering, other people's

248

pain, my own emotions are honed to a sharp point. I shift, sliding my other arm underneath Winnie, circling around her waist so I'm holding her even more tightly to me. Her arms band around mine, grasping my forearms.

It takes a few minutes and a lot of intentionally slow breaths for me to find my voice. "I am so sorry, Winnie. There aren't enough words for how horrible that is."

"The worst part is feeling like I lost my father twice. First, when he died, and second, when I realized he was never the man I thought he was." Her voice starts to wobble, and I swallow around the tightness in my throat. "I can't confront him. I can't work through my anger and hurt and betrayal. He's gone. I'm angry and hurt, and then I feel guilty about feeling that way. There is nowhere for my feelings to go. It's just so unresolved. I hate it."

"And you didn't tell Chevy because you didn't want him to go through the same thing."

One thing Winnie has shown me in the brief time I've known her is how she picks up on what other people need, how she watches for ways to be kind. Like what she did for me tonight—getting my family here, making shirts, celebrating my win. I keep insisting to everyone I don't need help. I don't need anyone but myself.

It's a lie. Probably everyone knows it, but Winnie most of all.

"You're only the second person I've told."

She doesn't need to tell me who the first is. I thought I felt rage before, directed toward her father. But it burns stronger and hotter now, thinking about Dale. Earlier, I'd seen him at the same time Winnie did, and watched as she made her way over, a determined and cheerful expression on her face. It made me relieved, honestly, to see that she seemed over him.

But things shifted when it became clear Dale had been with that woman while with Winnie. *You knew,* she said to him. I squeeze my eyes closed, feeling my nostrils flare. Winnie told her boyfriend about her father, while Dale was essentially doing the exact same thing.

I'm not a violent man, though I seem to have more of these urges around—or because of—Winnie. Throwing that guy in the pool last night, wanting to track down Dale and throw him off the roof of the building … this isn't like me.

I focus on breathing, on the feel of Winnie's hair tickling my chest. Sliding my hands to cover hers, I let my thumbs smooth tiny circles over Winnie's skin, the repetitive movement calming me. I press a kiss to the side of her head without stopping to think about whether or not it's a good idea.

I've moved firmly into the land of Who Cares If It's a Good Idea. Maybe it's the darkness or Winnie's vulnerability activating my protective side, but whatever hesitations and objections I've had are gone.

Winnie is mine.

Mine to protect. Mine to care for. Mine to …

I swallow hard again, my mind dizzy in reaction to the word I wanted to use there. Love. Mine to love.

It's way too early to know something like that. It's probably the late hour and the depth of Winnie's raw emotions. I'll wake tomorrow knowing this isn't—and can't be—love. I can worry about whatever emotion it IS then, too.

"You take good care of people, temp. I admire that." I lower my voice to the gentlest whisper. "But who takes care of you?"

Winnie trembles a little in my arms, and when I lift my head, I can see tears leaking from her eyes. A tight sensation pinches in my chest and I nuzzle closer.

"Don't cry, beautiful."

I shift my hold on her, lifting my arms until my thumbs slide over her cheeks. Emboldened by the way she closes her eyes, sighing with contentment, I replace my thumbs with my lips, leaning over her to kiss the wetness on her cheeks.

"James," she whispers, and I cannot take my eyes off her lips.

"I've got you," I say, and then I tilt my head, lean in, and brush my mouth over hers.

I am instantly vibrating with electric heat. The somber, emotional mood gives way to something completely different. I understand why people talk about making love during a time of intense grief, why physical connection can become a need, a healing balm.

The ragged feelings in my chest ease as my lips move over Winnie's. *Slow down*, I chide myself, wanting something different than the explosion in the elevator last night when I couldn't hold back any longer.

It takes all the control I have, but I keep my kiss a caress. Tender and light and soft. I want to soothe the ache in Winnie, smooth the rough, painful places as well as I can with my mouth. But when she makes a small sound and arches toward me, I release a little bit of my control, losing myself in Winnie.

I want my kiss to assure her of my intentions, though truly—I'm not sure what they are, other than to protect, to cherish, to keep her close and safe. I want to explore; I want to treasure. I want her to know her value and worth and how royally both her father and her ex screwed up.

But I'm also not ready for this to go beyond a kiss. When she wiggles and shifts, seeking more, pulling me closer, I press a last soft kiss to her lips and spin her back around so we're spooning again.

She groans in protest, but I only tighten my grip, chuckling. I press a kiss to her hair, then her temple, then bend to kiss her shoulder. "Sleep, temp."

I stroke her hair with one hand, holding her in place with the other. After a moment, I feel her sigh and relax against me. In no time at all, her breathing evens out. When I'm sure she's asleep, I lean closer in the darkness, whispering a truth I'm not ready to admit in the light of day.

"I knew one kiss would never be enough. Not when it comes to you."

I'll worry about what, exactly, this means later.

CHAPTER 26

James

I SMELL Winnie before my eyes are open, before I'm aware of her body curled into mine. *Caramel Perfection.* I don't know if it's a blessing or curse to know the name of her bodywash, because I can't get the name out of my head, like I can't get the scent out of my nose. Somehow, she still smells of it even though I used my body wash in her bath last night. I draw in a deep breath, closing my eyes to focus on her scent.

I haven't woken up many times with regret for something I did the night before. As sleep slowly lifts away from me, I refuse to feel regret now.

Not for the kiss on the elevator, not for the way I took care of Winnie after running into Dale in the lobby. Not for holding her after her nightmare or kissing her in the darkness. No regrets.

That doesn't mean I have any idea what I'm doing here or what to do with the woman in my arms.

Maybe you should listen to your dad. Try. Risk.

And maybe lose …

But at least TRY.

In what's an absolutely unwelcome intrusion to my thoughts, I suddenly hear Yoda's voice in my head, telling me there is no try. Do or do not. I bite back a laugh just as Winnie sighs softly, the sound sending a pulse of warmth through me.

She shifts, and I let my body move with her, not wanting to wake her. I'm not ready to let her go.

Her skin is so soft under my palms, and in the light peeking through the crack in the blinds, I get a chance to study her up close. I start with the tattoos on the arm I'm closest to.

It's delicate work, real artistry. The designs are not necessarily flowery, but thin, black lines flowing like ribbons or vines, twisted with the occasional flower, image, or word. I see a tiny anchor here, the word *hope* there, next to a rose. A secret garden of treasures on her skin.

I have one tattoo on the inside of my upper arm, a somewhat hidden spot because it's just for me, in memory of my mom. It's her name, written in Japanese lettering. I made sure to get the design drawn by a friend who grew up in Japan and moved here with his family when he was six. I didn't want to think I was getting my mom's name and really spell out something like *disco ball*.

Winnie and I talked about a lot of things last night, but I didn't ask about her ink. I wonder if there's meaning behind them, like mine for my mom, or if she based them on vintage tattoos or artwork.

The urge to press my lips to their lines, to trace the path with my mouth on her skin almost overwhelms me. But I'm not sure how Winnie will feel about the vulnerable things she shared in the night or about waking to my lips on her. The last thing I want to do is push her—or myself—too far, too fast. If I'm going to take this risk with her, it's going to be slow. It has to be. Especially considering her current employment status. I don't need to worry about getting in trouble with HR, obviously, like in a normal job. But there are reasons companies often put nonfraternization policies in place. If things go bad, they'll go bad on multiple levels. It's complicated.

Winnie stirs again, which probably means she's close to waking up. Ever so slowly, I begin peeling back my body from hers, pausing when she grabs my arm, nuzzling her face on it and leaving a trail of drool over the dusting of hair. I bite my lip, holding back my smile. She's adorable, and I know she'd be horrified if she knew she wiped drool on me. I wait again until she settles, then manage to extricate myself from her without stirring the bed too much. I take a big risk by running my fingers over a lock of her hair just before I step away.

I'm on my feet now, but the sight of Winnie with her sleep-creased face, her beautifully inked skin, her rumpled hair—it all tempts me to climb back into bed, to wake her with kisses.

Backing away, I decide to head to the lobby so I can grab a coffee to wake her with instead. I asked Winnie in the night who took care of her, and in the silence, through her tears, I heard what she didn't say: *no one*.

Sure, she has Chevy, who sometimes oversteps in his protection. She's got Val and Lindy, and probably half the town of Sheet Cake in her corner. But I'm realizing how much Winnie is like me—so busy taking care of other people that no one sees what she needs.

Until now. Until me.

———

The plan was to get coffee and return to Winnie. But that was before I spotted Dale in the lobby.

Plan A—take care of Winnie—has been temporarily set aside for Plan B—avenge Winnie by making Dale pay. Which, arguably, is part of taking care of Winnie.

Would she have asked me to do so? Probably not.

Would she stop me? I'd like to think no.

Either way, she's upstairs in bed, and Dale is down here handing his ticket to the valet. Anger rises hot in my throat, a flush I feel spreading through my limbs. Dale was the only one Winnie trusted to tell about her father. And it sounds like the whole time, he was with his fiancée. The thought makes my fingers curl into my palm and my throat tighten with anger. But I'm not getting physical. That's not my style —at least, other than with my brothers, and that's different. We know we love each other, even when we're driving each other nuts. Dale isn't going to get beaten up. He needs something else.

Something more creative.

I never thought I'd be glad to see clowns under any circumstance at all, but a small group of them selling balloons outside the coffee shop is exactly what I need. Especially because these aren't the little kid clowns. These are teenage clowns, which means they're without supervision. More importantly, they're more than happy to accept money for what I want them to do.

I hold out a crisp bill. "I'll give you twenty bucks to fill that guy's car up with your balloon"—I glance down at a netted bag filled with the things—*"swords."*

Right after we checked in, I pretended not to notice these guys making balloons into "swords" so phallic they deserve a ticket for public indecency.

"Make it fifty."

I pull two more twenties from my wallet. "Keep the change. It's that guy over there. The valet is bringing his car around."

"Dude, we won't have time," one of the clowns says, and I realize he's right. Dale and his fiancée are already moving toward the front doors as a silver SUV pulls up out front.

"If one of you can stall them for two minutes, I'll handle them. Just ... give me two minutes." The clowns scatter. One of them pulls out bowling pins, jumping in front of Dale and starting to juggle. Perfect.

Also perfect—a large group of the legging ladies, as Winnie calls them, emerging from the coffee shop, looking fresh and full of energy and, most importantly, like they're sniffing the air for the scent of desperation. I intercept them as quickly as I can without startling them.

"Good morning," I say. I'm met with giggles and hair tosses, even from the ones I see wearing wedding rings. I don't have much time, so I dive right in, pointing toward Dale and his fiancée. "My friends over there have been asking all weekend about what you do."

When I see six sets of hungry eyes turn that way, I go in for the kill, using terms I've heard snatches of while in elevators and hallways this week. "She said something about needing a purpose, wanting to invest in something to bring in extra income. I think she was too shy to approach anyone, but if someone were to ask before she leaves ..."

And they're off. Practically at a sprint, and just barely

intercepting Dale and his fiancée before they make it to the front doors. Which is a good thing, because just outside the glass, a group of teenage clowns is now filling Dale's SUV with balloon "swords."

Dale deserves worse. Much, much worse. But I'll hope his actions naturally catch up to him one day. For now, this will do. I'm whistling as I make my way back upstairs to find Winnie.

CHAPTER 27

Winnie

I GLARE AT JAMES AND, when that doesn't seem to have any effect, I *cross my arms* and glare. I use all the strength my eyeball muscles can muster to show him just how serious I am. "I'm not getting on that thing."

The *thing* in question being James's motorcycle, which he apparently swapped for his car the other night after the elevator kiss. I was all for going to have brunch with his family this morning ... until I learned how we'd be getting there.

James pinches the bridge of his nose, and I want to grin. I'm really serious about not wanting to ride on a motorcycle, but is it bad I also enjoy frustrating him? Especially when I know he's not JUST frustrated.

I've started to categorize James's levels of grump. There's the true grump, when he's legitimately mad or unhappy or stressed. He has an amused grumpy, where he finds something funny, but doesn't want to show it. Medium grumpy is kind of his comfortable resting state. A close cousin to amused grumpy, is the acting-grumpy-so-he-won't-appear-happy, which is exactly what it sounds like. I'm not sure why he can't just BE happy, but whatever.

Right now, he's the irritated-masking-slight-amusement grumpy.

"Get on the bike, temp."

"No."

It's a matter of safety. More accurately, it's about my self-preservation.

All morning, James has been *sweet*. In the grumpiest way possible, of course, but shockingly thoughtful and attentive. From waking me up by running gentle fingers through my hair to supplying me with coffee as soon as my eyes blinked open, he's been taking care of me. All this after rescuing me from my nightmare, holding me close, and listening to me spill my dark secrets. And let's not forget the spooning and the kissing. There was also that.

Now he's trying to get me on a motorcycle, all pressed up close with my arms wrapped around him? I don't think so. Not happening. I don't care what the books say. That's the way babies are made.

"Why not?" James finally asks, each syllable punctuated slowly, carefully, as though I'm trying his patience.

"You only have one helmet. That's why not." A valid reason, even if it's not the real or only one.

James holds out the shiny black motorcycle helmet to me. "You can wear it."

"And then *you* won't have a helmet."

"There's no helmet law in Texas. It's fine."

"And that's one stupid decision on Texas's part. Your skull is not getting cracked open like an egg on my watch."

"It's only a few miles. I'm safe."

Maybe he is a safe driver. Rider? Biker? Motorcyclist? I don't even know the correct term here. But James Graham is *anything* but safe.

He already owns the majority shares of my heart's stock and is angling for a hostile takeover. Maybe not THAT hostile. But I'm doing my best not to completely fall for this man who fired me once, ignored me at the conference, and then ran off after we kissed. He's made me all unsteady, and I don't like unsteady.

I cross my arms. "I don't trust the other drivers."

A true statement. But I also don't trust myself. I don't know why, but climbing on the back of this motorcycle with James feels like a point of no return. Like once I've wrapped myself around him during daylight hours and let this sexy man steer us through Austin traffic, it's all over. I'll be his forever, no take-backs.

"Let me worry about the other drivers," he says.

"How about you ride home, get your truck, and then come back to pick me up later in that. I'll just wait in the lobby. You have to come back with the truck anyway for our bags. No problem."

"Fine." James sighs and turns away. I immediately regret saying no.

He climbs on the bike in a move that deserves at least a PG-13 rating. I can barely drag my eyes away from his thighs and his butt in those dark jeans. He secures the helmet on the back of the bike.

"You forgot your helmet."

"No, I didn't."

Stupid, stubborn, infuriating man!

He fires up the bike, and the motor's deep purr is a sexy, sexy sound to match the sexy, sexy sight. He looks like the quintessential bad boy from the pages of one of my romance novels come to life. Only better. Because he's here, not a fictional man.

And, unlike a fictional man, you aren't promised a happily ever after.

But I CAN kiss him. Let's see a fictional man do that!

James begins maneuvering out of the parking spot, backing up slowly and using his feet to balance the bike. He pauses when we're eye to eye. I can't read his expression, but it's dark with a spark of something. A dare? A challenge?

I'm about ten seconds from caving in and hopping up there with him.

"Tank will be disappointed," James says, speaking louder to be heard over the bike. "He's making you crepes."

I am only as strong as my weakest part, and my weakest part is most definitely crepes.

"Crepes?" My question comes out like a wheeze. I don't usually get all fangirly about James's family. But the famous Think Tank, whose face has graced Billboards, magazine covers, and Sports Center, is making ME crepes???

Pardon me while my head explodes.

James shrugs. "I told him you liked crepes, so he's making them. Just for you."

My brow furrows. "How do you even know I like crepes?"

James doesn't answer, just blinks. It makes me want to yank out his dark eyelashes one by one. The thing is, he'd probably look just as good with bald eyelids.

"Jo told me," he says finally. "She said you took her all the way to Austin once for crepes at some food truck."

I blow out a breath. "What else did Jo tell you?"

James raises one brow. "Wouldn't you like to know? Come on. Get on the bike, Winchester."

Winchester. Why does it make me shiver when he says my full name? I'd always been secretly proud of my daddy naming me after his favorite gun, just like he named Chevy after his favorite truck. That is, until I found out the truth about my dad. I've hated my full name ever since. But when James says it … the name changes and feels different coming from his lips, from that low, gravelly voice.

"You could bring some crepes back when you pick me up," I suggest.

"I could."

But he won't. The implication is clear.

"He even bought Nutella. And heavy whipping cream for your coffee, though I can't promise he won't judge you for it."

The price of my self-preservation is not Nutella crepes! It is NOT. I am all too aware that whether he means to or not, James Graham is going to hurt me. Bad. I'm already way too invested in him, and he's shown me he doesn't know what he wants.

He revs the engine. "And Harper wanted you to meet Sergeant Pepper."

"Who's Sergeant Pepper?"

"A baby goat Chase rescued."

"A baby goat?" My resolve is like a bowl of Jell-O in direct sunlight. I'm watery, and any solid part I had left is melting into goo.

"He's not much of a baby anymore. Still likes to cuddle, though. Harper said she might bring some other babies. The woman who adopted Sergeant Pepper raises them."

I fist my hands on my hips, glaring. "You don't play fair, James Graham."

"Who said I'm playing?"

But he *is* playing. And he's doing so down and dirty, because talking about crepes and baby goats and cuddling goats is wholly unfair. The mental image of James Graham cuddling a baby goat has me feeling heat flush from the bottoms of my feet all the way up to the tips of my ears and my forehead.

One side of his mouth gives the tiniest fraction of a twitch as he studies me. "You okay? You look a little—"

"Shut up."

I unclip the helmet and attempt to swing myself on the back of the bike. I'm not as graceful as I intended and almost fall off the other side, but James reaches back, his broad hand spanning my thigh and holding me in place. He gives my leg a squeeze before letting go, and I'm practically panting from his touch.

"This is for the goats," I tell him.

"Sure," he says. "The goats."

"And the crepes."

"Understandable."

I get the helmet on but fumble with the strap. "And because I like your family."

James swivels, brushing my hands away. With masterful hands, he fastens the buckle under my chin, taking extra care to adjust until it's snug. His fingertips lazily trail down my neck when he's done, leaving a flush in their wake. Our gazes lock, and I'm met with a dark pool of desire.

"Just my family?" he asks in a low voice, eyes still fixed on mine.

Again—the man plays so, so dirty. But who's to say I can't do the same?

I let my lips part, dropping my gaze to James's mouth, then back up to his eyes, where his pupils almost eclipse the golden-brown irises. Leaning about as close as I can with the helmet on, I keep my voice low. He sucks in a breath.

"Just your family."

I pat his shoulder twice and lean back, feeling proud of myself when James chuckles and shakes his head. He revs the engine and pulls forward. My sense of smug satisfaction is lost when I squeal.

"Hold on to me," he orders, speaking loud over the engine as he starts to drive.

He doesn't need to ask twice. And I'm not just holding on for safety. I'm holding on because I'm a sucker for punishment. It's also why I slide my hands under his jacket, keeping them over his T-shirt, which is thin enough to reveal a lot of what's underneath.

I try not to count the abs. I really do. But I'm not made of self-control, so I settle for just making a mental note of the ones directly under my palms. I didn't get the chance last night during the shirtless cuddle-fest, so this feels like my due.

I barely catch the curve of a smile on his face as he tilts his head to speak over the roar of the engine. "I've got six."

"What?" I'm blushing furiously under the helmet.

"My abs. Trying to save you the trouble of counting."

I don't deny it, since it's obvious I was doing it. "Six, not eight?" I tease. "What are you—an underachiever?"

"It's genetic," he calls back. "How many abdominals a person has is related to their genetics and how many bands of connective tissue they have. Six is my max. And there is nothing underachieving about them."

And now I have a new category of grumpy: cocky grumpy. When he stops for a car backing out, I grab his sides seeking ticklish spots with a vengeance. He doesn't even flinch, though he does swat at my hands.

"I'm not ticklish," he says.

"Everyone is ticklish."

"Not me. Now, hold on."

Of course a man like James would have no weaknesses, not even a ticklish spot. Though I shouldn't, I issue myself a private challenge to find one. Because everyone is ticklish *somewhere*. No matter what James says. And if I have to do a full-body search to find it, well, that's a sacrifice I'm willing to make.

For science!

I'm able to get acclimated to the bike's movement on the slow turns out of the parking deck. It's simple, really—I just let my body move with James as he leans. Even when not on the bike, my body is attuned to follow him. He exits the garage, pausing to pay at the ticket booth, and a flutter of nerves moves through me as he pulls into traffic. It's Sunday morning, so fewer people are out and about, but I still feel so exposed.

In more ways than one.

Riding behind James, my body molded to his back, reminds me of how we slept. Only now, I'm the big spoon instead of the little spoon. I can't decide which one I prefer. Big spoons, little spoons, serving spoons, slotted spoons, plastic spoons—I think I'd like them all, so long as they involve James pressed against me.

He turns his head just before the light turns green. "You're safe with me."

I nod, knowing that he believes the words to be true. But I still feel certain that trusting James will mean the eventual evisceration of my heart. I squeeze him even tighter as the engine throttles and he pulls away.

Might as well enjoy the ride while I can.

Tank makes me feel welcome the moment I walk in the door with a hug that lifts my feet off the ground and I think also realigns my spinal column. "I'm so glad you came."

I don't get the chance to answer before James grabs me around the waist and plucks me away from his dad. James carries me through the spacious home like I weigh as much as a piece of mail.

"I'm not like a purse dog needing to be carried everywhere," I say, crossing my arms.

James only grunts and transports me an extra few steps into the open kitchen and family room. Out back there's a nice, sunny patio with a pool and a large yard, where Chase and Harper are playing with their two dogs and three goats—two babies and one larger one who must be Sergeant Pepper. The goats have on little sweaters or jackets. No—they're wearing *coats*.

"Goats in coats!" I squeal. "Awwww!"

"Food first, then goats," James says, steering me toward the table where Collin is setting out plates. He pauses to wink at James before giving me a hug almost as chiropractic as Tank's.

"Good to see you," I manage to wheeze from the air left in my lungs.

"You're breaking her ribs," James says, and once again, he yanks me from one of his family members' arms. This time, James deposits me in a chair, pushing it close enough to the table that I'll have a hard time getting out. He sits down next to me, scooting his chair closer as though to make absolutely sure I don't go anywhere.

My neck is getting sore from all the whiplash, though this

is nothing new with James. It's less a two-steps-forward, two-steps-back than a quick-step forward, a shuffle to the side, and a few hops back. We've been line dancing—that's what we're doing. Going this way, then that, and making no real forward progress because we're covering the same ground, over and over. But since last night, things have shifted, and it feels like we're moving in a singular direction. Together.

I don't even know what to do with this, with this new possessive caretaker side of him.

Tank calls out back and Harper comes in with Chase and the dogs, leaving the goats outside for now since they're still frolicking through the yard. There are loud greetings back and forth, a few licks from the dogs, and I realize once I've said hello to everyone, James has filled my coffee up and added heavy whipping cream, as promised. He gives me a little nod, and a little thrill goes through me.

"Let's eat," Tank says, passing out platters of bacon, eggs, and, of course, a platter holding crepes.

A girl could get used to this. ALL of this.

I love the big family dynamic. It was just me and Chevy and Mom and Dad, then just Chevy, me, and Dad. The Grahams household is something else, from the noise and playful bickering to the nonstop banter.

Collin teases James mercilessly, which I am fully on board with, especially now that I know James was kind of a nerd growing up. Apparently, he was a chemistry major in college and part of the chess club in high school. I know he taught Jo to play, but there's a difference between knowing how to play chess and being in the chess club.

"Did he have a pocket protector?" I ask Collin, earning a grin from Harper and a low grumble from James.

"He had a graphic tee with a picture of the periodic table on it," Harper says.

"Are there any photos?" I ask.

"No," James says, but Harper gives me a quick, secretive nod. Score! I'm totally going to find a good use for that photo. I'm thinking mugs, T-shirts, maybe posters …

"No." James nudges me with his knee under the table.

I blink in mock innocence. "What? I'm just enjoying this delicious breakfast."

He grunts and inhales two pieces of bacon.

"So, what did you two do after we left last night?" Collin waggles his brows suggestively, and before James can start growling, I jump in.

"I tried to get James to watch Tiktok videos."

That has them all laughing. Except, of course, James, who is busy still stuffing bacon in his mouth. I swear, feeding this family must take like a whole pig a day.

"How'd that go over?" Chase asks, barely holding back a smile.

I shoot James a quick look. "He took away my phone."

James shakes his head, pushing his chair back. "I'm going where I'm wanted. Out with the dogs and baby goats."

"I think you mean where you belong," Collin teases.

James has his brother in a headlock before I can blink. Collin grabs James's arms and the two thrash around, knocking over a chair. Harper moves a water glass out of the way and Chase scoots back, moving to the door.

"You know the rules, boys. Take it outside," Tank says in a bored voice, like this happens every day. Maybe it does. I definitely bet it did back when they were young.

Chase swings the back door open for James and Collin, who make their way to the back patio, still locked in a wrestling match. One of the patio chairs topples over. The dogs jump around them, barking like they can't decide if they want to break it up or join in.

269

"Don't worry," Tank says, patting my hand. "James usually comes out on top."

"I was going to put my money on Collin," I say. That earns me a deep booming laugh from Tank.

"I heard that!" James yells, just before he and Collin go right in the pool. Stormy jumps in after them.

"Did you ever get the pool heater fixed?" Harper asks, taking a bite of an egg white omelet.

"A week or two ago," Tank says.

"Too bad." Harper stands, grabbing her phone. "Better get some photos before they call a truce."

Tank and I are left at the table, watching as the fight continues in the pool. I steal a piece of bacon from James's plate, enjoying the show. Chase gets pulled into the fray—because Harper pushes him in—and the goats pick up on the energy, running and leaping on and over and off the lounge chairs.

"Is it always like this?" I ask Tank.

"Always." He smiles, but then his expression tightens, the smile lines around his eyes disappearing. "Other than the period right after their mom died. I heard you lost your mother young too. I'm so sorry."

This is an unexpected turn in conversation, a huge contrast to the laughter and shouts coming from outside. "Thank you. I'm sorry for your loss."

He nods, his eyes still on the melee outside. "They were all too quiet afterward, too well behaved. Like they thought they could somehow keep anything else bad from happening if they were just good enough."

My heart constricts and then makes a heavy thud. I remember having similar thoughts after Mom died. Not that I could keep the bad things at bay, but more that I needed to be the best daughter I could, to give my dad the least amount of trouble.

"James took the brunt of it on himself. He became more of a caretaker, more of a leader." He chuckles. "Even if his way of leading is silently shoving people in the direction he thinks they should go. Meanwhile, he's somehow untouchable, neither wanting nor accepting help. Which is why what you did for him last night, what you're *doing* for him means so much."

"Oh, I …" I swallow down my protests because Tank gives me a look that's all James. "I like a challenge," I say instead.

"James is that. You two are good for each other," Tank says.

"Oh, I don't know if we're together," I say, and the words feel false even before Tank gives me another look.

"Let's see how long you keep singing that tune. Just so you know, this is the first time he's brought a woman home."

Tank rises and begins clearing the table. I scoot my chair back, planning to help, but get waylaid at the sight of James climbing out of the pool, completely drenched. His T-shirt is molded to his torso, plastered there like a second skin. All the muscles I was snuggled up against last night but didn't get to appreciate, all the ones I felt as we rode here on his motorcycle are on full display.

He was right. There are six abdominal muscles, and they are NOT underachievers. They're like the Olympians of ab muscles. When he pulls the wet shirt over his head and begins wringing it out, a blush heats my cheeks. His torso is like a giant slab composed of overachieving muscles, from his sculpted shoulders to the broad pecs on down to those abs and the alluring vee where his hips narrow. Droplets of water skim over his tan skin, and I drag my gaze away just in time to catch him full-on smirking at me.

Busted! Before my cheeks can get any redder, I hop up and begin stacking dishes and carrying them to the sink for Tank.

"Are you okay?" Tank asks. "You look flushed."

"Yep. Totally fine."

Just, you know, thrown off by your son's hot bod. Just call me Miss Objectification.

James sticks his head in the back door, grinning, and I almost drop the empty serving platter in my hands at the sight of him so close. His wet hair drips, starting to form a puddle on the floor.

"Hey, temp. Before we go, come see where the magic happens."

"What?"

"Where I brew my beer," he says, still smiling that smug smile. "Don't worry. I'll put a shirt on first so you can concentrate."

Shirt or no shirt, I'm pretty sure my concentration is dead.

CHAPTER 28

Winnie

I PLAN to enjoy every second of the ride back to Sheet Cake. *Soak it up,* I tell myself. *Soak* him *up.*

Because I can't shake the feeling that the moment we cross the city lines, James and I will go back to what we were before, which was two people who maybe hated each other. Or pretended to? I can't begin to untangle my complicated emotions or when exactly I fell hard for the man I told myself was trouble the moment I laid eyes on him.

We've been living the past few days in a bubble. Away from home, away from nosy Sheeters and my meddling brother—who is going to lose his mind when he finds out about any of this. The bubble is going to pop. It *has* to. So the car ride is our farewell tour of sorts, the last moments I can enjoy James being tender and caring—albeit in his gruff caveman sort of way, which is apparently my own personal favorite thing. That and his thighs.

Instead of enjoying every moment, I fall asleep almost immediately.

When I wake up, James is pulling up to the curb in front of Chevy's house. I have drool on my face and a stiff neck from my awkward position. I feel heavy and realize the strange weight is the leather jacket spread over me. James's scent fills my nostrils, and my brain goes right to an article I read on dog training. A good way to help ensure bonding, especially when crate training, is to let a puppy sleep with his master's shirt. I want to snuggle down into James's jacket and breathe in the smell of him.

Those dog trainers really are on to something.

But we're here, my sleep-addled brain realizes. And James has already gotten out of the truck. Did he think I was still sleeping? Or is he just ready to be rid of me?

Frantically, I leap out, tossing his jacket toward the passenger seat. I grab my bag just as James rounds the back of the truck. I can't meet his eyes and focus on wrestling my unwieldy bag up the sidewalk.

"Thanks for driving and everything!" I say, much too brightly, wanting to avoid the word goodbye.

James says nothing, plucking my bag from me like it's nothing. He starts up the sidewalk with me like a yappy little dog on his heels.

"You don't need to carry my bag!"

He only grunts.

"I can get it!" I protest.

"Already got it."

Just before we reach the door, I trip over literally nothing. James reaches out a hand to steady me, gripping my arm without losing his hold on my bag.

"Need me to carry you too?" he asks, eyes sparkling.

Yes. Yes, I would like that very, VERY much.

I glare. "I've got it."

"Are you sure?"

He's smirking at me again, and I don't understand. Where's the aloofness? Where are the walls I expected him to put up?

Is it possible James hadn't planned to hit the reset button?

His hand is like a brand, burning my skin, even through my clothes. Hours from now, I'll still be able to see his handprint.

"Positive."

I try to snatch my bag from him. But James only moves it out of reach on the other side of his body.

"Stop it, temp. You'll tire yourself out." James hoists the bag above his head when I ignore him. Now, I have to jump, and that's exactly what I'm doing when Chevy throws open the door.

I stop grabbing for the bag, letting my shoulders droop. Chevy leans casually against the house in his uniform, sipping coffee from a travel mug.

"Oh, don't stop on my account," Chevy says. "This is highly entertaining."

"James, give me my bag." I stamp my foot a little for emphasis, which only makes me feel like the toddler I'm impersonating.

"No."

Chevy clucks his tongue. "A trip away and y'all are still going at each other?"

His phrasing has heat flooding my cheeks. "We're not— he's just—"

James moves past me, nodding at my brother. "Chevy," he

275

says as he deposits my bag inside the door.

"James," Chevy drawls. "Thank you for taking care of my sister."

Oh, he took care of me, all right.

Are my cheeks as red as I think they are? I really hope not.

James only grunts a response, but as he comes down the steps, his gaze meets mine and holds. *This is it,* I think. *This is the end. It was nice while it lasted.* My insides twist, like they're wringing themselves out.

I almost fall over as James pauses in front of me. With eyes bright and one corner of his mouth kicked up, he cups my cheeks and places a tender, lingering kiss on my lips. When he pulls back, that smirk is firmly in place again.

Meanwhile, I've forgotten how to breathe.

James drops his heavy hands to my shoulders and glances over at Chevy. "This is happening," he says. Firm. No question.

"Of course it is," Chevy says. "Do we need to have the talk again?"

"No," James and I say at the same time.

I wait for an argument or a fist fight or maybe for a gigantic sinkhole to open and suck me inside. Instead, James kisses me again, a quick peck this time, and strides back to the truck.

"See you at work tomorrow, temp," James says, and then he drives away, leaving me stupefied on the sidewalk.

"I hope you know what you're doing," Chevy says with a shake of his head.

I most definitely do NOT.

———

When I can't stand the thoughts stampeding through my brain, I do something desperate. I place a long-distance call to Lindy.

"Is it Jo? Is everything okay?" Lindy sounds sleepy but frantic.

I wince, only now remembering I don't know where she is or what time it might be. We were only supposed to call if there was an emergency. Does whatever's happening with James count as an emergency?

Yes. Yes, it does.

"Jo is fine. Sorry—did I wake you?"

A yawn comes before the answer, and I can hear Pat murmuring something in the background. "It's okay. What's up?"

I pause, not for dramatic effect but because I choke on the words. Which is why what comes out of my mouth is: "I slept with James."

"What?!" Lindy's screech is ear-splitting and makes me realize what I've said or more how it *sounds*.

"Like, in a bed."

"Winnie! I don't need details!"

I slap a hand to my forehead. "No! I'm not saying this right. What I mean is we slept in the same bed. Just for the sleeping. Not the sexing."

Hi. I'm Winnie. I'm twenty-eight, and I just referred to sex as The Sexing. I need more sleep or more coffee. Maybe more of both.

Lindy yawns again. "Okay. I know it's like the middle of the night here so I'm having trouble computing. But can you start over, speaking softly and using small words? Also, please say what you mean. No idioms or euphemisms."

It's a relief to tell Lindy everything—and I mean *everything* —about the weekend's events. Kyoko, whom I hugged in a tearful goodbye a few hours ago, is the only other person I talked to about James, and our conversation at the restaurant hardly counts for much. It feels like everything has changed since then, and the need to talk about it has been building with volcanic pressure inside me.

The only thing I leave out are the details about my nightmare and my dad. Confessing the truth to James made me realize I need to tell my best friends ... but not yet. One big, emotional thing at a time.

Lindy squeals at periodic moments, which is very uncharacteristic of her. I chose to call her rather than telling Val, because I assumed I'd get a more analytical, maybe even cynical, response. But maybe being with Pat has changed her genetic makeup. By the time I finish, her deep sighs make it sound like she's melted into a puddle of goo.

"I expected more from you, Linds. If I wanted the reaction of a teen girl at a K-Pop concert, I would have called Val."

She scoffs. "I'm on my honeymoon. Forgive me if I'm in a mushy romantic place right now."

"You're supposed to be the voice of reason. You should tell me James is a bad idea and remind me that Dale and I just broke up."

"You and Dale were DOA. You just waited an excessively long time to call the time of death."

"Have you been watching *Grey's Anatomy* again?"

"It's so funny dubbed into Italian!"

I'll bet.

"I don't want James to be a rebound."

This makes Lindy laugh. And laugh and laugh. I don't know how much this call will cost her with the international plan she set up, but I hope it's a lot. She totally deserves it.

"James—a rebound for *Dale*," she says. "That's rich."

Okay, fine. The feelings I have for James are not rebound

feelings. And I think she's also right about me and Dale being over long, long ago. Did we ever even start? Knowing now about Celia, I'm grateful I held so much back.

But am I really ready to risk myself for James? He's the kind of man who probably has *Heartbreaker* and *Commitment Issues* tattooed somewhere over his heart. Though I didn't notice any such tattoos when he was walking around shirtless ...

"So, you think I should forget about the fact James and I work together, forget all the mixed signals from him and just go for it?"

"I think it sounds like you're looking for a reason to object," Lindy says. "That's why you really called me, not Val. You expected me to shoot this down."

Okay, maybe she's got a point here too.

"It's just ... complicated."

"When is love not complicated?"

"Whoa, whoa, whoa. Calm down, son. No one here mentioned love."

Lindy laughs. "I just wanted to see how defensive you'd get if I said *love*. Pretty dang defensive, Winnie. Which tells me you may not be in love yet, but *yet* is the key word."

Love is a massive, terrifying word. It's a monster underneath my bed, and I've got the covers pulled tight over my head. But as much as I'd like to hide from it, that word more than any other describes the depth of feelings I'm grappling with. They're not just like. They're not just lust. They're beyond infatuation or attraction or any of the other -ions.

"You're the worst when you're happy and in love," I tell her.

"I miss you too. Lucky for you we're coming back early."

"You are? What about your amazing honeymoon?"

"It *is* amazing. But I miss Jo. And can I just say that my

insides are not loving all this rich food? Plus, the toilet paper over here is weird. It's very chafey and—"

"You lost me at *chafey*. When exactly will you be back?"

"In time for Feastivus. Will you make sure someone invites the Graham clan? I don't know what their plans are, but Pat wants them to come."

With everything going on, I'd forgotten about Feastivus, Sheet Cake's unique take on Thanksgiving. A few women from the Ladies Literary Libations Society started the tradition the fall after Mom died and Val's mom ran off. Someone decided there were too many people around town with missing family members, so they established a big feast on Thanksgiving Day. It's like a dysfunctional version of a church basement potluck with better food.

It was originally The Feast of Us, but got shortened over time—and because of accents—to Feastivus. I didn't have the heart to tell anyone that the name is shared by the game Plants vs Zombies. Most of the older Sheeters wouldn't know what that is anyway.

"I'll ask them. So, any actual, practical advice, my terribly lovestruck friend? I mean, I have to work with James, and I don't even know what's going on."

"You're only working with him temporarily, though, right? I mean, this was never the long-term plan?"

"Right." The word tastes wrong, like coffee with bitter, over-roasted beans. *I'm looking at you, Starbucks.*

This job for James was never supposed to be long-term. And actually, before we left brunch this morning, Harper said she's going to get me in contact with one of her friends' husbands who has launched several successful apps. Which means I could move from just thinking about selling Neighborly to actually doing so. Even if I get a modest price, it would mean I don't need to work with James.

But I WANT to work for him. After this weekend, I'm practically burning up with ideas for Dark Horse. I've got a whole notebook full of session notes and to-do lists. I want Dark Horse to succeed. I want *James* to succeed. And I want to be a part of it all.

NOT as a temp but as more of a partner. Not, like, officially, like a partner making equal pay. More that I want to be fully on board, to have James see me not as a temp, but a part of what he's doing.

The issue is ... I don't know where I stand with James, personally or professionally. He kissed me in front of Chevy, which was a declaration, but not a DTR. And his favorite nickname for me only emphasizes the fact that he doesn't see me as a permanent part of the team.

Maybe what I need to do, at least in terms of the job, is make sure James knows I'm indispensable to him, both personally and professionally. And I think I have the perfect idea of where to start.

Lindy yawns again. "You want my advice, Winnie? Stop freaking out. Be open and just see where this goes."

Easy for her to say. She's on the other side of her happily-ever-after. Me? I'm the heroine hoping she's not betting on the guy who's going to really and truly break her heart.

TEXT THREAD

Winnie: What time should I report to work tomorrow, boss?

James: Meet me at Dark Horse at 9

Winnie: Do I need to wear anything special?

James: A lot of things come to mind …

Winnie: I mean, like, clothes to do manual labor in vs my regular clothes, dummy.

James: Wear whatever is best for catching the orange cat

Winnie: Are you seriously STILL going to make me do that?

James: Of course

James: We can't have a cat living in the building. It's unsanitary

Winnie: But is that really the best use of my time? Cat wrangling?

James: The website's done, isn't it?

Winnie: Yes …

Winnie: But I have tons of ideas from the conference I'd love to discuss and need to finalize the logo design

James: The logo is perfect

Winnie: Thanks! Maybe as a reward for perfect logo design, I could NOT catch the Orange Cyclops. I got 99% of the cats!

James: Your math doesn't work. Unless you got rid of 99 cats

Winnie: Fine. I got rid of 75.7% of the cats

James: That's a pretty exact number

Winnie: Focus on the fact I got MOST of the cats out.

James: Don't you want to complete a job rather than just 75.7% of it

Winnie: Ugh. You're the worst.

James: Take it up with the management

James: Speaking of the management, we should probably find a way to separate business and personal

Winnie: I'm open to suggestions ...

James: Maybe during working hours, we just keep things focused on work

Winnie: I think I can handle that. The question is: can YOU?

James: Guess we'll see tomorrow

Winnie: Feels like a challenge. I like it.

James: Goodnight, temp

Winnie: Sweet dreams, boss!

CHAPTER 29

James

"HELLO? JAMES?"

Winnie arrives exactly three minutes early. I got here an hour ago to set things up and have been hiding behind a bunch of boxes for fifteen. The boxes contain the metal shelving units that will hold supplies in the back, and I probably should be putting them together, not lying in wait for Winnie.

And no, I don't want to talk about how ridiculous this is.

I hear the scuff and clack of her heels on the concrete as she walks inside the building. I stay put, peeking around the doorway where I can just make out Winnie's profile. My heart does an embarrassing flip and leap at the sight of her high ponytail and the way her glasses rest against the curve of her cheek. So far, she hasn't seen the chalkboard window where I left it propped against the wall.

From wherever he's been hiding, the one-eyed orange cat saunters across the room, stopping just out of Winnie's reach. He might not want to be caught, but he sure wants to be seen. If I didn't know better, I'd say he's taunting her.

"You! My nemesis," I hear Winnie hiss. "This is the week. I'm going to catch you. I will."

The cat licks one paw, watching Winnie as he does. I don't hide my chuckle well enough, and Winnie spins in a slow circle. "Come out, come out, wherever you are! I can hear you breathing."

That's an exaggeration, but it makes me chuckle again. Winnie turns my way. I step out from behind the boxes with my hands up. "I come in peace."

Winnie's hands go to her hips. "Is that so? Then why are you hiding?"

"I wanted to surprise you." I tilt my head toward the chalkboard as I walk closer. In my blocky writing I've scrawled *Answers* in one windowpane, then written—you guessed it—answers to questions she didn't ask me in the three others.

"Like *Jeopardy!*," Winnie says, grinning. "Okay, I'll play. Fresh basil, roasted garlic, and black olives. Let's see … favorite pizza toppings!"

"In the form of a question, please."

She rolls her eyes, but she's smiling. "What are your favorite pizza toppings?"

"Yep." I slide my hands in my pockets, unsure if I should touch her but wanting to all the same. I was the one who said we should be professional at work. Stupid me. My finger finds the seed Winnie gave me, transferred into these pants just this morning. I know one day it will get lost or disintegrate, but until then, I'm keeping it close.

Winnie beams at me, then returns her gaze to the chalkboard. "Dancing—hm. What is something you do surprisingly well?"

I scoff. "Yeah right. One of my biggest fears."

Crossing her arms, Winnie narrows her eyes, studying me. "There's no way. I saw you dance at Pat's wedding. Your hips didn't lie, Graham."

Normally, knowing someone watched me dancing would make me flush with embarrassment. The thought of Winnie watching me, noticing me, makes a primal part of me very, very happy. From her comment, she clearly liked what she saw. It makes me want to pull her into my arms now.

Slow dancing—THAT I can do.

I take a step closer, still not touching her, but definitely invading her space. It's slight, but I don't miss the way Winnie shivers. I love having an effect on her. Seeing her react does something similar to me as a tingling electric feeling zips up my spine.

My voice is low and husky. "Have you been watching me, temp?"

Her attention moves from my eyes down to my lips and back up. "You're kind of hard to miss, big guy." She blinks a few times, then clears her throat. "Back to dancing—is it really one of your biggest fears?"

I nod, slowly. I wasn't thinking about how vulnerable this question actually makes me feel when I jotted it down. "I'm not good at it. And I feel like everyone's watching me."

"A *fear* though? Dancing—not bear attacks or falling off a cliff or dying?"

As she asks, I realize there one thing I fear more. Losing someone I love. My chest tightens, and I clench my hands into fists in my pockets.

"Bear attacks definitely aren't on my radar, and I don't tend to frequent cliffs."

287

Winnie smiles. "Touché. For the record, I thought you danced well. And yes, I might have been watching you. I'll admit it."

"So, you didn't hate me then?"

"Did you think I hated you?" Winnie asks, tilting her head.

I shrug. "You didn't seem to particularly *like* me."

"I didn't not like you. I just thought you were ... dangerous."

Well, that's an interesting tidbit. I want to ask more, but she keeps going.

"My question is, if you hate dancing, why did you do it?"

"Jo asked me."

Winnie's eyes soften, and she bites her lip. She must like this answer because she steps forward, closing the last bit of distance between us and to wrap her arms around my waist. I hold her against me, stroking one hand up her back while the other gives her ponytail the lightest tug. She feels so perfect in my arms, like all her curves and angles were designed to fit mine.

"You're a big softy under all these layers of grump, James Graham," she says.

"False. I am not a softy."

I'm really not. That said, I would do just about anything Jo asked. I'm beginning to worry the same might be true of Winnie.

I nuzzle my nose into her hair, inhaling her sweet caramel scent. *Definitely perfection.* Sliding my palms down her arms, I bend and press a soft kiss to Winnie's temple, then to the curve of her ear, then to her neck. Her eyes flutter closed.

"Is this how it's going to be?" she asks

"How what's going to be?"

I kiss the edge of her jaw.

"The job. Your text said you wanted to keep things professional at work."

And now I'm totally rethinking my stance on that. "You hugged me first."

"And you kissed me. And smelled my hair."

I take another deep inhale. "Caramel perfection. My new favorite scent."

Winnie hums, tilting her head to give me better access to her neck. I take full advantage, leaving a line of soft kisses up her throat.

"I'm not so sure I can work under these conditions." Her voice is breathy, almost a pant.

"Perhaps you should write a strongly worded letter to the management."

"I don't think my boss would care."

I kiss the corner of her mouth, and she exhales a soft sigh. I want to capture each of these sounds. Even more, I want to spend more time exploring, seeing what kinds of sounds I can draw out of her with my lips, with my hands.

"Oh, I think your boss cares. He cares very"—*kiss*—"very" —*kiss*—"much."

"Well, then. I'll get to work on that strongly worded letter —in a minute."

I place another teasing kiss just shy of her lips, and she groans.

"Maybe ten minutes," she says.

With that, Winnie pushes up on her toes and covers my mouth with hers. The kiss is searing and desperate, making me think she missed me the last seventeen-and-a-half hours as much as I missed her. I cradle the back of her head, drawing her closer as her fingers trail up and down my spine.

I don't know what I was thinking—mixing a relationship with work is actually pretty fantastic. I can see a lot of benefits to this arrangement. Especially considering we're the only two people here in this whole empty building.

When I pull back, we're both short of breath and looking a little dazed. Winnie chews her lip and looks up at me with those fathomless blue eyes.

"James?"

I grunt a response, then press a kiss to the tip of her nose.

"I was thinking maybe we could revisit this cat-catching assignment."

Cupping her face in my hands, I skim my thumbs over her cheeks and push her glasses back up into place from where they slid down. "Sorry. That part of your job is nonnegotiable."

"James," she pleads, and I'm tempted, I really am. But what I want more than to say yes is to enjoy watching Winnie continue her epic battle with the one-eyed cat.

"It's character-building."

"You don't like my character?"

"I love your character. But I'm pretty sure all those self-help gurus say we should always keep developing."

Winnie closes one eye, studying me like I'm a blueprint. "You listen to self-help gurus."

"Oprah is my BFF."

"Right," Winnie says, drawing out the word.

"How about this," I say, brushing a loose strand of hair behind her ear. "I'll put in a good word with your boss. But from what I've heard, he's not a very understanding guy. Best of luck, temp."

With a final quick kiss, I force myself to back away before I change my mind and say yes to whatever she asks.

CHAPTER 30

Winnie

THE REST of the week leading up to Feastivus goes something like this: try to catch a stupid cat, make out with James, work on my secret project for Dark Horse, make out with James some more, try to catch a stupid (okay, fine, he's smarter than me) cat.

In addition, I've become very familiar with every area of the building—mostly because James and I have made out in all of them. With my eyes closed, I could create a blueprint, plus report on the sturdiness of the walls and flat surfaces like countertops and tables.

For example, the outer wall in the back room feels like it needs reinforcing and creaks loudly when someone—or some*ones*—are pressed up against it. And the small wooden table in the storage closet was NOT meant to hold a human's weight. It has been relocated to the large dumpster outside. In pieces.

What we have NOT done is discuss the particulars of our relationship. Honestly, though, I'm fine letting things be nebulous for now. DTR talks are so early 2000s. Do adults even still have these talks? I'm so out of the loop I'm not sure what typical is anymore. And so long as we're just kissing, I'm okay putting off some official talk about what we are and what we want ... for now.

Aside from all the kissing, James and I really are pretty consumed with work. The contractor has had his crew in, prepping the plumbing for the brew tanks and starting to frame out the bathrooms. There's some issue or headache every hour, it seems, and if James isn't talking to the contractor, he's on the phone with suppliers. It's a lot of people and paperwork for him, and I wish he'd let me help. Especially if it would get me out of trying to catch the Orange Cyclops.

I'm choosing not to be hurt when James refuses my offers for help. I feel like this will change when I can show him I'm serious, show him I don't want to just be a temp, show him my ideas for Dark Horse. I've spent a lot of time on the phone with Kyoko, pestering her with questions and getting more ideas. What started as a small document has turned into a large document with an accompanying slideshow presentation.

Yeah. I'm not obsessing AT ALL.

Every day, I arrive to find new answers scrawled on the chalkboard in James's so-very-James handwriting. Just like him, it's hard to read. This is a twist on my daily question requirement, but I love it, mostly because it was James's idea. Also, if I guess correctly, I get rewarded, and I really, really like the rewards.

If I miss? I'm punished by being tickled until I'm breathless. Which ... I don't mind either.

James doesn't make this easy. On Tuesday, his answer was seventeen. I guessed how many women he's kissed—though the idea of his lips on anyone else makes me feel more unhinged than an old screen door. Thankfully, it was how many stitches he's gotten in his lifetime. Some were from surgery, but the rest he said I'll have to find myself. I can't wait for more exploration.

Today, Wednesday, he simply wrote *a pilot*, and I correctly guessed this was what he wanted to be when he grew up. The mental image of James in a pilot uniform behind the controls of a jet is pretty hot.

"Thayden said he'd give me lessons in his private plane sometime," James says, brushing his lips against my jaw in a spot I've discovered I really, really like. We're in a storage closet, the sound of hammers hammering and country music crackling over a speaker offering a soundtrack to our private moment.

"Who's Thayden again?" I shiver as James drags his mouth up, up, up. I care less about the answer and more about extending what was supposed to be a five-minute break.

"He's our family lawyer ... and sort of friend." His lips close around my earlobe, and I squeeze my eyes closed, gripping his shirt in my fists. When he kisses the apple of my cheek and backs up, resting his forehead against mine, lips just out of reach, I want to groan.

I try to locate a coherent thought. "I think I met him the day y'all got arrested for disrupting the peace at Backwoods Bar. Expensive suit, smug grin?"

James snorts. "That would be Thayden."

He kisses me, slow and soft and sweet. I'm seated on a

stack of pallets with James standing between my knees. The heat of his body is delicious against the chill bite in the air. I draw him closer, kissing a zigzag line up his throat—payback for making me dizzy minutes ago. I feel him swallow against my lips, and there's something so powerful in knowing how I affect him.

"If I get my pilot's license, I promise to take you up," he says, swallowing heavily again.

With the way James makes my stomach flip and swoop, I feel like I already know what it would be like to fly with him. "I'll hold you to that."

"It took convincing to get on a motorcycle, yet you'll get in a plane with me behind the controls?" He sounds amused.

"There are more motorcycle crashes than plane crashes." I'm pretty sure this statistic is true. I'll need good old Mr. Google to be sure.

"So you say. But I think—"

"Too much talking."

I slide my glasses on top of my head and pull his face down to mine. The warmth of his lips, the bite of his stubble, the strong grip of his hands on my hips—I don't think I'll ever tire of these things. His fingers tighten, pulling me even closer as his mouth moves over mine.

"Winnie," he says, my name sounding like a plea on his lips, his breath mingling with mine.

I drag my hands through his hair, nibbling a little on his lower lip. He groans and starts to pull me closer still when the door slamming open and a booming voice makes us jerk apart.

"Pat's back, baby! And wow—okay. Y'all are making out. I see we've got some catching up to do."

James drops his head to my shoulder, groaning. "Didn't you see the closed door?"

294

"Yeah, but no sock on the door handle."

James growls and presses a last kiss on my collarbone before standing up and moving away. "I'd say welcome back, but you're not really welcome."

Pat holds out his arms, and with a heaving breath, James hugs him. It looks less like an embrace and more like a struggle for dominance. There's a lot of squeezing and back slapping and grunting.

Finally, Pat taps James on the shoulder twice, wheezing out, "Okay! You win! You're the biggest and baddest and strongest. And, let's not forget the oldest!"

James gives him a last, painful-looking squeeze, making Pat squeak, before letting go.

I slip off the stack of pallets. "Welcome back, Patty."

"Good to see you, future sister-in-law."

A flash of panic crosses James's features. It has the immediate effect of making my stomach twist, but I don't have time to study James as Pat envelops me in a hug. When I glance at James again, he's back to his normal gruff and possessive look, making it easy for me to forget what I think I saw.

"Where's Lindy?"

"She's picking up Jo from school. I'm meeting them at Mari's in a few."

Pat squeezes and lifts, my feet coming off the floor. The Grahams could teach masterclasses on giving bear hugs. I feel the breath whoosh from my lungs as James snaps, "Don't be so rough, Patty."

"Winnie's not a delicate flower, brother. This one's a fighter. I can tell." Then, in a low voice near my ear, Pat whispers, "Welcome to the family."

James practically rips me out of Pat's embrace and shoves his brother back a few feet.

"I was going to say congratulations on taming the grump, but never mind," Pat says, laughing.

James tucks me under one of his arms, and I slide my hand up to his chest, smiling at Pat. "Grumps aren't meant to be tamed, Patty. They're meant to be enjoyed as is."

Pat's eyes twinkle. "Well, don't let me stop you from enjoying. I'm headed out to meet Lindy and Jojo. Feel free to meet us at Mari's. That is, if you aren't otherwise occupied."

Pat winks, and James tenses, like he's debating whether or not to give chase. When he lunges forward, Pat squeals and darts out of the room.

"You're a brave woman, Winnie!" he calls.

His voice echoes from the other room and rattles similarly around in my head. Am I brave? Maybe so. But only on the surface. Because as much as I'm enjoying all this getting-to-know-James stuff and definitely the kissing, I can't shake the feeling I had driving back after the conference, like I'm still in a bubble set to burst any moment. And deep down, I am completely terrified.

CHAPTER 31

James

"WE HAVE A PROBLEM," Winnie says through the phone.

Dread coils up my spine as a thousand terrible possibilities career around inside my skull like loose pinballs. "Are you hurt? What's wrong?"

She laughs, short and stressed. "No—sorry. I'm not hurt. Nothing like that. Smaller scale emergency."

I set down the can of green beans on the counter with a little too much force, and Tank gives me a look of concern. But it's hard to take him seriously when he's mashing potatoes while wearing an apron that looks like a sexy French maid uniform. A gift from Pat, of course.

It's Thanksgiving Day. Which in our family has always meant a small gathering where Tank, Harper, and I make most of the food while Collin and Pat handle the arguments. Then we eat and round out the day watching football. This year, though, we're joining in Feastivus. To say I'm not thrilled about being around a ton of people after spending the weekend around a ton of people—well, it would be a grand understatement.

"Tell me."

"It's just ... our location for Feastivus lost power."

The tightness in my chest eases, and as Tank mouths, *You okay?* I give him a nod and step into the bathroom. I need a moment of quiet. The green bean casserole can wait. I pass Pat and Lindy, who are engaged in a noisy discussion about the history of Thanksgiving with Jo while the TV plays some movie with an animated turkey.

Winnie is going on about Judge Judie's house and something about the size and heat and double ovens. I'm listening but don't need all the details. I need the favor I can tell she's winding up to ask.

"What do you need from me?" I can't help but admit a little relief that maybe this means we won't be celebrating the holiday with the entire town.

"Do you trust me?" Winnie asks, and my chest goes tight again.

Trust is a currency with a very high exchange rate for me. This feels somehow like a trick question. Of course I trust her, but I also am scared of where this is going.

"Yes?"

There's a long pause on the line. "I wanted to see if we could hold Feastivus at Dark Horse."

I blink. Tell myself to breathe steadily. Then realize I'm gripping Tank's bathroom counter so hard either my knuckles or the granite are going to crack.

Right now, Dark Horse is little more than an empty warehouse, halfway under construction. We have electrical now, but that's about it. A lot of burned-out industrial bulbs

298

needing to be replaced. No heat or HVAC system. The bathrooms are framed in, but there is no plumbing. Duct tape on the floor marks out plans for the contractor. Boxes of things like shelving units are stacked in corners, waiting to be put together.

My thoughts go straight to worst-case scenarios like lawsuits and electrical fires. Even the idea of having half the town traipsing around the outside makes my skin feel warm and prickly. It was bad enough on the workday, and that was only a dozen or so people. I haven't minded the work crew, obviously, but random people?

"How would this work, exactly?" I ask carefully. "There are no tables or chairs. No heat."

"You wouldn't need to worry about it. I'll handle everything."

"No bathrooms."

"I've got a plan. Trust me, boss."

I pinch the bridge of my nose, trying to force my pulse to slow. Everything about this spells disaster. Or maybe just my worst nightmare. Either way, it's not what I want.

And yet … I already know I'm going to say yes. Unless there's another solution.

"What about Tank's place?"

"It's not big enough."

"How many people are we talking about?"

Winnie sighs. "James, I love you, but you're a giant buzzkill. You know that?"

My brain stops functioning at the words *I love you*. Winnie threw the phrase out casually, like a joke. I know she doesn't really MEAN the words. I'm honestly not even sure she realizes she's said it.

But hearing the words come out of her mouth immediately forced me to realize something: I think I do love her.

Not casually.

Not like the way I love a good steak or being alone or the feeling I get finishing a table or bench or something I've built with my hands and hard work.

Love love.

And I have no idea what to do with that knowledge. Or the ensuing sense of panic. I close my eyes, gripping the counter again with my free hand. "Okay."

Winnie squeals. "Thank you, thank you, thank you. And to think, your favorite word used to be no."

The problem is: no still is my favorite word. And now there are two people in the world, in this little town even, I can't seem to say it to. One is pint-sized and can school me in chess. The other has a sassy mouth, inked skin, and her hand wrapped around my heart.

––––––

Probably to keep me away from whatever dark magic she's working at the warehouse, Winnie sends me on an errand. It's one I'm pretty sure does not require both me and Big Mo, but here we are—driving around town in a borrowed shuttle bus, picking up elderly people for Feastivus.

"Well, aren't you a big boy?" A smiling woman wearing a pink wig and bifocals lets go of her cane long enough to pat my chest. I hand her off to Big Mo, who grins at me before helping her up the bus steps.

I head back to the front of the nursing home for two more ladies. They each take an arm, giggling as we shuffle toward the bus. The one on the left is massaging my bicep, and before Big Mo takes her arm to help her up the shuttle steps, she sniffs me.

The one on the right pats me on the butt like an athlete

might for a teammate. "You'd fetch a pretty penny at the livestock show. And I would know. I was in the FFA. Raised some prize heifers."

There have been times in my life, most especially when I played college ball, where I absolutely felt like a piece of meat. Never has it been so LITERAL. Technically, in this situation, I'm not a piece of meat but a side of beef.

We get the last few people loaded up while I'm gritting my teeth and Big Mo is trying to hold back laughter. Before we pull away, he waves to the woman in scrubs standing by the entrance to the assisted living center.

"You'll bring me back some pie, Big Mo?" she calls.

"Yes ma'am," he says, even though I'm pretty certain the woman is younger than he is. Though, with the big beard and bushy eyebrows, it's hard to pinpoint exactly how old Big Mo is. I'd guess around Tank's age, mid-fifties, maybe a few years younger.

Once we're buckled up and back on the road, he gives me a wide smile. "You sure are a hit with the ladies. I can't say I don't appreciate it. Usually it's just me fending off indecent proposals."

"Glad to help."

One of the women calls from the back, "How about some tunes?"

I fiddle with the radio, locating a station that's jumped the gun playing Christmas music. The bus fills with complaints.

"Blasphemy!"

"No Christmas music until tomorrow!"

"Turn it off!"

I switch to a country station, which elicits a similar reaction. So does the soft rock station. The back of my neck starts to heat from all the heckling. At a red light, Mo reaches over and presses one of the preset buttons. A sugary pop song with an electronic beat blares over the speakers. Already, my ears are starting to bleed, but there's a cheer from the back, along with one lone male groan.

"Not Justin Beiber!"

"Shut it, Mort. Jealousy is unbecoming."

"I can't compete with him!" a man, who I'm assuming is Mort, protests.

"Few can," another man says.

"He's got his original hips and knees," one woman says appreciatively. "And all that ink!"

"The young feller up front certainly gives him a run for his money."

"His hips definitely seem to be in working order."

"I'm adding him to my freebie five list."

I turn to Mo, who is laughing silently, tears pooling in his eyes. "Is the freebie five list what I think it is?" I ask.

"I'm afraid so. Congratulations."

I shake my head as arguments about various celebrities continue. Better them than me. But already, I'm feeling twitchy from all the voices and the full shuttle. I can't wait for the end of the day when I can lock myself in Tank's guest room, though I'd really prefer my own empty house. One where I could be alone, or alone with Winnie.

I debated about calling a real estate agent twice this week after I found an empty but not terribly run-down farmhouse not too far from where Pat and Lindy are building their place. But the idea of taking on a house right now, especially one that might need some renovations, would be just one more thing. As soon as the brewing tanks come in, I'm going to be pulling fifteen-to-twenty-hour days as I set things up and start brewing the first batches.

So, no. I need my own space, but I'm not ready to take that on yet.

"You get roped into this job every year?" I ask Mo.

He shoots me a quick glance, a smile still in his eyes. "I *volunteer* for this job every year."

Now I feel like a jerk. "That's very kind of you."

"It's what they do here."

The *they* catches my attention. I see Big Mo as a fixture in Sheet Cake, someone who would be part of a *we*, not see it as a *they*. It's hard to imagine this town without the man who is a fixture in Mari's kitchen and pretty much everywhere, a big, steady presence.

"You didn't grow up in Sheet Cake?"

He's quiet for a moment. "I ended up here after my wife and daughter died."

The tightness in my chest, which has been coming and going a lot lately, returns with a vengeance. I can't help thinking of Mom, then of Winnie and Chevy losing their mom and dad. This town has a way of wrapping around people, taking them in and holding them close. I don't have a chance to fumble over rote words of condolence before he continues.

"I showed up at the diner, weary and not sure I wanted to go on. Mari fed me, forced me to stay in the apartment above the diner, and kept offering me a job until I took it. Been here ever since."

I want to ask more questions, but I think better of it. More like, my own emotions are much too close to spilling over to carry on conversation. My mind goes back to the dark days after Mom died. To listening with my ear pressed to Tank's door, hoping for a sound other than sobbing.

To fixing everyone frozen pizza or mac and cheese from a box. Breaking up fights between Collin and Pat. Tucking

Harper into bed. Waking up when she had nightmares and holding her until she stopped crying. Washing clothes and dishes and making sure everyone had on pants without holes or stains when we caught the bus for school.

Grief has a long memory, and a way of leaping up to surprise you. I always miss Mom on holidays. She's been on my mind a lot more since my talk with Dad. I love the sense of togetherness of Sheet Cake. It's a good thing to include people who wouldn't have family or a celebration.

But at the same time, I hate how we're giving up our Graham family traditions for people I barely know.

Mo tips his head toward the back of the van where a lively discussion about compression socks sounds like it's about to turn into a full-on brawl. "Stay long enough, and it'll be you too."

That, I don't know about. But I don't have much time to consider because someone in the back calls, "Settle a debate for us, big fella. Boxers or briefs?"

———

The knot of tension in my chest has tightened into a solid mass by the time Big Mo and I finish collecting various older folks and those with limited mobility from around town. It's been about three hours, but knowing Winnie, anything could happen in that time.

A fact highlighted by the giant Dark Horse banner featuring Winnie's final logo concept hanging out in front as we pull up to the curb. I narrow my eyes. Winnie couldn't have whipped that up today, since it's professionally printed. Which means she's been working on this and who knows what else without asking me. The idea comes with a sharp pinch of discomfort.

The sign looks great. Be thankful not irritated, I tell myself. But I don't like details out of my control, much less out of my knowledge. I really hate secrets and surprises, especially when it comes to things like my own business, where there should be zero surprises, even good ones.

"You coming?" Big Mo asks, and I realize I'm frozen in my seat, staring at the sign and what lies beyond.

There is a flurry of activity and people, way more than I thought would be here—and that's not including those we need to help off the van. I climb out, taking in everything I can at a glance. I see folding tables, portable space heaters, and twinkling lights strung across the courtyard outside of the main building.

It's hard to breathe. Somewhere, under the rising sense of panic, there's a sliver of excitement, humming like a live wire. This is a tiny foreshadow of things to come, of what this place could be.

What it will *be*, I mentally amend. Tank and Wolf Waters appear at the shuttle steps helping folks out of the van. I stop just inside the gate to take in the full effect.

Tables are set up for at least fifty, maybe closer to seventy-five. There are candles and tablecloths and pitchers of water and mason jars of what I'd guess is Judge Judie's moonshine. Collin is tossing a football with some kids. There are a dozen or so dogs running around underfoot, and a loud hum of conversation and laughter as the tables fill up. The Bobs, who apparently moonlight as a bluegrass band when they're not obsessing over the high school football team, are setting up drums on a makeshift stage.

Dark Horse feels very alive. The air practically vibrates with joy and anticipation. My insides feel like they're vibrating with exactly the opposite emotions.

I spot Winnie, floating between tables, calling out hellos

as well as orders, pointing to where platters of food can go while stopping one of the dogs from eating a stick of butter right off a dish on the table. She's glowing brighter than all the twinkling lights, an easy smile on her face and a radiant energy practically following her in a cloud.

My heart shudders once, then struggles to find its rhythm, like a half-capsized boat wobbling its way back to upright. Winnie is so incredibly, indescribably beautiful—totally in her element. This is her JAM.

But it is not mine. Not even a little bit.

Nope. I'm ready to run, where she looks ready to grow roots.

"Can you give us a hand, James?" Big Mo passes me, an elderly woman on each arm, and I head back to the shuttle, clenching and unclenching my jaw.

I help a white-haired woman off the shuttle, trying not to flinch at her touch as she wraps her hand around my arm.

"Well, isn't this lovely," she says as we shuffle through the gates, and all I can manage around the knot in my throat is a grunt. I think she said her name is June, but my mind is stuck in January.

That's when I'm supposed to have this place at least in some semblance of working order, even if not fully operational. The Sheet Cake Festival brings thousands to this town, and Tank wants least a half dozen shops and restaurants up and running, even some of the lofts to show people what this place could be.

More people. More activity. More noise.

"You all right there, big fella?" June eyes me with an assessing gaze behind her thick glasses.

"Yep."

She harrumphs and looks ready to press me for more when Winnie appears suddenly. Just the sight of her makes the tension let up a tiny fraction of a bit. Then I see the light in her eyes, a massive contrast to the dark cloud pouring rain over my head, and my shoulders tense.

"Don't mind him." Winnie helps June into one of the folding chairs. "He's a man of single syllables."

"Don't need words when you've got a body like that," June says.

"Agreed." Winnie gives me a smile I wish I could return and loops her arm through mine. Leaning close, she says, "Come with me for a sec. I need your help with something."

I don't fight as Winnie drags me toward the building. Each time a person stops her to say hello or ask a question, it's like a kick to my gut. My mouth is desert-dry by the time we make it into the building.

More lights are strung across the ceiling here, and a series of folding tables have been set up with the food. There are several turkeys, Tank's brisket, and a whole platter of sausages along with multiple dishes of potatoes, rolls, and the green bean casserole I made earlier, slightly singed on top.

My stomach rumbles at the smell, but I'm not really hungry. Instead, I feel shaky and sick.

We reach a storage closet, the only one with a chair. Winnie pushes me down into it and closes the door, leaning her back against it.

The room is dim, lit only by the afternoon light coming through the dirty window. The room feels too small, too hot. I shrug off my jacket and toss it over the back of my chair.

Memories of making out with Winnie in this room yesterday shoot to the front of my mind, then fade under the weight of my overwhelm.

Winnie studies my face with a look of concern.

"Why are we here?" I bite out, my voice rougher than I mean for it to be.

Winnie doesn't flinch at my tone. "You looked like you could use a breather."

My shoulders loosen a little. But only a little. Winnie reads me like she wrote the manual. Right now, though, I'm not sure I want to be read.

"There are a lot of people." I don't mean to sound accusing, but it slips into my tone.

"I may have downplayed it a little." Winnie's mouth tilts up in a small smile. "I know this probably wasn't an easy yes for you, the King of No. But it's a really nice thing for you to do for the town."

I didn't do it for the town.

I swallow those words down. It's not the right time to discuss the feelings I have for Winnie. How they've grown wild as weeds and taken over my lawn. How earlier, I had the realization all those unfamiliar feelings might fall under the heading of one Very Big Feeling.

And then, after seeing her in the midst of everyone outside, a dark thread of doubt stitched its way through me.

I realize she's waiting for my answer, so I nod.

"What do you think?" Winnie twists her hands, then seems to realize she's doing it and balls her hands into fists.

I see a crack in Winnie's tough shell, a breathy whisper of vulnerability. I chew the inside of my cheek as I fumble for the right words. On the one hand, what she managed to pull together in a few hours is almost impossible. Dark Horse for the first time, feels like a real, living thing. More than a possibility.

But my worry speaks louder. Thinking of all the people outside leaves me feeling like I've stepped in a fire ant pile. They're swarming up my legs, preparing to bite. I scratch at my arm. Is this even what I want—to work in a business filled with people? I've known that's what I'm creating, what I'm working toward.

But it was always a concept. An idea. Now, the all-too-real reality is right outside the doors, and I'm not sure it's what I want.

Seeing all the people, getting a real picture of what this business will be like if it succeeds has me fearing success as much as failure.

I want to brew beer. Do I want all *this*?

I really didn't think through the logistics of having the tasting room being an extension of the brewing area. It sounded like a great idea, something many breweries are doing to create that sense of authenticity, to let the patrons really get the full experience. But now, I can imagine working at the tanks while just a half-dozen feet away, patrons drink beer while music plays and stools scrape over the concrete.

My hands tremble at the idea of adjusting temperature, checking valves, and filling kegs with an audience. It's too late to change the layout now that the drains are in place and the plumbing and electrical has been set in place for the bar area.

The room is cool, but sweat prickles at my hairline and along my spine.

"James?"

More than a sliver of vulnerability colors Winnie's eyes now. She's genuinely worried, and knowing her, I bet she's more concerned about how I'm doing than about receiving some kind of praise for a job well done.

The light that radiated so clearly from her outside has dimmed.

I did that. I put out Winnie's light.

Guilt gnaws at me like a dog with a bone. I sift through

possible responses, trying to find one that's accurate but also doesn't broadcast all the volatile things brewing inside me. I breathe deep, thinking of Mo's words from our ride earlier. How he lost his family, showed up in Sheet Cake, and was given a new lease on life. How he volunteers to drive old folks to this event. I know for a fact he baked no less than a dozen pies for today.

In contrast, I'm a big bunch of sour grapes. I am a claustrophobic man inside an airplane bathroom at cruising altitude. There is nowhere for me to go.

Seeing Winnie's excitement, her vulnerability, her hope for this place, for me, makes it all worse. I may love her, but am I the kind of man she needs? Disappointing her doesn't feel like a possibility; it feels like a sure thing. She's betting on me, and the odds are five hundred to one.

I swallow and wrangle my lips into something like a tiny smile. "You pulled off the impossible, temp. Well done."

My tone could use some work, but the words are true. I can say them, even if I don't *feel* them.

To be very clear, I definitely do NOT feel them.

And, as Winnie's eyes brighten and she launches herself at me, wrapping her arms around and clinging to my body for a hug I probably need but definitely don't want, I do my best to pretend here too. The act of running my hands up and down her back is just that—an act.

I've read about people having skin hunger—the need for more touch when there hasn't been enough. I've got the opposite problem. Mine is skin *overwhelm*.

And if Winnie doesn't step away from me soon, the hot, itchy feeling clawing its way up my spine is going to end in an eruption this woman in no way deserves.

Maybe she senses it, or maybe she just needs to get back outside, but Winnie lets go. She pats my chest twice, then a few more times with an appreciative smile. If she notices me tensing, she probably thinks I'm just flexing for her. I'd prefer she think that than realize I'm an overfilled balloon about to burst.

"Stay in here as long as you need." Winnie backs toward the door. "I've got things under control out there. Okay?"

I nod, not able to access words over the tornado siren that is my head. And then Winnie's gone, leaving me alone, slumped over and breathing heavy in this tiny, airless room.

CHAPTER 32

Winnie

I SCAN the crowd again for James's dark head and broad shoulders. My gaze catches on Collin, then Tank and Pat. Similar frames, wrong men. Unease coats my stomach, dark and thick like the bottom of a coffee pot that's been left on too long.

I'm aware the man doesn't like crowds. And today is definitely a crowd. At the conference I saw the way he closed up like a Chick-Fil-A on Sunday. The tension didn't leave his shoulders and neck until we got out of the crowded areas and into an empty hallway or the hotel room. Even with his family at brunch, I could see the strain in his eyes.

Today is a risk. I thought it would excite him to get a sense of how things could be—how they *will* be. I also hoped James would see *my* potential. What it would be like to give me a little more control, allow me to help him more. (Okay, yeah, and maybe to make him see it's a waste of my time to try catching the Orange Cyclops.) But his expression was stunned, then closed off like he was more statue than man. He seemed wrong, even when I left him.

Should I not have left him? I got the sense he needed a moment alone, even from me.

Should I not have asked this of him? That's perhaps the bigger question. I think of Chevy telling me I push people too hard. Is that what I'm doing? I thought this might overwhelm him a little, but also allow him to get a preview of how amazing Dark Horse could be once the doors are officially open.

Instead of catching the excitement I feel buzzing in the air, James seemed to shrivel up and fold inward, smaller and smaller.

Maybe this is pushing him too far.

I glance around at the smiling faces, the twinkling lights, the collection of Sheeters who have gathered. The smell of turkey and brisket coats the air and the band is warming up, an acoustic guitar strumming over the rest of the noise. It feels like home.

To *me,* it feels like home.

But maybe this isn't what James envisioned for Dark Horse. I thought I've been reading him well, but maybe I've missed his vision, given that I'm trying to pick up on it by context clues and reading the man who is as closed a book as I've ever seen.

I'm grateful Eula Martin chooses this moment to whistle through her fingers. The sound is piercing and shuts up the people, though several of the dogs bark. Harper brought her two, and Lindy's got Amber and Beast, plus a few other people have their dogs running around. Most are off leashes and ready for any scraps to drop under tables once we start eating.

The Orange Cyclops, still eluding capture, has wisely stayed hidden today. Or maybe he decided to take up a home somewhere else. I should be so lucky.

"Y'all take your seats now," Judge Judie says, waving a hand. "Go on."

Chairs scrape back as the stragglers find their places. Only then do I realize I've been so busy setting up I didn't pick out my own place to sit. I crane my neck but still don't see any sign of James. Lindy, Pat, and Jo are seated with Val, Mari, and Big Mo, the table where usually I'd be. Only right now, there are no open seats.

For just a moment, loneliness bites at my heels, the left-over vestiges of showing up to the cafeteria on the first day of school and not being able to locate my friends.

"You're with us," a familiar voice says, and I glance up to see Tank's easy smile. He guides me with a gentle hand on my shoulder to a table with Chevy, Collin, Harper, Chase, and Chase's sister. Molly—I think? She's some kind of big-deal influencer Lindy was shocked I hadn't heard of. I make a mental note to ask Chase if it would be weird to ask her to post something for Dark Horse. Next week, assuming James okays my plan, I'm going to start working on Dark Horse's social media.

But first, the man needs to come out of the storage room.

"He'll be here," Tank assures me, as though reading my concern.

I slide into the seat Tank pulls out for me, adjusting as he scoots me in. Though Pat has more of Tank's affability, James absolutely got his manners and gentlemanliness (is that a word?) from his dad. Collin gives me a wink and a nod from his spot just across the table. I manage to smile back, but my focus is on the empty folding chair next to me as Judge Judie begins her Feastivus blessing.

While her husband, Burt, looks on adoringly, Judie raises her arms above her head, not unlike a preacher giving a benediction. "Dearly beloved, we are gathered here today to celebrate the three Fs: family, friendship, and FOOD!"

The word *food* is shouted out by everyone except the Grahams, whom I forgot to warn about our traditions. Then again, it's entertaining to watch their faces as they take it all in. Tank's grin is huge, while Collin is frowning, and Chase whispers something to Harper, who gives him a small smile. Still no James.

Is he mad at me? Is he really so unhappy about the number of people here? The idea that I pushed him too far with this has me digging my nails into my thighs. I realize too late that I've torn the tights I have on under my black skirt.

Take a breath, I tell myself. *This is amazing. You did an amazing job pulling this together. James will see that.*

I fiddle with my glasses, trying to fight back tears as Judie finishes her thankfulness list, which starts with the basics like the weather, general health, and another year of life, and then extends to the specifics of Big Mo's pies and Burt getting on medication for his IBS, which has lessened the amount of gas in society by at least twenty percent.

"Hear, hear!" someone calls at the last one, eliciting chuckles around the dining area. Even Burt raises his glass at this.

A big hand lands on my shoulder, and the knot of worry in my chest loosens, even if only a slight amount. James slides into the chair beside me. His lips brush my temple, making goose bumps pop up on my arms and legs and a smile on my face.

"What'd I miss?" His voice is husky, and my goose bumps get goose bumps. He isn't smiling, but I don't expect that from him. His expression is tight, but his eyes thaw slightly as they skim over my face.

"Not much," I tell him. "But I sure missed you."

I press a quick kiss to his cheek and adjust my chair so I can lean back against his broad chest. I need the contact. After a brief pause, one of his arms snakes around my waist, and only Chevy coughing—or, fake coughing—loudly keeps me from crawling right up into James's lap. I toss a glare Chevy's way, and he only shakes his head.

As Judge Judie continues, James leans close to my ear again. "There's a turkey," he whispers.

There are multiple turkeys on the food table—two fried, one smoked, and at least two oven-roasted. But I know the one he means, and it's the actual, living turkey strutting his way through the tables like this is HIS event. Which, technically, one could make the argument it is. Stormy, the younger of Harper's two dogs, is following at a semi-safe distance, trying to sniff discreetly. He yelps and bolts when the turkey lunges at him.

"That's King," I whisper back.

"But it's a turkey ... on Thanksgiving."

"Yeah, and?"

James tilts his head a little so he can meet my eyes. His expression is so serious I almost laugh. "We're eating his friends," he whispers.

I force my face into a concerned expression. "Oh, no! Do you think King saw?"

James gives me that James look, patent pending, and now

I do laugh, but quietly because heaven forbid someone interrupt the benediction. But this moment feels almost normal with James, so I'm willing to risk the wrath of Judge Judie. I'll cling to this scrap like a junkyard dog. Just try and take it away from me—I DARE YOU.

"I don't remember whose idea it was, but years ago, we started having a live turkey as our way of honoring the bird."

"While *eating* the bird."

"Other birds, but yes," I whisper.

"How long has King been attending Feastivus?"

"Technically, we're on King the third. But we just call them all King."

"Did Kings one through three end up on a plate?"

"Oh no. All the Kings get to live out their natural avian lives. Just turns out those lives aren't very long."

"I see." He pauses. "I'm not going to be the one scrubbing turkey droppings off the cement when this is over with."

I sigh. "I volunteer as tribute."

James nods, jaw clenching. But this time, as he turns away, I realize it's because he's trying to hide a smile.

Okay, then. Maybe this is okay; maybe *he's* okay. Relief pours over me like water, and I sigh deeply.

"Finally," Judge Judie says, clearing her throat and turning her gaze directly on our table, "I would be remiss if I didn't acknowledge the Graham family."

James tenses behind me, and something shifts in the air, leaving a very weighty silence. I swallow past a lump in my throat, hoping this is going to be a good blessing and not a complaint. Most of the people present have already offered grudging support after Tank bought the town. Pat marrying Lindy had a lot to do with it, as most people are suckers for a happy ending, especially if it involves one of Sheet Cake's own. And no one can argue that he didn't come in and take great care of Lindy and Jo.

Judge Judie continues, "While their introduction to Sheet Cake certainly has not been without its share of drama and several arrests, I think many of us have begun to see the good these interlopers have brought."

"Who are you calling an interloper?" Pat calls out. "I married Sheet Cake royalty!" As though to demonstrate, he tips Lindy back, planting a kiss on her lips that has people giving wolf whistles and Jo covering her eyes.

"Get a room!" Chevy shouts through cupped hands.

Judge Judie rolls her eyes but otherwise ignores the outbursts. "Today, James Graham showed real Sheet Cake hospitality by allowing us to meet and congregate here, at the site of what I think we all know will be a successful brewery. Though we can all agree it'll never be as good as my family's moonshine." She raises her mason jar.

There are several shouts of agreement, mostly from other people holding glasses of said moonshine. James relaxes a little with the attention off him.

"Raise a glass of whatever you've got," Judge Judie says, and around the space, people lift glasses in the air. I hold up my water, but behind me, James is still impersonating a corpse. "To the Grahams and their first Feastivus. We hope you'll stay to see many more!"

"To the Feast!" a chorus of voices rings out. One more part of our tradition I should have prepared the Grahams for. But that's okay. By next year, they'll be old pros.

The thought of next year or the future in general makes something drop inside my stomach. What will the next year bring? Will I still be working alongside James? More importantly—will I still be *with* him? Will the brewery be open and successful, the town of Sheet Cake revived?

A part of me can see it, a future with all my hopes bundled together like a present tied up with a ribbon. But at the moment, it feels a little like my perfectly wrapped present has been mistakenly dropped off at a toddler's birthday party and grubby hands are going to rip into it—or maybe rip it apart. I shove away the dark thoughts and turn to press a kiss to James's stubbly chin.

"You did good, temp," he says.

I glow under his praise, preening. I almost toss my hair. "So did you."

His expression tightens. "I didn't do anything."

"You opened up your sacred space to a bunch of strangers—that's something, especially for you. And you earned your badge for helping elderly ladies while being ogled."

"Is that an official badge now?"

"Yep. I'll help sew the patch on your vest later."

Eula Martin rings one of those old timey dinner triangles and there's a loud gong—because someone also brought a full-sized gong. As one does.

But as people start to push chairs back, another sound rises over the crowd. A much, much worse sound.

First, there's something like a yowl/howl. Then a chorus of snarls, a loud crash. That's when the screaming starts.

I whip my head toward the building just in time to see an unfortunately familiar orange blur bolting from the table—an orange blur with a whole turkey leg in its mouth. That stupid, one-eyed orange cyclops just stole a turkey.

The cat streaks outside with two dogs in hot pursuit. It leaps on the nearest table, which happens to be ours, knocking a pitcher of water all over Chase and Molly. The dogs must hit the legs of the table just right because one side gives out and everything from pitchers of water to glasses of moonshine slide down into a heap of plastic picnicware and shattered glass.

People are jumping up, chairs tipping over as the cat plays a mean game of Frogger across the tables. Another crash sounds from inside the building and I look in time to see two dogs I don't even recognize ravaging the food table. A pug mix is literally ON the table while a German Shepherd wrestles the whole brisket from the platter to the ground. Tank gasps as a yellow lab grabs the other end of the brisket.

"The dogs have gone wild!" someone shouts, and then there is only chaos.

Stormy, Harper's dog, runs by carrying a whole fried turkey by the leg. Another small dog I don't recognize is hot on his heels, and right as they pass our table, the second dog makes a grab for the bird. The two of them wrestle, taking out a second table, even as Chase jumps into the fray.

Stormy ends up with just the leg, leaving Chase holding the bird aloft—with the little dog holding on to the breast by its teeth, legs pedaling in the air. While I watch, a big golden retriever jumps up, paws landing right near Chase's shoulders. The dog rips the bird right out of Chase's hands, sending the smaller dog flying into Eula Martin's lap. The retriever takes off out of the gate, the whole bird dragging along the ground.

Big Mo is waving a set of serving spoons at the remaining dog pack, trying to herd them outside of the building, but it's like they've all gone mad. Ducking between Mo's legs, two medium-sized mutts jump up and the whole main food table goes down with a crash. A splatter of sweet potatoes hits Mo on the face, a bright orange spot on his cheek.

But how are there SO MANY DOGS?

King gets spooked, and, though he doesn't fly well, he takes a hop and a flying leap, landing right on one of the few tables still standing. Mort Hammecher swings a cane at the bird but knocks over a pitcher of water instead, soaking Lynn Louise, who calmly pulls a hanky from her coif of hair.

King gobbles his way down the table, a terrified turkey version of Godzilla, stepping right on a stick of butter and knocking over glasses and pitchers. People jump up as rivers of water and wine and moonshine flow over the edges of the plastic tablecloths. Before Burt can chase King off, the bird leaves a fresh deposit of turkey droppings right on Judge Judie's plate.

There are people chasing dogs, dogs still tearing apart the food from the floor, and in the chaos, the Bobs somehow decide now is the perfect time to start playing a bluegrass version of "America the Beautiful."

This is beyond the worst-case scenario for the day. There isn't a defcon level for this kind of disaster.

"Protect the pies!" someone shouts, and I realize the only table untouched is the dessert table.

Tank jogs over to help Big Mo dispel the pack of dogs, but as I watch, both men slip in a butter-slick pile of mashed potatoes and go down hard.

I haven't glanced at James even once, but as I do so now, I wish I hadn't. His jaw is working, and I can practically hear the sound of his molars grinding even over all the shouting and the growling and the ridiculous music.

"James—" I start but am interrupted as a siren starts to drown out the noise.

A fire engine roars up to the front gate, and my stomach sinks. I can't look at James. I can feel the frustration crackling like electricity from him.

Gamble Briggs, the fire marshal, climbs down from the passenger side of the truck, followed by a few other guys in uniform. The fire marshal is wearing a navy suit and has a cloth napkin tucked into the front of his shirt, like he just came from his Thanksgiving table. He probably did.

And based on his deep frown, he is NOT happy about it.

No one pays him any mind as he tries to shout over the din because King the turkey has taken up residence in June Elliot's lap and the Bobs have inexplicably moved on to play what sounds an awful lot like Lady Gaga's "Poker Face."

Gamble cups his hands around his mouth and shouts even louder, "HEY, EVERYBODY!"

Chevy manages to wrangle King off June's lap in a flurry of gobbles and flying features. Thankfully, the Bobs give it a rest.

Gamble's gaze travels over the total disaster that is now Dark Horse. He looks one part irritated and one part flabbergasted. "Y'all know I support Feastivus, but unfortunately, I've got to shut this down."

The reaction to this is stunned silence and some light gobbling from King, who is pecking at a pile of dropped biscuits. Shame rolls through me, hot and thick. I absolutely did not think about permits. And I should have, especially given the way Billy Waters shut down Lindy and Pat's reception in the town square for a similar reason. I'm sure Billy alerted Gamble in the first place.

But I'm the one who should have thought about this, who should have known it might be an issue.

Gamble waves a hand toward the front gates. "Go on, now. Y'all need to disperse, and I need to figure out whether I'll have to cite the owner with a violation."

Even better. I squeeze my hands into fists, wishing one of the dogs had dragged me off like a giant turkey leg. My stomach is in a freefall down my body. I try to catch James's expression without meeting his gaze, and the man looks like he's turned into a statue.

"For what?" That's Pat, sounding indignant and about two seconds from starting a brawl.

The fire marshal glares. "For starters, you have a permit for construction but no certificate of occupancy for a group of this—or any—size. Now, if you'd all start moving in an orderly fashion toward the gate, I'd like to get back to my meal."

Well, there goes the holiday.

CHAPTER 33

Winnie

THE SCENT of fried turkey and failure hangs in the air when I sneak back over to Dark Horse. Most of the Feastivus-goers moved to Mari's diner to eat what was left. Which was, essentially, a lot of pie and anything Big Mo and Mari could whip up from the kitchen. The people of Sheet Cake always find a way to soldier on.

I suspect that James Graham, however amazing his shoulders are, may not be similarly equipped.

It's why, when I sneak back over to Dark Horse, I come armed with two very important things. The first is pie, and the second is my laptop with the presentation I've been working on with plans for Dark Horse. I hope the pie will provide enough drugging sugar to pacify James. And the presentation is my redemption for the disaster of today—

showing him how I can be an asset to the future of Dark Horse, rather than the harbinger of disaster like I was today.

I've mentally crossed all my fingers and toes, accepted a pat on the back from Tank, and sat through a mini pep-talk from Lindy and Val while shoveling pie into my face. Is this the ideal way to go out on a limb asking James to keep me on in a more full-time capacity?

Not even in the slightest.

It's more like I was thrown out of an airplane and I'm pulling all the cords I can pull, hoping one of them goes to a parachute.

I squeeze my way through the closed gate, equally careful with the pie and laptop. The outside is still in a state of disarray with toppled tables, broken glass, and paper plates blowing like tumbleweeds in the cool breeze. The strings of lights have been unplugged, but from somewhere inside the building, there's a dim glow.

Cautiously, I walk inside, shivering a little. Darkness has fully fallen, and without the heaters fired up, the night air definitely has bite.

Though the outdoor space is still a mess, inside, the floor has been swept, the tables removed, and James is running a mop over the concrete. I take in the stiff line of his shoulders, the ticking muscle in his jaw, and debate my approach.

I know James is overwhelmed. Irritated. Frustrated.

I could just offer him pie and an apology tonight. Maybe a massage to work out some of the stiffness in those shoulders.

But I can't shake the idea that my presentation will give him something *more*. It's me, offering myself up to James. Telling him I want more—not only with the business but with *him*. I want to be more of a permanent fixture, both at

Dark Horse and in his life. This is my grand gesture, an apology, and an offering all rolled up into one.

"Need a hand, boss?"

James stiffens. His gaze flicks to me, then back to the spot on the floor he keeps going over and over. I have a very vivid mental image of Tank, Big Mo, and a mound of mashed potatoes that I hope will one day be funny.

"No," James says.

Ever since I pointed out that this is his favorite word, James's lips have curled up when he says *no* to me. Right now, his mouth is in what looks like a very permanent frown.

Again, indecision crowds my brain. James is in a MOOD. I would be too, honestly. I could wait—maybe I *should* wait. But everything that happened today is my fault. I asked about using Dark Horse. I brought in all the people without thinking about permits—which is ridiculous. Billy Waters had Pat and Lindy's vow renewal shut down in the center of town a few weeks ago. I have zero doubt he's the one who called up the fire marshal and reported Feastivus.

I'd like to toss Billy into a vat of mashed potatoes.

But back to James—maybe he just wants pie and a hug? Or pie and then to be left alone? Or … just to be left alone?

Maybe it's that part of me that just has to push, but I'm not satisfied with that. I wanted today to be about a preview for James, showing him what could be. I simply can't leave things as the epic fail they were.

Decided, I square my shoulders. "Could I talk to you for a minute?"

James stops mopping and leans on the handle, looking as exhausted as he does frustrated. I want to walk over and brush the hair out of his eyes. But my James Graham manual tells me touching him right now isn't what he needs.

"I'm really sorry about earlier," I say. "I should have anticipated—"

"It's not your fault." The way James says this seems to imply he thinks it's *his* fault. Which is wrong, wrong, wrong.

I shake my head. "We can agree to disagree on that. Anyway—I've got pie to go along with my apology." I hold it out, but James only eyes it warily. So much for softening him up. I set it down on the table which, only an hour ago, held all the desserts. Fishing my laptop out of my bag, I locate a folding chair and set it up in front of the table.

"Can I show you something?"

James seems to be thinking, and his eyes soften a little as his gaze moves over me. With a bone-weary sigh, he says, "Sure."

I indicate the chair. "Want to sit?"

"Standing is fine." He leans the mop against a wall and crosses his arms over his chest.

Tough crowd. Guess this is as receptive as he's going to get. I can only hope he'll lighten up when he sees what I've made for him.

"First of all, I want to say thank you for being willing to host today. I had hoped it would be a preview of things to come." I grimace. "Without the whole fire-marshal-kicking-everyone-out bit."

James doesn't smile. I draw in a breath and pull up the presentation I've been working so hard on this week.

"Since today didn't go as planned, I have something else to show you." I click the mousepad to pull up the slideshow fully on the screen. "I've been working on something of a launch plan for Dark Horse."

He flinches at the phrase *launch plan*, but I still think it's going to be fine. I mean, who WOULDN'T flinch at the idea of a launch plan after a disaster like today? I start moving through the slides, walking him through each point of the plan, the timelines, the budgets, my suggestions—all of it. I have an outline for all the social media, for PR, and other grassroots marketing.

There is a whole section on different themed events Dark Horse could host, as well as ideas for the tasting room and a potential expansion into the connected back building, which as of now, will be empty. We could have a whole wall of board games for people to play or a collection of vintage arcade games—functions for the space itself beyond the beer to keep people here and happy. I am nothing if not a fount of ideas, and after the conference, I have been overflowing with them.

I'm not sure how it's possible for a person to grow MORE silent, but I swear, James's silence is expanding like some kind of black hole. It's sucking all the air out of the room, which I'm sure is why I'm practically panting as I reach the just-over-halfway point. His silence is starting to suck away my confidence too, and I mess up the slides, accidentally skipping ahead to one showing financials, which finally gets a reaction out of James.

Not one I'd like, since his eyes go wide and his jaw finally opens. It's more of an unhinging, and I'm thankful when he snaps it closed again. I was a little afraid it was going to hit the floor.

"Don't worry about those numbers just yet. Pretend you didn't see them." I wave my hand in front of me, Jedi style. "Those weren't the numbers you were looking for," I say, realizing I am not simply crashing and burning like a plane. I'm crashing and burning like a meteor passing through the earth's atmosphere. I'm about to make impact, and I think the crater from my landing is going to be visible from space.

"Harper and Collin helped with this part, so we just made

some projections based on Collin's gym." I had spectral phone calls with James's siblings this week, getting help with some of the finer details regarding finances and expenses James never shared with me.

"You talked to my family about this?"

The harshness of his tone hits my bloodstream like an infection, like a poison. I've been able to stave off his bad vibe with the force of my hope. But now, everything in me sinks as I realize the colossal misjudgment I've made.

I shift on my feet, digging my fingernails into my palm. "They were able to fill in the blanks on some of the things I don't know offhand," I say, knowing how defensive I sound.

"You didn't think to ask me if I *wanted* them involved in that?"

"They're your family. On top of that, they're investors and had the original business plan with all the numbers I haven't seen. I just thought—"

"You thought wrong."

I swallow and take a step back, my hand hovering over my laptop. My brain scrambles, seeking a way to salvage this. If I could just get back on track, I could show him the examples of other successful breweries I put together and the—

James slices a hand through the air. "Just stop."

"But I haven't gotten to the part where—"

"Just … stop." James's hands drag through this hair, and his eyes are wild. "I can't do this with you."

BOOM. Impact of my crashing and burning is more painful than I thought. I swear, those few words from James have my teeth rattling and my bones aching. Because they sound much, much bigger than a reaction about my slideshow. There is a finality to them, a resignation that has my nerves firing and my stomach bottoming out.

James walks toward me, his face still a hard blank, his jaw

329

and shoulders tight. When he lifts his hand to slam my laptop shut, I flinch. The sound is so incredibly final.

The thing is, even in his state of silent fury, James is wildly beautiful. Maybe wild *and* beautiful is a more apt description. He's like the big grizzly bear you really wish you could hug even though you know it would probably rip your face off.

"Do you want me to—"

"Why did you do this?" he asks, stepping back and crossing his arms.

"I did it because I wanted to. For *you*. I like thinking this way, planning, visioning. Going to the conference really helped me get an idea for what this place could be, how to bring your dream to life."

"*My* dream."

"Yes." I'm agreeing, but it feels more like surrendering, and not in the peace treaty way. More like a surrender preceding imprisonment or maybe banishment. My mouth itches to find a smart comment or a sarcastic retort. Protection for myself. But I know that would make it worse.

"I didn't ask for you to do this," James says.

"I know."

"I didn't want you to do this." He sweeps a hand toward my closed laptop. "I didn't want this at all. I don't want any of it."

He gestures now to the room at large, and I'm consumed. He doesn't want this building? The brewery itself?

"All of this got away from me." James is muttering now, not looking at me, not really looking at anything, his eyes wild and unfocused.

So, yeah. Clearly, I should have listened to the part of me saying it would be better to wait for this conversation. This is like the fake website times a thousand. Or a few hundred thousand. I categorically underestimated how upset James was or overestimated the power of my presentation.

I have no more words. At this point, it seems best to just let Mount St. James erupt and assess the damage later.

"You talked to my family about Dark Horse. About the financials, the business plan. You showed them this presentation?"

His voice is so full of hurt, so calm, so deadly, so painful. I feel like James has taken a spoon out of a drawer and is using it to scrape out everything in me.

I swallow hard and nod. Another miscalculation. I thought I could get some confirmation from James's family about my ideas. I thought it would give me the last bit of courage needed to show James.

"Did you have, like, family meetings?"

"No. Nothing like that. A few phone calls." I clear my throat. "And a video chat."

The harsh lines of his face hurt to look at.

"I like your family," I add in a small voice.

"I like them too. Doesn't mean I want you talking to them without me about Dark Horse." He shakes his head. "This is what happens when I'm not in control. When other people make decisions. I end up here." James laughs, short and humorless. His gaze fixes on the floor, and he scuffs the toe of one boot across something only he can see.

I don't fully understand what he means or what's so wrong with talking to his family, with accepting help from people who care about him. "Is here so bad?"

He raises his head then, slowly, like it's being pulled up by a puppeteer who's mid-yawn. He doesn't need to say the word. I see the yes in his eyes. Hear it in his silence.

"Why won't you let the people who love you help you?"

If he knows I'm counting myself in that group of people who love him, he doesn't react, which is probably all the answer I need.

"I don't need help."

I grab my laptop, sliding it inside my bag, gathering my purse. "I think I'll go."

Please come after me, a part of me begs, even as the bigger, smarter part of me knows he won't. Nothing good will come of that now. James needs ... well, I don't know what he needs.

I thought I could read him. Tonight showed me how wrong I was.

I'm almost to the door, my chest suffering from a psycho-somatic gunshot wound, when I hear two quiet words that make me pause.

"You're fired."

The bubble I was worried about since Austin? I'm pretty sure it just popped. I turn slowly. James isn't looking at me, but I wait an almost unbearable length of time for his eyes to meet mine.

"Firing me once wasn't enough?"

James says not a word. Makes not a sound. Moves not a muscle. Just one blink is all I get.

And for some reason, this infuriates me.

Maybe I chose a poor time to present this idea to him. Maybe I should have waited until a day or two had passed from this horrible disaster. But still!

"Well, you're fired too—as my boyfriend, or whatever you were."

The words feel like the perfect circle, the exact revenge, and also a huge mistake. Breaking up isn't what I want.

Neither is being fired. I feel like a double loser. And yet, I don't feel like James is giving me a choice.

The man wasn't lying when he said he wasn't soft. He's a grump through and through. A grump whose biggest fear is dancing but will do it when a little girl asks. A grump who held me close and offered comfort when I had a nightmare. A grump who threw a man in the pool for touching me. A grump whose kisses could melt the polar ice caps.

Not that we want that—I'm just saying, his kisses could do it.

But the thing I'm realizing as I taste regret on my tongue, is that for all he's opened up, James is still closed up tight. To me and to everyone. Right now, it's the to-me part that matters.

Nothing between us can ever work if he gets upset and fires me because of his own personal issues.

I wish he'd argue. I wish he'd apologize. I wish James had any expression on his face other than what appears to be cool disinterest.

But if that's how he feels, then my decision is absolutely the best one. Even if making it feels like walking barefoot over a mix of hot coals and broken glass.

Because I'm right and he's wrong and because he needs my help and maybe because I've fallen in love with this giant prickly pear of a man, I absolutely cannot help myself from getting in the last word.

"I'll send you an email with the slides and the other documents I've made. Just in case you realize you're wrong. Because you absolutely are, James Graham. So wrong."

I honestly don't know if I mean this as an olive branch or firing a parting shot. Maybe a little bit of both.

FROM THE NEIGHBORLY APP

Subject: BIG BREAKUP

DeltaDeltaDelta
NEWSFLASH! Winnie Boyd and James Graham broke up! Haven't heard reasons yet, but obvs she's not good enough for him.

MegaB
Plus, that's her second breakup this month. Take a break, honey.

The_Real_Shell-E
Dibs!

BagelBytes
I don't think we should be celebrating any breakups OR be posting about them here. Let everyone have their privacy.

DeltaDeltaDelta

I'd love to have some privacy … with one of the Grahams.

SweetPea23

I don't know why someone hasn't claimed Tank yet. That is one handsome fella.

Cal_45

If that man's smart, he'll stay away from the likes of you

SweetPea23

Was keying your car not enough? Need me to key your house too?

Cal_45

Keep talking and I'll keep taking screenshots for my lawyer

GrahamFan

I made a poll. Who did the breaking up with who? I think Winnie broke up with James. He was a rebound for her—and he deserves better! Vote below!

BagelBytes

I think you mean, *Who did the breaking up with WHOM*

The_Real_Shell-E

Thanks for the grammar lesson Mom

BagelBytes

That would be: *Thanks for the grammar lesson, Mom.* There's a punctuation lesson too.

Neighborly Mod

    [This thread has been closed and marked for deletion]

CHAPTER 34

James

AFTER WINNIE LEAVES, the pounding in my head doubles in intensity. Needing a break, needing speed and distance and wind in my hair, I drive my truck back to Austin so I can take the bike out. I spend a very sleepless night in Tank's house, where the emptiness seems to mock me. It's a reminder of all the events that have swept me along the past few months.

I'm Dorothy, carried off by a tornado of my own making. In my story though, I landed in Oz only to have my own house fall on me.

When I fired Winnie for the second time, it wasn't so much of a conscious choice as a knee-jerk reaction. The over-whelm of the day—and the last few weeks, really—grew and mounted into a fever pitch I could only silence by lashing out.

Every time I try closing my eyes, I see Winnie giving her presentation. As the slides advanced, every page, every line, every number I'm sure Winnie carefully researched crowded into my brain, jostling for position. I kept picturing how Dark Horse looked with all the people there—smiling, happy people. But I wasn't smiling. I wasn't happy. It was someone else's dream. Not mine.

All the worries I've had, and new ones I hadn't even thought of began shouting all at once. My brain filled with high-pitched static, a painful shriek of anxiety until I couldn't even hear what Winnie was saying.

Her lips were moving; my head was imploding.

When she mentioned talking to Collin and Harper, though, the static narrowed to a very fine point.

She was only trying to help, a distant, far too logical thought tells me.

And that's what makes all this even worse. I know Winnie wanted to help. Because she cared—about the brewery and, for whatever reason, about me.

Except, losing Winnie silenced nothing. The voices in my head are louder than before, and they all sound like her.

I hope you're happy now.

Spoiler alert—I'm anything but happy.

Is this really what you want?

No. But I have no idea what I DO want.

Do you think you can really do all this on your own?

I have about zero percent confidence I can pull this off.

How does it feel to be totally, totally alone?

After being with Winnie, getting a taste of her, it feels pretty much terrible.

That's what I thought.

I leave Tank's empty house the next morning, my skull

throbbing, my muscles aching. It feels like any minute, the pressure is going to make my head pop right off.

I screwed up. I know I did. But I've been screwing up for months, a slow slide into failure as I let myself get carried along by someone else's dream. I can't run the brewery. Now that I've had a tiny taste, I don't even *want* to do it. I want to go back to my solitary life—living alone, brewing small batches to distribute on a small scale. Alone.

Only … Winnie has ruined alone for me. Because I've seen what life is like when I'm not alone. I've gotten a taste of being with Winnie, and already, her absence feels like a festering wound.

Gross analogy, but I said what I said.

It's for the best, I tell myself. For HER best. I watched Winnie at the conference and at Feastivus. Being around people is like plugging Winnie in—she lights up. Whereas my circuits overload and my system shuts down. We don't work together. Better we end things now before they go any further—as far as both Winnie and Dark Horse are concerned.

I can hand over my recipes, hand over everything to my family. They can run it. Or not. I'll even give them the launch plan Winnie sent me, which of course I looked at last night, being a glutton for punishment. It's perfect.

Perfect for someone else.

When I hit the newer part of Sheet Cake, a stabbing pressure assaults my temples with every beat of my pulse. My chest feels like it's been clamped inside some kind of medieval torture device, and I can't stop sweating.

I stop at a Walgreens next to a Shipley Do-Nuts and a tanning salon. There's a blood pressure machine right next to a locked glass cabinet full of birth control options. Somehow, this juxtaposition seems fitting.

After I manage to cram my arm into the metal loop with the cuff, I listen to the computerized robot voice tell me super obvious things like how to sit still as I wait for the cuff to inflate. Despite the mounting pressure I feel, I get two thumbs-up from the cartoon dog.

Yay—my heart isn't in danger of exploding.

My head, though, tells a different story. My night away has done nothing to ease the throbbing.

I'm not an idiot. Or, not too much of one. I've known that my stress level has been rising. It's only been getting worse since I moved to Sheet Cake. No, since Winnie started working for me.

The start, though, was when I let myself dream too big, when I accepted seed money from my family and basically put all of us at risk over a stupid idea. I should have known I'd never be able to pull it off. Not alone, as I'd been trying to do it. Not with my family backing me. Not with Winnie beside me.

Not at all.

A lanky, over-eager employee appears beside me. His name tag reads Clark. He is a total Clark and reminds me of Gumby, especially as he bends unnervingly close to look at the screen.

Isn't this some kind of privacy violation?

"Looks like you passed the blood pressure test with flying colors! Bravo!"

He adds a little round of applause, clapping in a circle the way you learn to do when you're in elementary school. I cannot get out of the cuff fast enough.

No, actually, I can't get out of the thing.

"Let me give you a hand," he says. "I think if you just—"

"I've got it!"

And I do. Literally, I've got it, because when I wrench my

arm, the whole cuff comes with me, ripping clean off the machine.

Then, of course, it slides right off my arm with ease and clatters to the floor.

Great. Now I've broken Walgreens.

Clark takes a few steps back, looking like he thinks I might break him next. "Don't worry about it," he says with a nervous laugh. "This kind of thing happens all the time."

Doubtful. But I pick up the broken cuff, place it in his palm, and make a swift exit.

Convinced that physically I'm fine, even if ONLY physically, I drive straight back to the warehouse and park out front. I don't have a plan, but when I see the banner Winnie purchased hanging outside the gate, I fixate on this.

Hopping out of the truck, I stride toward it and yank it down with one hand. If it weren't made of vinyl, I'd rip it into pieces, but I settle for tossing it in the long, low dumpster I rented. The banner flutters and lands neatly on top of the mound of black trash bags from the mess of Feastivus.

Just thinking of the disaster of yesterday has the pressure increasing in my skull and my chest growing tight again.

"What'd that sign do to you?"

I whirl around, taken aback to see Pat standing behind me with his trademark grin—the one that looks like the Cheshire cat who ate a cage full of canaries. I hate that grin. Now, more than ever.

"I'm just cleaning up some trash." I brush past to walk inside, hoping he'll go. Knowing he won't.

"Doesn't look like trash to me. It looks like a perfectly good banner."

"It was temporary." It was all temporary. And a mistake.

Pat leans over and starts to pull the banner out, but I grab his arm. "Leave it."

He searches my face, and I hope my expression gives nothing away. Pat steps back and crosses his arms.

"Why?"

"Don't need it."

"But why, James?"

A challenge lights his eyes, and the very last thing I need today, when I'm barely holding it together, is my youngest brother stirring up trouble.

"Why are you here?"

The subject-change tactic sometimes works with Pat. Today, though, I know he sees right through it. "I came to fetch you," Pat says.

"For?"

"Black Friday afternoon poker? Come on, Jamie. Don't tell me you forgot. It's *tradition*."

I absolutely forgot. Squeezing my eyes closed, I mentally count to ten. I get to three. "Just family?"

"Lindy won't even be there. She's catching up with her girlfriends. And Jo is getting pedicures with Mari." Pat's gaze sharpens. "Why? Who are you trying to avoid?"

"Everyone."

———

"Bid's to you, James," Collin says, rapping his knuckles on the table. "Where's your head at today?"

Definitely not here. Not in this game and not in this town. I've done my best to lose my chips or, when I've got a hand like I do right now—pocket aces—to fold so I don't stand a chance of winning.

"Fold." I lay my cards down on the table and lean back in my chair, crossing my arms over my chest.

Pat eyes me. "Same." He slaps his cards down and mirrors

my pose. His eyes have a gleam I don't like. He elbows Chase.

Chase's eyes dart between the two of us. "Uh, I will also fold?"

"Me too." Collin pushes his cards away and gives me a long stare.

"You can't all fold because I fold," I snap.

"Sure we can," Pat says, grinning. "We just did."

Tank sets his cards down and puts his elbows on the table, leaning forward. "Anyone want to explain why I'm about to win the pot with nothing but a five-high hand?"

Chase shifts in his seat. "I don't know why we're folding. I just don't want to get punched."

"No one is getting punched," Harper says from her spot on the couch. She sets down her book. "What's going on?"

I glare at Pat. "Nothing. Get back in the game. All of you."

My most infuriating brother only grins. His face looks more punchable by the second. "Where you go, I go, brother."

"Me too," Collin says. "Where are we going, exactly? Just so I'm clear."

"Down," Pat says. "We're going down."

"No, *we* are not going down." I glare.

"Like it or not, we're in this together, Jamie," Pat says.

Tank clears his throat. "Will someone please explain—"

"James is folding." Pat gives me a pointed look, a smug look. It's the look that says he's figured me out.

"I think we can all see that," Chase says.

"Not this hand," Pat says. "Or, not *just* the hand. He's folding Dark Horse."

Way to throw me under the bus, then back up and run me over a few more times for good measure, Patrick.

344

A barrage of questions and exclamations follow, all of which I ignore. Leaning my head forward in my hands, all the noise becomes an indistinct wall of sound.

I'm cocooned inside of it, completely still, untouchable. Only a high-pitched whine fills my ears, the rest of the sun in the room muffled beneath it. I close my eyes and jam the heels of my hands into them.

It's not until I feel a soft hand on my shoulder and a voice says, "Jamie?" that I snap back into the room.

Harper is standing just behind me, one hand lightly on my shoulder. Miraculously, she seems to have shut everyone else up, but my head is still buzzing, still overfull. Their faces are a blur around the table.

I rub my eyes. "What?"

"Want to take a walk?" Harper asks gently.

"No. I don't know." I run a hand through my hair. *Yank* it through my hair, is more the truth. A few strands come out, and I shake them loose from my fingertips, watching as they fall to the floor.

"Come," Harper says, lightly tapping my shoulder. When I flinch at her touch, she backs up. "Sit over here with me for a second."

"I don't need to—"

"*Come and sit.*"

At Harper's fierce tone, both dogs jog over and sit down at her feet. Ignoring the rest of my uncharacteristically silent family, I let Harper somewhat forcibly lead me to Tank's new chair, a buttery leather one he doesn't like anyone else to sit in. Right now, though, he doesn't say a word. I collapse in the chair and meet Harper's eyes as she kneels in front of me.

"There you are." She gives me a soft smile and pats my

knee before thinking better of it and clasping her hands. "Want to tell me what's going on?"

Winnie's face flashes before my eyes. Not her smirk or the fiery anger from earlier when she left. I see the vulnerability when she woke from the nightmare, remember the way she felt so small in my arms. I rub my eyes again until she disappears.

"I messed up."

I shove a hand into my pocket, my fingers brushing Winnie's seed. I press it under my fingernail, and the tiny pinch of pain grounds me, reminding me of what I can't have. I tried to throw the seed away last night when I got undressed for bed, but I couldn't bring myself to do it.

Harper gives me a kind smile, one I definitely don't deserve. "Nothing you did can't be fixed."

I only wish that were true.

"Do you not think you'll be ready in time?" Tank asks. He stands from the table and walks over to the living area. Chase and Collin follow, and Pat flops onto the couch, putting his feet up on the table. "Because the timeline doesn't matter. If you're not fully up and operational by the festival, it's fine."

I'm already shaking my head. "I can't do it."

"What do you need help with?" Collin asks. "I could take some time off from the gym if you need me."

NOW he wants to help. I'm already shaking my head. "It's too much."

"It's too much because you're trying to do it all on your own," Pat says. "Just like you always do. Stop trying to be a one-man show. You can't shoulder it all."

"Exactly," I snap. "I can't do it all, and I'm done trying to hold it together. This isn't what I wanted."

Tank frowns. "What isn't what you wanted?"

I wave a hand, feeling that same rise of hot volcanic pressure I did last night when I exploded on Winnie. "None of this is what I wanted. This town. A big brewery with a bar and events and people."

All the people. I picture the crowd from Feastivus, imagine trying to pay attention to temperatures and timing and shutting off the right valves while a crowd of people look on. I shake my head.

"I don't—I can't."

"What can't you do?" Harper asks softly.

I stare down at the worn knees of my jeans, where the deep blue has given way to white. "Any of it. I'm screwing it all up. It's not what I want, and yet, I can't fail. I can't let you all lose everything because you bet on me."

"We care more about you than we do about the money," Tank says.

"Speak for yourself," Pat chimes in. "I care about the money."

"Shut it, Patty," Collin says.

"No," Pat says, getting to his feet. "Superman over here doesn't get to try and save the day all alone, then torpedo the whole world when he realizes he can't save it by himself. He hasn't wanted our help. Now, he's realizing he can't do it by himself, like we've been saying all along, and rather than *try*, he's walking away. I'm not okay with this. Sorry, not sorry."

I lumber to my feet, spinning to face Pat even as the blood pounds in my head. "When did you ever offer anything other than opinions I didn't ask for? All I really wanted was to brew beer and make furniture. A simple, quiet life."

"The life of a hermit," Pat says, and the comment barely registers because he just never stops.

"I only wanted this for you." I sweep my arms out, not even sure who I'm gesturing to. Because if this isn't my dream, whose is it? I'm all tangled up, unsure of anything

347

except my own failure. "I didn't want this for me. And now, it's too late, and it's too much, and I can't keep holding things together for everyone else."

"No one asked you to hold things together!" Pat shouts.

"No one had to!" I shout back. "But someone had to make sure you all ate, that your clothes got washed, that you got out of bed in the morning and got on the bus. It all fell on me. It always feels like it's on me, and I can't do it anymore!"

There is silence when I finish, in the room and, for the first time in a day, in my head. Shame curls up and takes residence where all the anger and pressure had been building.

When I speak again, my voice is a whisper dragged over broken glass. "I can't do it anymore. I've wrecked it all—the brewery, my family, *her* ... I'm done. I'm done."

I collapse back into the chair, dropping my head in my hands, my breaths heavy and my eyes burning. I'm exhausted. I'm not on edge anymore because I've gone so far *over* the edge.

I'm a disappointment. To myself. To Winnie. To my family.

Not only have I failed everyone in my life I care about, but I just dredged up a bunch of long-buried things and dropped them like a dirty bomb in the middle of a family poker game.

And then there's the fact that everyone has money on me.

A heavy arm comes around my shoulders, and I can't help it—I flinch before I relax under my dad's touch. I don't pull away, but I can't manage to unlock my jaw or untense my shoulders.

"Son, I am so sorry. Sorry so much fell on you after we lost your mom. I don't think I realized how much you had to carry. I was just ... grieving." His voice catches in his throat.

"You were allowed to grieve."

348

I'm not looking at him, but I still see his head shaking. "Not at the cost of my children. I didn't realize how all this felt for you. I was so grateful for you helping—I *am* so grateful. But James, you were never supposed to pick up all these burdens and carry them around."

"It's fine," I mutter.

"It isn't fine. You are a caretaker, James. You've always been so strong—for yourself and for those around you. Even when you didn't think anyone noticed. We did. And we don't thank you enough."

"Maybe because he'd probably fight us if we tried," Harper says, but her voice is gentle.

I raise my eyes for just a moment, taking in her soft gaze. She suddenly, more than she ever has, resembles Mom.

"We see you, James. But sometimes we forget that you need help because you're so capable. I never meant for you to carry so much, son. It isn't your burden to carry alone. It never was."

Tank's words fall over me softly. I am reminded of the one time we went skiing together in Colorado as a family. A storm rolled in, and I paused at the top of a slope, temporarily alone. As the flakes drifted down, it was with a quiet, blanketing hush.

I keep my head in my hands now, remembering that moment, feeling peace settle my restless thoughts like the quiet snow.

"Do you hear me, son?" Tank squeezes my knee.

I nod, because words have escaped me.

"We'll figure this out. Together. You won't have to carry this alone."

"Is that why he's bigger than the rest of us—because he's been carrying around so much extra weight?" Pat. Of course.

I shake my head, but my lips twitch with a smile as I stare

349

down at the floor. Some things never change. Like Pat's big mouth. Even in a moment like this—and there's comfort and familiarity in that.

"You just don't know when to shut your mouth, do you, Patty?" Surprisingly, that's Chase.

"Those are fighting words. I'm shocked." Collin sounds impressed.

A sigh. "You've all rubbed off on him too much," Harper says.

"Or not enough." Again, it's Pat with the big mouth.

I stand, pulling Tank up with me and into a hug. I don't know why I don't do this more, because my dad's hugs have the power to shake everything loose that needs to be shaken loose and put it all back together. It might even squeeze out a tear or two I've been trying to hold back.

The sound of a phone taking a picture makes my eyes fly open. I catch Pat, grinning down at the phone in his hand.

"Did you seriously just take a photo?" Collin asks.

"Had to capture this sweet moment for Instagram."

"Do you mind if I kill him?" I whisper to Tank, giving him a last squeeze.

Dad rumbles out a laugh. "Nah. Chase makes a pretty good replacement."

"Then with your blessing ..." I release Tank and leap over the chair, going straight for Pat.

He screams like the little girl he is and darts to the kitchen, still tapping at his phone even as he giggles. Is he really posting on Instagram? The dogs follow at my heels, barking, as I round the end of the kitchen island, grabbing Pat just as he tosses his phone on the counter.

"Mercy!" he cries as I lift him off his feet, throwing him over my shoulder like a giant sack of rotten potatoes.

"It's too late for mercy, little brother. You're getting

justice instead. Door," I order, and without any further prompting, Chase throws open the front door.

I manage to make it down the steps, Pat wiggling and trying to escape. Not this time.

My family follows behind as I cross the street, headed for the warehouse.

"Put me down, you brute!" Pat punches me in the back, and I let go with one hand, long enough to give him a charley horse in the thigh.

He howls. "Tank! Call off your dog!"

Dad only chuckles. "I'd kinda like to see how this plays out. Sorry, son. Your mouth got you into this, but it won't get you out."

"Where are you taking me? Why are you so freakishly strong?"

I don't answer him, because he really is heavy and I'm getting tired. "Collin," I bark as I near the front gate—and the dumpster. "You get his ankles."

With a wicked grin, Collin grabs Pat by the ankles just as our youngest brother realizes what we intend to do. His fight intensifies, but now there are two of us on him. Chase steps in to help me get a solid grip on Pat's wrists.

"On three," I say, meeting Collin's eyes. He nods, tightening his hold on Pat's ankles. We start to swing Pat, who gives up the fight, probably realizing the inevitability of it all. I count, and on three, we let him fly—right into the low, industrial dumpster outside the warehouse. Pat lands with a muffled crunch on top of the banner and all the garbage bags of food from Feastivus.

The orange cat yowls and leaps out, barely missing Chase.

"It smells like rotten turkey in here!" Pat yells. "Ugh! One of the bags broke and I'm covered in … gravy? I really hope that's gravy."

Pat's head pops up over the side of the dumpster. He has brown goop—and I also really hope it's gravy—dripping down his cheek. He swipes at it with the side of his shirt.

"And these are my favorite jeans. You are officially the worst brother."

"Thank you."

"Is anyone going to help me out of here?"

"No," several voices chorus at once. The dogs are the only ones eager to help, probably because of all the dumpster food.

Harper nudges me. "Did you say something about wrecking things with Winnie too?"

I stiffen, then drag a hand down the side of my face. "I did. I really did."

"You're not going to give up that easily," Harper says. "Are you?" She raises an eyebrow in challenge, and I feel something stirring in me.

"I don't know if she'll want to see me." I grimace. "I might have … fired her."

"Again?" Harper asks.

"Again."

She bites her lip. "Well, looks like you've got some groveling and grand gesturing to do."

Tank comes to stand on my other side as we watch Pat try to wrestle his way out of the dumpster. "Too bad you threw our groveling expert in the trash."

"Yeah, I'm not helping you now," Pat says.

I lunge for the dumpster and he squeals, falling back into the trash bags. "You'll still help me," I say. "If I need help."

His laughter echoes from inside the metal dumpster walls. And then he tosses the banner Winnie made out onto the sidewalk. Other than a streak of some unidentifiable food, it looks okay.

"Trust me, brother. You definitely need my help."

"That's what I'm afraid of," I mutter. But at this point, I'll take whatever help I can get.

"Um, hi?" I turn to see a woman it takes me a moment to place out of context. She's standing next to a Prius—probably why none of us heard her pull up—looking between Pat in the dumpster and the rest of us.

"Kyoko?"

She waves. "That's me. Is this a bad time? It kind of looks like a bad time."

"If you came to see Winnie, she's not here."

Kyoko walks over, then picks up the banner by one corner, wrinkling her nose. "Actually, Winnie told me to come. I'm here to apply for a job."

CHAPTER 35

Winnie

SOMETIMES, I really really hate my best friends. Especially when I told them not to come over but they do anyway and then try to get me to talk about my FEELINGS.

Feelings? What feelings?

I don't have feelings.

YOU have feelings. And you can keep them. Because I don't want them. I have a zero-feeling carbon footprint. Doing my part to help the environment!

"Remember," Lindy says, patting my thigh, "just a few months back, you were telling me to go for it with Pat. And look how that turned out?"

"I remember. It filled your practical head with romantic nonsense, which you're now spewing at me."

I shove Lindy's hand away with a grumble that reminds me way too much of James and his constant rumbly, grumbly, growly sounds. Not that I miss them as the soundtrack to my life. The stubborn man can keep his stupid grump noises. I need to find my own noises. But right now, all mine would be wimpy ones like sighs and whimpers and sniffles.

"You're supposed to be on my side," I whine.

"We *are* on your side," Val pipes up from my other side, bumping her shoulder into mine. "Every couple has fights. You'll get through this."

They've made me the meat and cheese in a very squished sandwich, both practically sitting in my lap on Chevy's couch. It's like they suspect I'll run if they don't bodily keep me here.

They know me too well. Though, honestly, none of us are going anywhere because we're drinking. Lindy and I are sipping jalapeno margaritas I made, while Val has a strawberry wine cooler that looks like blood.

"We aren't a couple. We never were." I've made this argument already. Several times, in fact. It doesn't stick now any better than it did when I first said it. Even if it's the truth.

"It was an unspoken coupling," Lindy says.

I roll my eyes. "That's worse than an unconscious coupling."

Val frowns. "How does one become a couple while unconscious?"

"Go google Gwyneth Paltrow and her conscious uncoupling. *Later*," Lindy adds when Val pulls out her phone. "But seriously. Just because you and James didn't have an official conversation, a DTR, if you will—"

"I won't."

"That doesn't mean you weren't a couple. You *kissed*."

"Quiet! Chevy is probably listening with his ear pressed to the bedroom door. He doesn't need to hear details about me kissing." I don't want Chevy going all big brother again and trying to take on James. "Plus, people kiss all the time who aren't in relationships."

"Not you," Lindy points out.

"Not me. But *some* people."

"You kissed a *lot*," Val adds in a loud whisper, waggling her dark brows at me. "Didn't you say you kissed him in every square foot of the warehouse? That's a lot of square feet."

"Not helping."

I don't want to think about kissing James while pressed up against the storage room door. Or behind that stack of pallets. Or while perched on top of the pallets. Or while— NO. Must stop thinking of kissing. I want to think about *despising*.

Even though, in truth, I don't despise James. Even now.

I can still see the pain on his face as he lashed out at me. I didn't deserve it. But I also made an error in judgment trying to show him my presentation when I did. I know that. I think I knew it then too. James is working through something else, something bigger, something that probably has little to do with me. I just happened to be the one who buzzed around him like an annoying fly until he slapped me away. I get it.

Does that mean I want to forgive him and keep going as we were?

Nope. But I did already do something to help him because, as Chevy often tells me, I just don't know when to quit. Kyoko texted me late last night, groaning about her bosses being impossible. I told her to come interview for a job. *My* job.

Is James hiring? No.

Does Kyoko want to take my job? No.

But were either of those reasons enough to stop me from

convincing Kyoko she needs to drive here and interview for a job? No, they were not.

James and Kyoko can both thank me later.

Or, in James's case, he can NOT thank me, because I'm not planning on talking to him again. I'm just going to ignore the whiny voice saying I miss him already, and I'm a hundred times more heartbroken over this than I was when things ended with stupid Dale. I mean, not that there was any heartbreak involved in that relationship.

But thinking about Dale has me thinking about what he did, which has me thinking about my dad, which makes me remember the truth of the matter.

"I don't want a relationship anyway. Men can't be trusted."

"Not this again," Val groans. "Why do you keep coming back to this?"

I haven't told my two best friends the reason I can't trust men. Not about seeing Dale in Austin. Not about my dad. Which is very un-best-friend-like of me, and they will absolutely give me grief about keeping this from them. "It's a long story."

"We've got nothing but time, chica."

Lindy looks at her phone. "Or, we have an hour. Then I need to pick up Jo."

There's a knock at the door, and when I try to get up, Val holds me in place. "I'll get it," Lindy says, giving me a pointed look. "You're too much of a flight risk."

"Hiya," Kyoko says when Lindy opens the door.

"Oh, good. Reinforcements," Lindy says.

"I'd get up to hug you, but I'm being held hostage," I tell her.

Lindy ushers Kyoko inside. I make quick introductions, and Val pours Kyoko a jalapeno margarita.

"Can you talk sense into her?" Val asks.

"Doubtful," Kyoko says, plopping into the chair across from the couch. She grins when Lindy practically sits down on top of me again. "But I'll do my best."

"How was the job interview?" I ask.

"I officially got the job. But I won't say it wasn't without some enthusiastic family involvement. Also, I think it was … your husband—Pat?" She looks questioningly at Lindy, who nods. "Yeah, he was in a dumpster for some reason. No one explained why."

I can imagine several reasons, and all of them involve Pat running his mouth to James. I'm happy to hear about the family involvement though. Maybe it means they're jumping on board to help James with his crisis of overwhelm. Good.

"A dumpster, huh?" Lindy makes a face. "I love Pat, but he probably deserved it. Hopefully, he showers before I get home. Anyway, Winnie was just about to tell us why she doesn't trust any men."

"Was I?"

"Yes," Lindy and Val say at the same time.

"I don't remember ever agreeing to that."

Kyoko takes a sip of her drink and hums appreciatively. "Now. You've fixed my life. You've tried to help James fix his. Your turn!"

"I don't need fixing." When they all laugh at this, I glare. "I'm fine."

"You've had two breakups this month," Lindy says.

"You've been fired twice," Kyoko adds.

"You're living on your brother's sofa," Val says.

"You could sell your app at any time but for some reason, refuse to do so. You keep helping everyone else with their lives, while ignoring your own."

I stare down into my drink. "If your goal was to bring me

down, it's working. My life is a lot sadder than I realized. I guess I'm not fine?"

Val pats my knee. "No, you're not fine. But you will be."

I really, really hope she's right.

"What kind of sad sack convention do we have here?" Chevy emerges from his room, glancing at the limes, tequila, and scattered glasses on the table. I swear his eye starts to twitch.

And, of course, seeing my brother makes Val spill her drink all over her shirt. It looks like she's bleeding from a gunshot wound to the chest.

Chevy winces as he looks down her shirt, then, as though realizing he's staring at Val's chest—honestly, it's hard to miss—his gaze shoots straight to the ceiling as he rocks back on his heels. "Sorry. Is that my fault?"

"It's fine," Val says in an overly bright voice. She holds her shirt out from her body.

"You can borrow one of my shirts," I tell her.

"Or one of mine," Chevy says. "Here."

And while we all watch, my brother strips off his T-shirt and holds it out to Val. She stares at him for a long moment, her gaze traveling over his bare chest. My brother is built like some kind of oversized-teddy-bear-linebacker hybrid. He's big and sturdy, not ripped or cut like the Grahams, and has a pretty impressive coating of chest hair. If you're into chest pelts.

Apparently, Val is very, very into them. Stocky and hairy must be exactly her fantasy, because her eyes have gone all glazed. She's holding Chevy's shirt but making no move to put it on.

Still looking at the ceiling, Chevy says, "If you, uh, want to change, I can get that stain out for you."

"It's one of his better qualities," I say. "His ability to

remove the toughest stains from a variety of fabrics." When Val still doesn't move, I nudge her. "Maybe go change in the bathroom?"

"Change! Yes. I'll do that." With a last look at Chevy, Val hightails it to the bathroom, her cheeks flushed a deep red. I hate to tell him, but Chevy is never, ever getting that shirt back.

"I hope you didn't forget," Chevy says to me, and I obviously did forget, because I have no idea what he's talking about. "Going to visit Mom and Dad?"

I groan. This is usually something we do on holidays. With all the Feastivus craziness, we didn't get to the cemetery yesterday.

Which is just fine by me. Every one of these visits has been torture, knowing what I know. And knowing Chevy doesn't know.

"Do we have to?"

"Yep. You can go like that if you want to," he says, eyeing the pajamas I've been wearing for almost twenty-four hours now. "But … your smell might make someone mistake you for a corpse." With a grin, my brother disappears into his room, presumably to grab a new shirt.

"Well, as fun as this has been, friends, I've got a sibling date with the cemetery."

———

A sibling date at a cemetery the day after you've been fired and broken up with a man you're pretty sure you're in love with is just about as miserable as you'd imagine.

No—MORE miserable.

Because I'm standing here in front of my parents' shared headstones, thinking mean thoughts about my unfaithful, lying two-faced jerk of a dad, while my brother stands next to me, sniffling. Because he doesn't know our dad is an unfaithful, lying, two-faced jerk.

And maybe it's that I don't feel like my dad deserves Chevy's sadness or maybe it's my own emotional overwhelm or possibly even the jalapeno margaritas, but whatever the reason, I blurt out: "Dad was having an affair."

Like he's in a movie with special effects, Chevy's head turns to me in slow motion. His blue eyes, mirror of mine, blink. "What?"

"For years. He had a … girlfriend, I guess?"

Chevy just keeps blinking. And I just keep talking.

"And he was also paying for her kid's college tuition. Or part of it."

This is officially the quietest my brother has ever been. I take my role as silence-filler VERY seriously.

"Which is why I'm so broke. I gave the woman he was having an affair with the little bit I inherited because she kept calling and I didn't want her to harass you too. Ta-da! Happy Thanksgiving. Now, it's officially the worst holiday ever."

Chevy's jaw works. I consider touching him, but he looks tensed to spring. "You knew about this … and you didn't tell me."

I shake my head. I should feel bad for springing this on him. Maybe I will later. For now, I don't have room to feel bad because I'm just so furious with our father. He doesn't deserve Chevy's tears. If I could afford it, I'd have him moved to some separate plot at the back of the cemetery and get his name chiseled off the headstone. Telling Chevy honestly feels … freeing.

Except for the part where I've tainted his memories of Dad with this information, just like it totally trashed mine. Only … he looks more concerned than upset. He slides an arm around my shoulder and pulls me close. I wrap my arms around his waist. My brother could be an honorary Graham for the way he hugs.

And this thought, of course, has me thinking about James and the way he picked me up after my nightmare, curled around me, and held me there all night. My eyes burn. I haven't let myself cry, and I'm not about to start now.

"How long have you known?" Chevy asks.

I squeeze him tighter. "I found out right after he died."

Chevy sighs, relaxing against me. "I'm the one who should be apologizing."

"Why? You're not the one who had the affair."

When he's quiet for a long time, much too long, I pull back and stare up at him. His blue eyes look gray and overcast. He rubs a hand over his jaw, looking … really guilty.

"Why are you apologizing, Chev?"

"I found out about Dad's affair when we were in high school."

I almost fall over. My mind reels, rewinding backward all the way to high school, trying to make sense of this statement.

"Why didn't you say anything?"

"Probably same as you—I wanted to protect you. Lot of good that did." He sighs. "Amelia contacted me after he died. I gave her money so she wouldn't tell you."

Shaking my head, I shoot a glance at the headstone, where Chevy placed fresh-cut daisies for our mom. I realize he's never brought anything for Dad, but I always assumed it was because Mom loved flowers. "We're like that awful Christmas story—the one where she sells her hair to buy him a watch chain and he sells his watch to buy her hair clips or something."

"I always thought that was a sweet story."

"It's a depressing holiday story. If they had just talked—if *we* had just talked …"

"What would have changed?" Chevy asks.

I shiver as a breeze lifts my hair off my neck. The sun has just dropped down over the trees and the light has turned to a soft gray. "We wouldn't have been so alone."

Chevy slings his arm over my shoulder. "We've never been alone."

"I felt alone," I admit quietly.

We probably need to go. The cemetery officially closes at dusk, and it's definitely dusk. Though I don't think Chevy is going to arrest us. Still, it's cold, and I feel like an old shirt that's been through the spin cycle twice.

Chevy glances around, then gives me a little tug. "Time to go."

Neither of us say goodbye to Mom or Dad, though I silently toss out a *love you* to Mom and an *I'm still mad at you* to Dad. As we walk, little solar lights begin winking to life all around us. I'm not sure who started the tradition, but almost every plot and most of the paths have little solar lights—the kind you can pick up at any Walmart or dollar store. It makes the Sheet Cake Cemetery look magical, like some kind of fairy garden.

"Did your breakup have anything to do with Dad?"

For the second time in half an hour, Chevy's words almost bowl me over. "What breakup?" I ask, WAY too cheerfully.

"Nice try. I saw the post on Neighborly before you deleted it."

"Stupid app," I mutter. We reach Chevy's truck, and he holds the door open for me. "Why would you think my breakup has to do with Dad?"

Chevy closes my door and waits until he climbs in his

side of the truck before answering. "Don't think it escaped my notice that you've been dating totally safe guys like Dead-Eye Dale. Then you bolt from a guy I could actually see you with."

"Shouldn't you be happy? I thought you tried to scare him off." Chevy turns on the car and I crank up the heat, holding my fingers in front of the vents.

"No, I talked to him because I thought things could get serious with you two."

I scoff. "Well, you were wrong there."

"Are you sure you aren't just running?" He assesses me, and I can't meet his gaze.

"If I am, it's because he chased me off."

"And what happens when he realizes he's an idiot and starts chasing after you?"

"He won't."

"He will."

"Well, I'll just keep running."

"That!" Chevy turns, putting his back up against the door and pointing at me. "That's what I mean about Dad. You're running because you're scared of getting hurt. You're scared to trust."

I point right back at him. "This goes both ways, brother dear. Is it because of Dad you keep dating terrible women?"

He makes a face. "They aren't terrible."

"They are."

Sighing, he faces forward and puts the truck in drive. "Fine. They're terrible."

"About time you admitted it." I don't feel the sense of elation I should. I just feel … sad. "So—do you think Dad is part of why?"

"I just—" Chevy's jaw clenches as he turns out of the cemetery and heads back toward his house. "I just don't want to be like him, you know? What if I can't be with just one person? What if I suck at commitment? What if I—" He pauses and swallows, that same muscle clenching in his jaw. "What if I hurt someone the way he hurt us?"

Oh, Chevy. My heart aches for my big brother. Who, besides being a giant pain in my butt sometimes, is really pretty amazing.

"Not that I have tons of experience in this department, but I'm pretty sure you can't have a relationship without hurting someone. Or being hurt. I think that's what happens when two imperfect people are in a relationship."

He hums a noncommital response.

"And if you're thinking you share his DNA, so you can't be trusted, well—if that's true for you, it's true for me too. Do you feel like I'm going to screw up every relationship just because I'm his daughter?"

Chevy shoots me a sideways glance, one corner of his mouth tilting up. "I mean, you *do* seem set on screwing up your relationships …"

I shove him from across the console, and he laughs. "Fine. No. I don't think that just because of Dad, we're both doomed to bad relationships."

"So, maybe we should try acting like we believe it," I suggest.

Chevy grunts, which only reminds me of the man who perfected the art of grunting.

I hold out my hand, extending my pinky. Chevy looks at my finger like it's a cockroach—the giant flying kind Texas is famous for, which my brother doesn't ever have in his house because he's too much of a neat freak.

"Pinky swear," I say, giving my hand a little shake. "Come on."

"What exactly am I swearing on?" he asks.

"That we're not going to torpedo our relationships because of Dad's mistakes."

Chevy takes one hand off the wheel and hooks his pinky around mine, grinning. "Fine. Consider me unarmed. Weapons down."

"I never thought this day would come," I tease, and he gives me a look I don't like one bit.

"You realize this means you have to stop running from James."

My stomach does a little flip, and I tell it to stand down. Just because my friends and my brother think there might be some chance for James and me doesn't make it a reality.

"I wasn't the only one responsible for blowing up our relationship."

"Good to know."

"Chevy," I say in a warning tone. "You're not going to do anything stupid to James, right?"

The smile he gives me is straight-up wolfish. "I don't do stupid revenge, sister. Only smart revenge."

"Well, in that case, I should tell you about Dale."

CHAPTER 36

James

TRYING to catch the Orange Cyclops feels like the perfect penance for me. And the perfect apology for Winnie.

"A cat is a terrible grand gesture," Pat tried to tell me last night. "Just like you don't give puppies as birthday gifts or baby ducks and bunnies at Easter. Plus, he's not doing your arms any favors."

I run my fingernail lightly over one of the long scratches on my forearm. No, OC, as I've started calling him, is not doing my arms any favors. But is it bad that Pat's disapproval only fueled my determination to catch and tame this cat for Winnie? If only determination were enough to capture the dang thing.

In case anyone wanted to know, it's not enough.

I hold out the plastic bowl filled with canned cat food,

giving it a little shake toward the cat. "Come here, you big, orange—"

"He's not going to go for that."

I curse under my breath as the cat backs away, tail twitching. Big Mo stands over me. I really need to get the gate fixed so I can lock people out.

It's been three long days since I fired Winnie and she broke up with me. And at least once a day, some Sheeter wanders in here to check in, which usually turns into a good hour of conversation I don't want. Yesterday, Judge Judie sent moonshine by way of Burt on his lunch break from security at the courthouse. The day before that, it was the Bobs, who gave their two cents times ten about beer.

Today, I guess it's Big Mo, here to critique my cat-catching.

"What won't work?"

"That canned stuff." Big Mo crouches near me, then opens a small container, pulling out something I can't quite identify. It smells disgusting. Mo makes some kind of quiet whistle with his teeth and holds out his hand.

Talk about not working. There's no way this one-eyed orange cat is going to just walk right up and—Oh my gosh! It IS working.

It's more than a little infuriating to see the Orange Cyclops sidling up to the tall, bearded cook within seconds. As I watch, OC sniffs Mo's outstretched hand, then starts eating from it.

Right from his hand!

"What is that?"

"Raw liver," Big Mo says.

Disgusting. "I wouldn't have thought to try that." I tried canned cat food. Canned human food—tuna and salmon and chicken. Catnip. Today I came back full circle with a more expensive kind of canned food, the one with the fancy cats in all the ads.

The Orange Cyclops apparently has an even more refined palate. Because he dines on raw liver.

"Your turn," Big Mo says. "There's more in the little container."

I stare down at the liver. I'm not sure I've ever looked at liver. I've definitely never touched it. And I don't want to now.

You're doing this for Winnie. You can do this for Winnie.

When Meatloaf sang his famous song, proclaiming he would do anything for love except for THAT, I have to wonder if the *that* was *pick up raw liver in his hand to tame a stray cat for a woman.* If so, that would be oddly specific ... and where Meatloaf and I differ.

Because I'm going for it, despite the way my stomach turns as I pick up the raw meat. Raw organs? Whatever.

Trying to ignore the texture, which will give me nightmares for months, I remember my goal: to get Winnie back. Getting Winnie back is worth touching raw liver. Fact.

Am I ridiculous for fixating on this scrappy, stray cat as a way to apologize to Winnie? Probably. Pat told me I'm being stupid, and if Pat says it ...

But this cat is Winnie's white whale, as she refers to him. Maybe it's extreme (or extremely stupid), but I feel like catching and taming this cat is symbolic of ... something. I just can't shake the idea. Which is why I'm crouching in my warehouse, holding out a slimy hunk of liver.

"Just sit," Big Mo says. "Let him come to you on his terms."

I sit, grumbling silently about the idea of doing anything according to a cat's terms. But Big Mo knows what he's doing because the Orange Cyclops approaches me, his one eye wary. My heart starts to thud in my chest, and sweat beads on my lower back. I'm not nervous about the cat. I've already got claw marks up my arms and one on my cheek. It's more the idea that this might not work. And, really, the bigger picture of what's at stake here: Winnie might not want to forgive me, orange cat or no. Or, she might forgive me, but not want to try a relationship with me for real.

The Orange Cyclops sniffs my hand, but he's taking longer to warm up to me than he did Big Mo. "What am I doing wrong?" I ask, keeping my voice low and even.

"Just relax. He's checking you out."

"No offense, but you're a lot scarier than me."

Big Mo chuckles. "Yes, but I'm not the one who's been terrorizing him and trying to trap him in a cage."

Touché. Trap him in a cage, trap him in a bag, shoot him with a tranquilizer dart—which was totally Collin's idea. It ended with Pat shooting Collin in the leg with the gun, which didn't knock him out, but did make him loopy—and also strangely good at chess—for a few hours.

He ended up spending a few days here, taking the first break from his gym since he opened years back. We all sat down and had a conversation about Dark Horse, and everything felt … lighter. As though just telling them all what I'd been holding inside for so long loosened something in me.

I don't look forward to dealing with my family more, but with the addition of Kyoko—one more instance of Winnie pushing in the best way—I think it will be fine. I almost keeled over when Kyoko showed up for an interview that I hadn't scheduled for a position I didn't plan to fill. But within five minutes of being in the space and talking to me, she suggested a glass wall between the brewing tanks and the bar. It will still give people a full view of the process, but it will allow me to brew in peace.

I hired Kyoko on the spot.

"You've got to earn back trust," Mo says, drawing me back into the moment. I don't point out that I never had the cat's trust to begin with. I'm not sure Mo is still talking about the cat. "It starts with you taking initiative, putting yourself out there. Then, sometimes there's a lot of waiting."

The Orange Cyclops delicately takes a bite of the raw meat in my hand. His whiskers tickle my palm, and I do my best to stay very, very still until he's finished. His rough tongue licks my hand clean. It's a weird feeling, but surprisingly, I don't mind.

Instead of backtracking like I expect, the OC stands in front of me, sniffing the air and staring with that one yellow eye. I'm wholly shocked when Big Mo swoops in, grabbing the cat by the scruff of his neck. The cat goes limp.

"What was all that about earning trust?" I say, getting to my feet as Mo secures the cat in the carrier I purchased earlier this week. He hands it to me.

"Wasn't talking about the cat."

I glance in the carrier and the thing hisses at me. "What do I do now? The thing hates me."

Big Mo chuckles, getting his empty liver container and heading for the door. "Rome didn't fall in a day. It's going to take more than one bite of liver to endear him to you."

Is it going to take more than a groveling apology, a declaration of love, and a one-eyed cat to endear Winnie back to me?

"Any other advice?" I clear my throat. "About cats."

"Baby steps," Mo says. "Patience and discipline."

"I don't want her to think I'm ignoring her."

"So, don't ignore her," Mo says, and I feel like a total

punk kid being schooled by Mr. Miyagi. Mo meets my eyes again. "Baby steps," he repeats.

And when he's gone, leaving me alone with a hissing cat in a carrier, I slide my phone out of my pocket and spend way too long composing way too dumb of a text to Winnie.

Baby steps.

TEXT THREAD

James: Hey

Winnie: Seriously? You're gonna lead with hey?

James: Greetings

James: Hello

James: Aloha

Winnie: You forgot hi.

James: Hi

Winnie: *gif of Stanley from the Office rolling his eyes*

Winnie: Hi.

James: How have you been?

Winnie: I'm sure you don't need to ask. There was a whole Neighborly thread on my emotional well-being or lack thereof. The poll is 50/50 on who broke whose heart.

James: There's a poll?

Winnie: There was until I deleted the thread.

James: Well, I don't believe the rumors. I'd rather hear from the source.

James: So, how are you?

Winnie: Is this your weird version of an apology? Because it kind of sucks.

James: No. An apology will be made in person at a date as yet to be determined

Winnie: Okayyyy

Winnie: Be sure to send me an evite so I can clear my very busy schedule.

James: Oh, you won't miss the apology. Trust me

Winnie: Now I'm scared.

James: Speaking of Neighborly, congratulations on the big sale

Winnie: Thanks. I think.

James: How do you feel about it?

Winnie: Since you asked, Dr. Freud, I'm feeling a lot richer.

Winnie: And I negotiated to keep control of the Sheet Cake part of the app.

James: You are an excellent negotiator

James: But you really WANT to keep moderating this town's gossip?

Winnie: No. But I don't want a stranger doing it either.

James: Control freak

Winnie: If I'm the pot, you're the kettle. Or vice versa.

James: Ready for your question of the day?

Winnie: That deal expired when you fired me the second time.

James: Sorry about that

Winnie: I thought you were giving me an apology at a later date? That was a little underwhelming.

James: I owe you multiple apologies. Consider that a teaser

James: How about a new deal?

Winnie: You think I'm interested in making a new deal with you?

James: I've given you every reason NOT to be

James: But I'd like to reopen negotiations

Winnie: Ugh

Winnie: Fine. One question a day.

James: An hour

Winnie: What??????

James: One question per hour for twelve hours daily

Winnie: You're crap at negotiating.

James: Is that a yes?

Winnie: NO

James: Six questions per day

Winnie: Three

James: Done

James: First question. How do you like your eggs?

Winnie: THAT'S your question? EGGS?

James: Breakfast is the most important meal of the day

James: And can also be had for dinner

Winnie: I prefer my eggs (breakfast, lunch, or dinner) inside baked goods. Cakes, muffins, waffles, etc.

James: Noted. Have a good morning, Winchester.

———

James: What's your favorite book

Winnie: Good morning to you too.

James: Morning

Winnie: Not good? Just a morning

James: Just a morning. What's your favorite book?

Winnie: I have too many to list them.

James: Try me

Winnie: Okay. You asked for it …

———

James: Night owl or morning person

Winnie: Hello to you too. I'm having a great day, thanks for asking.

James: Hi, temp

James: How's your day?

Winnie: Thanks for the muffins! I assume those were from you?

James: You're welcome

James: So night owl or morning person

Winnie: Night owl. You've seen me in the mornings. I'm surprised you even asked.

James: You look beautiful in the mornings

Winnie: Even before coffee?

James: Especially before coffee

Winnie: Liar!

Winnie: I look like a troll's ugly stepsister before coffee!

James: No

James: Before coffee, you look like the truest version of yourself. Fierce, strong, soft, real.

Winnie: I … thank you

Winnie: When is this apology happening? Just, you know, so I'm prepared.

James: Soon

James: But not soon enough

CHAPTER 37

Winnie

"HE'S WOOING YOU. You're being wooed. Stop moping and enjoy it, chica."

Val sounds distracted, or maybe even annoyed. She's trying to finish the same painting that's looked finished to me for a week. I'm slumped on my usual stool, whining about James, like I've also been doing for a week.

I guess I'd be annoyed with me, too. It's been seven days since I walked out of the warehouse, sure the unofficial nonrelationship between James and me was over for good. It's been six days since he started his texts and his barrage of questions. Five days since I started finding things like freshly baked chocolate chip muffins or the new novel by my favorite romance author on the porch.

I'm not sure which day I was ready to cave. Maybe ... on the second day?

Look—I don't want to complain about being wooed. Wooing is amazing. And the word is fun to say: woo, wooing, wooed, woos. Woo woo!

In all this time, though, I haven't laid eyes on James Graham. And I miss the big hunk of grump. Badly. His growly voice and his intense eyes and the back and forth we have.

His near-constant daily texts are A-plus material. But they are no replacement for in-person banter.

"Would I be desperate if I—"

"Winnie, *please!*" Val spins around to face me, and I almost fall off my stool at her tone. "I love you. You know that I do. But I cannot work like this! You love James."

I swallow, my throat suddenly feeling tight. "I don't love him. I just—"

"Fine! Don't admit it's love." She throws up her hands. But since there's a brush in one of them, it sends a splatter of paint across her cheek. She doesn't seem to notice, and I won't point it out. "Call it what you want. I'm calling it love. Because you are one lovesick woman, and I cannot listen to it for one more minute! Go to him and let him grovel. Wait for him to come and grovel. I do not care so long as there is groveling of some kind, an amazing kiss, and a happily ever after. But I have to get this painting done today, and you're killing my vibe."

For now, I'm ignoring most of what she said. Because I'm processing. There were a lot of big ideas in there.

Instead, I'm going to focus on what's most interesting to me in an immediate sense.

"Why do you need to finish today? Are you finally going to talk to the new gallery owner?"

Val's mouth clamps shut, and she turns back to the canvas. "I don't know. Stop changing the subject."

Touchy. So, maybe she *is* going to the owner of the new gallery setting up on Main Street. I saw the sign up the other day, though the windows were papered over so I couldn't see inside. Not that I've been hanging around downtown, hoping for a glimpse of James. I totally was just visiting Lindy. Because that's what friends do—they visit their friends.

Maybe excessively so, given the fact that Lindy finally passed me off to Val, who seems just as tired of my moping.

I'm about to say something else about the gallery, because I'd rather focus on anything other than James, when Lindy's dogs start barking like mad. I hear the sound of tires crunching over gravel.

Val groans. "Can you go see who it is? And tell them to go away?"

"Gladly."

Only, when I walk out of the side door, I'm shocked senseless. Because standing there in all his gorgeous grumpiness is James. The sight of him after a week is enough to make my breath catch, but then I see why Amber and Beast have gone so wild, and I'm not sure I believe what I'm seeing.

The Orange Cyclops, as we call him, my one-eyed white whale of feral cats, stands in the driveway, hissing at the dogs. That part is unusual enough. But the leash and collar he's wearing, complete with a tiny bow tie? THAT has my jaw dropping.

"Go on, Amber," James says to the dogs. "Scram, Beast. Get!"

After fending off a last swipe from the cat, the two dogs run for the house and settle on the porch. James hasn't noticed me, and so I continue to watch him. Because what in the ever-loving WORLD is going on?

"All right, OC. Are you ready for this?"

James is talking … to a cat. *The* cat. While holding its leash in his hand. OC, as I guess he's being called now, looks up at James with his one eye, then gives his front paw a good licking.

"Sure. No problem," James says drily. "I'll wait. Not like I'm in a hurry to tell the woman I love I love her or anything."

I bite my lip to hold back a gasp. James just used the L-word! About me!

… TO A CAT!

The Orange Cyclops sees me first, his one eye zeroing in on me before his entire body tenses. Oh, he definitely hasn't forgotten me, and I'm not sure that's a good thing. His attention draws James's gaze, and now I'm engaged in a five-eyed stare-off with a man and a cat.

I finally break the silent *whatever* kind of moment we're having. "I have so many questions."

James, using the Ultimate James Graham Starter Pack, does not answer. He grunts.

"Not starting in order of importance, but what kind of voodoo magic did you work on the Orange Cyclops?"

"I call him OC now."

James glances down at the cat, and I swear, there's the tiniest hint of pride in his expression. Like James is suddenly this proud cat dad. I wouldn't have EVER predicted this, but I am here for it.

Looking back my way, James gives me the smallest smile —one I feel all the way down to my toes. I lean on the garage wall for support, needing something to ground me. Otherwise, I'm liable to skip the talk we need to have in favor of the kissing part I hope will be coming right after.

"It took some doing, and some help from Big Mo. I didn't

come out unscathed." He tilts his head, and I can see a healing scratch along his cheek.

"Bad kitty," I say, but my tone sounds a lot more like praise.

James's lips twitch. "I took him to the vet to get him, uh, fixed. But Doc Maddie said he already had been. I guess this guy was less feral and more … abandoned. She got him all cleaned up and up to date on his shots."

"Did she also get him the bow tie and leash?"

At my question, James tilts his head as though issuing a challenge. "He likes it."

Shockingly, the orange cat does seem to like it. Or, at least, not mind it. "Me too. But I didn't think you were a cat person."

"I did it for you, Winnie. It felt like something I needed to do to show you—" He stops himself here, and I can see the thoughts whirring in his head. "How much did you overhear when you were eavesdropping?"

I love that he sounds irritated. I know he's here to apologize, but James wouldn't be James without this bit of rough edge to him. I happen to *love* that edge. Even if I'm more than ready for the apology he promised was coming days ago.

"I wasn't eavesdropping. I came out because the dogs were barking. Then I heard you talking to the cat."

His frown deepens. Is it weird I find him hotter frowning than smiling? Are frown fetishes a thing? If not, I'll gladly be the start of this trend.

"You weren't supposed to hear it like that."

"Like that as in, you telling a cat you love me?"

Groaning, James tilts his head back to face the sky. "I've ruined this," he mutters, almost under his breath. Then he takes a breath and meets my gaze. "I'm going to leave. Then

I'll come back. You'll pretend I was never here, and I'll do this right."

Of their own volition, my hands go to my hips. "Don't you dare get in that truck, James Graham! You're going to stand there and apologize, maybe grovel a little. Or a lot. The level of grovel is up to you. Then you'll tell me, not the cat, you love me. Do you understand me?"

"So bossy," James says, not sounding like he minds a bit. "And what are you going to do?"

"I'm going to stand here, pretend like I'm still mad, and like I wouldn't have forgiven you five days ago."

He shakes his head, fighting back a small smile. "It was the chocolate chip muffins, wasn't it?"

"They were excellent muffins. But I think I liked the book better. It showed you paid attention. And I found some pages with turned down corners—which, I'll have you know, is a capital punishment—but it made me think you actually read the book."

That, or he got it at a thrift store or drove to Austin for one of the used bookstores. But the copy he gave me is in great shape, and it's a new release, which is hard to find used. I'm hoping my guess is correct.

He rubs a hand over his jaw. "Capital punishment, eh?"

I nod.

"Well, that's unfortunate. I'll have to plead my case before the court for not using a bookmark. Yes, I read it. Not saying I've got a new favorite genre or anything, but I ... like romance."

"Romance and cats. Who knew?"

We seem to have come to a conversational impasse. Or one of those silences I heard occurs every seven minutes. For now, we stand here. Not speaking. Not moving. Just staring like it's our sole purpose in life.

382

Finally, I cross my arms and raise a brow. I'm trying to keep the semblance of cool. Call me a head of iceberg lettuce fresh from the crisper. A mountain stream after winter snow melts. Liquid nitrogen.

"About that apology ... need some pointers on how to get started?"

"No."

"You sure?"

James takes several steps forward, and I bite the inside of my cheek to keep from laughing at the way the Orange Cyclops saunters along next to him. They have matching strides and wear the same intense expression. It is ... a-freaking-dorable. I've seen dogs that resemble their owners—Lindy wrote a whole article on that once—but I've never seen a cat match the attitude of its owner.

James stops a few feet in front of me. The cat stops next to him.

"What's funny?" he demands.

Apparently, I'm not hiding my amusement over his new feline twin well enough. I take off my glasses and buff the lenses on my shirt, giving me a brief reprieve from seeing them in focus.

"Nothing. Just preparing for this stellar apology."

"Winnie," James growls.

I hold up both hands. "Don't let me stop you."

He sighs. "Now there's too much buildup. It's going to be disappointing."

"Trust me. Nothing about any of this"—I wave a hand over his body, the cat, all of it—"could possibly disappoint me. Go, James."

"Winnie, I am so sorry. Truly." His words are agonized, and even if they weren't, his eyes show his sincerity.

Still...

"For?"

James huffs out a breath. "Even when I'm trying to apologize, you're giving me a hard time."

"Want me to stop?"

"No."

James takes another step forward, until we're just shy of touching. The heat of his body does wild things to mine, but I manage to keep still. I'm not just maintaining a poker face here. I've got full-on poker *body*.

James clears his throat. "I don't want you to stop. I want to go head to head or toe to toe—"

"Or mouth to mouth?" I suggest.

James drops his gaze to my lips. "Especially that. I want to wake up every morning and kiss that smart mouth of yours. And I want to go to sleep the same way."

My heart has decided to stop doing its job and is now beating erratically, making me feel short of breath. "What about the middle of the day?"

James's nostrils flare, and he puts one hand on the garage beside my head, caging me in. "All. Day. Long." His gaze trails from my eyes to my lips and right back up. "I want this, Winnie. This back-and-forth. This … thing we have. It's *life* to me. It's everything. I know I'm a lot to deal with on a good day. I'm not good at accepting help or working with others. I don't have much practice being a partner. I'm so sorry for unleashing my stress on you. It wasn't your fault. It wasn't yours to take."

There are so many smart retorts zinging through my mind, but I want to save them for later and, just for once, bask in this sincerity and the surprisingly tender moment.

"I forgive you, James. And I understand, at least, a little bit. I'm sorry for putting pressure on you. I got overeager and—"

"No." James stops me with one firm word and a shake of his head.

"Okay, so now I can't even apologize?"

"No. Not when you were trying to help me. You supported me in a way I'm not used to, even from my family. You aren't allowed to apologize for loving me so well."

I swallow. "Who said anything about love?"

James leans closer, his brown eyes darkening as his pupils dilate. "I did. I *am*. I love you, Winchester. Maybe you're not ready to say it in words because this is fast, but I *feel* it." James removes his hand from the wall and taps his chest, right over his heart. "I feel your love in all the things you've done for me."

Okay, this is entirely too much. The cat. The proximity. The words—oh my gosh, who knew when James decided to use more than one-syllable words it would be so devastating?

"I know you just came out of a relationship," James says.

Did I? Dale is hardly more than a foggy memory. A blip. A contrast to show me exactly how love *really* feels. I open my mouth to say this, but James is still going. And I'm not about to stop him, because who knows when I'll get this again.

"We can go at your speed. I'll be … as guarded as I need to be. As long as you know what's waiting for you."

"What's waiting for me?" My voice is husky. I sound like I could do voice-overs for a young, sexy ingenue character. But who even cares? If James isn't hiding, neither am I.

"This," he says, and then his mouth covers mine.

James kisses me like a man who knows exactly what he wants, like a man not afraid to declare it. The way his hand curls around the back of my neck, holding me in place, is possessive, but in a way that makes me feel *free*.

Free to let go.

Free to trust.

Free to *love*.

Val wasn't wrong, and neither was James. I DO love him. The realization hits me square in the chest. It's not a scary thought, but rather one that seems inevitable, unavoidable, impossibly perfect.

My hands slide up James's broad shoulders, loving the way his muscles move and flex at my touch. His lips are demanding, but no more than mine. The man made me wait agonizing days for this, and I'm fueled by pent-up desire and an urge to punish him.

Though the kiss is nothing like punishment. James rumbles out a groan, proving my point. I let my hands roam up his neck, dragging my fingers through the hair that's always falling over his eyes. James deepens the kiss, wrapping an arm around my waist and pulling me flush with his body.

And then, James changes pace from frenzied passion to languid delight. He nips and teases and trails kisses from my lips to my jaw, then back again. His mouth is masterful, just as amazing when slow and soft as it was wild and unrestrained.

When he pulls back, resting his forehead on mine, his breath is ragged, matching my own. I close my eyes and rest in the feel of his body, so huge and yet so perfectly matched to mine. James pulls back to meet my eyes. When he cups my cheek in his big, warm hand, I nuzzle into it, craving the connection I've been starving for.

"I need to ask you something, Winnie," he says, and my heart does a little stutter at his seriousness.

"Well, you've certainly put me in a mood to say yes."

"I hope so." His smile lasts only a moment, shifting right back to serious. "I'd like you to call me boss again."

I can't help but grin. "Easy. I always loved calling you

boss, *boss*." I let myself indulge in running my fingertips lightly over the stubble on his jaw. I love the gentle tug of it on my skin. The roughness that's so very *James*.

He steals a quick kiss, then seems to think better of it and lingers for a longer one. The corner of his mouth lifts as he pulls back. "I love it as a nickname. But I meant in more of an official capacity."

A laugh escapes me. "I don't want to be your temp, James. And I think we saw how that worked out. I don't want work to come between us."

Even if I loved working alongside him. This week, while I've been missing James, I've also been missing the work I was doing for Dark Horse. I'm right back to not knowing what I want to do next with my life, especially now that I've sold Neighborly.

James crowds me, running his nose over my cheek, and I barely hold back from diving right into another kiss. "I don't want anything about you to be temporary, Winnie."

His voice makes a shudder pass through me. "Still. I'd rather have this"—I press a teasing kiss to the corner of his mouth—"than *that*."

"I think we could have both. I'm not saying I'm suddenly perfect at this, but I'm learning to give up control and to trust other people."

"So, maybe you'll rethink that rainbow unicorn site design?"

His fingers find my ribs, tickling, and I squirm, unable to escape when his other hand wraps around me.

"No unicorns. No rainbows."

"Okay! Okay! Uncle! No unicorns!" I take a breath as he stops the tickle assault. "What would this look like?"

"I haven't thought much more past wanting to get you to forgive me and come back to work with me."

"Don't you mean *for* you?"

His eyes catch mine. Then he slowly shakes his head. "No. Definitely *with* me. You're too brilliant and too valuable not to have more say."

I'm about to ask more, when something touches my leg. I almost jump, but then there's a plaintive meow. I'd forgotten all about the orange cat. THE cat. At some point during our make-out session, James must have dropped the leash. Glad he's got his priorities straight.

"I think someone's a little jealous," I say. "Sorry, OC. Priorities."

The cat sneezes, and I laugh, then reach down, holding out my hand. James watches as the OC sniffs me, then sniffs me again. I'm about to stroke the top of his head when he hisses and swats at me. I jerk my hand out of claw range and straighten, glaring at James, then the cat.

"Hey! I thought you said you tamed him for me! He still hates me."

James's grin is smug. "I put in the time. I guess you'll need to do the same thing to earn his affection."

I step up on my toes, pressing a soft kiss to the smug mouth I love so much. "As long as I've got yours, that's all that matters."

EPILOGUE

James

MY NERVES ARE like tiny gnats, buzzing through my bloodstream. Which is a truly disgusting analogy, and something that would totally make for a great sci-fi movie, but should be banned from my brain forever.

"Are you all good, son?" Tank appears beside me and squeezes my shoulder. It feels like it's part warning, part encouragement, like he doesn't know which I need more.

But if he thinks there's any chance I'm running from this, from today, then he hasn't been paying attention the last few months. Sure, I've got nerves—any man on his business's opening day would feel the same way. But that's not why I'm nervous.

I scan the patio area until I find Winnie. The pressure in my chest loosens. Knowing she's here, knowing she's mine.

Correction—*almost* mine.

I give Tank the side-eye. "I'm good. Don't you have other things to worry about? Perhaps other *people?*" I watch as he squirms.

"Naw, I'm all right," he says, a little too casually, even as he searches the crowd the same way I just did.

If that's how he wants to play it. *Fine. Keep telling yourself that, Pops. And we'll all keep pretending we believe you.*

"I'm proud of you, son. Opening day already looks like a success," Tank says.

It does. And though I care—a LOT, actually—there's something even bigger on my mind.

"It's in no small part to the people standing alongside me. So, thank you."

It hasn't been what I'd call easy relinquishing control and letting other people step up and do more with Dark Horse. Winnie has been integral in helping me, running interference as needed, and putting me in time out when I got over-whelmed with all the peopleing. The time-out closet got a lot of use in the past few months. And not just for me to calm down alone. The make-out closet would be just as apt a name.

My eyes find Winnie again. She's talking to Kyoko and gesturing to something at the bar. I watch her lips as they curve into a smile, the tiny flash of her tattoos peeking out from one sleeve, tattoos I'm now *very* familiar and maybe slightly obsessed with. Winnie tugs on her ponytail, some-thing she does when nervous or excited.

When she sees me looking this time, she throws her arms wide and mouths, *WHAT?*

I smile, a full one, loving the way even from afar it seems to melt her. I point toward the building and mouth back, *Closet.*

Her brows shoot up, and I can see the hesitation that

quickly gives way to something else as she bites her lip. I can read her next word clearly since I'm already staring at her mouth.

Now?

I nod, my expression turning serious, giving her no room for argument. She smiles, a secret one just for me, and begins to cut her way through the crowd, slowing only a little to say brief hellos.

"Well, looks like you've got somewhere to be," Tank says with a sly grin.

He grabs me in one of his famous hugs. Ever since I've gotten as tall as he is, our hugs have been more of a friendly competition.

He squeezes. I squeeze back harder. He chuckles, which gives me room to tighten my hold. He grunts and his arms become pythons around my middle until my feet are off the ground. This is new.

"Have you been … working out?" I grunt, struggling to breathe.

He gives me a last squeeze and drops me, grinning. "Maybe."

There's a sheepish look about him, and I don't need to ask why he suddenly feels the need to hit the gym again. Why does any man start doing wild things? A woman.

And maybe it's because I've found my own that the idea of my dad with someone doesn't sting the way it might have before.

"Well, isn't this cozy? Two of my favorite Grahams having a hug-off." Chevy sidles up to the both of us.

Over the past six months, he and I have formed a mostly easy friendship. I say *mostly* because keeping his sister happy—and paying her enough so she could move out of his house—has made Chevy happy. He's also given me two speeding tickets, I think as a way of keeping me on my toes.

Also, I was speeding. So that's on me.

Tank gives Chevy a hearty back slap and then some kind of complicated handshake the two of them developed. I'm still rolling my eyes when Dad steps back from Chevy, then leans close to my ear.

"Don't be nervous," Dad whispers. "She'll say yes."

When he pulls back, I stare at him, stunned. No one knows. No one.

"How did you ...?"

Tank winks. "It's a dad thing."

Chevy glances at me and then at Tank's retreating back. "Hm. A dad thing?"

"Yeah ... just brewery stuff," I say.

Months ago, I took Chevy out to Backwoods Bar, asking for permission to marry Winnie. I just never said *when*. He made me wait two days, saying he needed to *mull it over*. And I unorganized his pantry the next time I was at his house with Winnie. We're in no way even, but I'm trying not to escalate things. Pat and Chevy can have that as *their* thing. And if I don't tell exactly when I'm going to propose to his sister, well, that's just too bad.

"Today's the day, huh?" he asks.

Chevy can't know too. There's no way I'm *that* obvious. "What?"

His smile shifts into a smirk. "The brewery opening?"

"Right. Yes. Hey—I've got to ask Winnie about ... the servers."

"Sure. The servers. I'm sure she'll say yes to whatever you ask about the *servers*."

Chevy winks, and okay, so fine. Two people have guessed

I'm about to propose. Better get on with it before someone posts about it on Neighborly.

"James," Chevy calls as I'm starting to walk away. "You still have my blessing. So long as you keep looking at my sister like she's the only woman in the world."

I raise my brows. "Isn't she?"

His laughter fills my ears as I make my way through the crowd to the inside of the building, which is still roped off.

We're almost out of time, and I'm feeling sweat gather at my lower back as I reach the closed door. My hand slides into my pocket where my fingertips first brush against the seed from Winnie's very first day of work. So far, it's made it through multiple washes and outlasted several pairs of jeans.

Today, the seed has company. I was too afraid to carry the ring around in my pocket for too long, though I bought it the same week I asked Chevy's permission. It's been hidden in one of my boots in the closet.

I hesitate outside the closet, which means I get noticed.

"Hey!" Kyoko calls from the bar across the room. "Shouldn't you be ..." Her eyes go to the closet door, and she smirks. Hiring her at Winnie's insistence might be the single best decision I've made. "Never mind. I can stall for a few minutes if needed."

I nod, but before I can answer, the closet door flies open and Winnie drags me inside by my shirt collar. I let her move me where she wants, happy to be manhandled by this woman. She slams the door before pushing me up against it and yanking my mouth down to hers.

She's greedy and desperate—or, knowing Winnie and her detailed brain, just very aware how little time we have.

She pulls back, breathing heavy. "You ask me to meet you five minutes before opening and then hesitate outside the door. Pull it together, *boss*."

393

I'm torn between wanting to kiss her some more, wanting to drop to my knee immediately, and wanting to postpone this for a less rushed time. I catch sight of OC, now the official Dark Horse brewcat, by the window, licking one paw and staring at me with a look that says, *Get on with it.* I thought about attaching the ring to his bow tie, but that felt like a few steps too far.

Winnie's eyes contain an ocean of meaning, an ocean of love, behind her glasses. Her fingertips trace my jaw, one of her favorite things to do. I can't say I mind it either.

And in that moment, I know I can't wait.

"Winchester Boyd, you're my everything. My fire, my tender warrior, my brilliant partner."

"Aw, I love it when you go all mushy on me."

"I'm not mushy," I say, putting the deep growl in my voice I know she loves. "Okay. Only a little. Only for *you.*"

"Well, is that all the mush, or do I need to prepare to be more twitterpated?"

"I don't know what that means. But no, I'm not done." I draw in a deep breath. "Winnie, you've been the best partner I could ask for with Dark Horse. You're creative and full of brilliant ideas, resourceful and scrappy. I couldn't have done any of this without you. But I think it's time for you to take on a new role. This one just doesn't suit you anymore. Which is why—"

Her eyes suddenly go wide and she interrupts me. "I quit."

My hands tighten on her hips. "What? You … don't want to work with me any more?"

"I promised myself I wouldn't let you fire me again, that I'd quit first. This sounds like a firing speech. Much nicer than the other two, but still."

Her eyes go a little watery, and I sigh heavily, digging in

my pocket for the ring. I manage to get it and the seed, too, and I grab her hand, dropping both into her palm. She stares down at the ring, a square cut black onyx in a vintage setting —what I thought was the perfect ring for Winnie's signature style.

I drag a hand through my hair. "Clearly, I still fail with words. I was trying to ask you to marry me, not firing you."

"Oh," she breathes, taking a small step back.

Still cradling the ring in her palm, she picks up the seed between two fingers.

"Is this—"

"What you gave me on your first day. I've kept it in my pocket ever since. It grounds me when I'm stressed. Just like you ground me. And you help me …"

I jam my mouth closed, and Winnie tilts her head. "I help you what?"

"It's stupid."

"Tell me."

I can't deny her. Especially not when she gets bossy. "You ground me, and you help me fly. See? It sounds stupid."

"It's not stupid," she whispers. "I love it."

Winnie's eyes well up with tears, and I want to wipe them away, to wrap her in my arms. But this whole conversation has gone in a very different direction from what I imagined, so I'm still not sure where we stand. I did propose, right?

When she holds out the seed to me, my stomach drops. "You're giving it back?"

"Only so you can keep it in your pocket. And so I can better examine this gorgeous ring."

I take the seed, tucking it safely back in place. Winnie turns the ring over in her hands, and though I don't think she's the type to say yes or no because of the size or kind of jewelry, I really want her to like it.

I'd also REALLY like to move to the part where she says yes.

"So, you just thought you'd spring this on me five—now TWO—minutes before the grand opening?"

Okay, so yeah. The timing sucks. So does my proposal. If I were grading, I'd give me a solid D+.

But I'm done waiting and second-guessing. I step forward and wrap my arms possessively around Winnie's back. "I don't want to take one more step toward my future without securing you as a part of it."

"Oh," she says again, a little breathlessly. But then she smiles up at me, an overwrought, vulnerable smile that shoots straight through me in the best way. "In that case, same."

"Same? Does that mean yes?"

Winnie slips the ring on her finger, and it is a perfect fit, just like I hoped it would be. I've been sneaking measurements and secretly working on the design with Val. Winnie slides her hands up my chest and around my neck, beaming with the brightness of an exploding star.

"Yes. James Graham, I would love to marry you."

I can breathe. I mean, obviously, I was breathing, but it was like going through the motions. Now, I take in breaths of air that feel fresh and new. Because Winnie said yes to being my forever. And I do mean forever. I want the kind of love my parents had. Hopefully, Winnie and I will have more time.

"I love you," Winnie says, leaning up to press a kiss on my lips. "But I have to ask—can I unquit?"

"I'll take it under consideration with the board. Collin may have paperwork for you to fill out."

She groans. "Collin and his paperwork."

There is a frantic banging on the door. "Guys!" Kyoko

says. "I held off and now Pat has the mic. I think he's about to start singing."

Now I groan, starting to pull away, taking Winnie with me. Because this woman definitely isn't leaving my side anytime soon.

"We're coming," I say, but Winnie pulls me to a stop as my hand grabs the doorknob.

"One last question," she says. "How do you feel about VERY short engagements?"

———

THE END
(but keep reading for a bonus epilogue…)

BONUS EPILOGUE

Val

I THINK I've given Winnie and James enough time to kiss and make up. Or make up and kiss. Either way. He pulled up outside my studio fifteen minutes ago, so surely that's enough time?

It's killing me to pace inside the studio, both because I want to congratulate them on finally figuring out they belong together, but also because I have twenty minutes to get paintings loaded up in the truck and to the gallery. I'm barely going to make it as is. And Mr. Silver, the gallery owner, gave me a tiny window of time, I think honestly because he doesn't want to carry my pieces in the gallery at all. I got the impression this is one of those things where he's just humoring me.

Actually it was more than an impression. Mr. Silver all

but said he was doing so as a favor, which can only mean Tank asked him. Probably because Lindy asked Pat who asked his dad. That's the kind of thing the Grahams do. The kind of things friends and family do for each other.

And honestly, it's because of this, because I don't want to disappoint anyone else that I'm actually considering showing my work at all.

I know Lindy and Winnie think I'm just nervous or that I'm not confident in my work. They think with enough mama-birding they can push me out of the nest to fly.

But they don't know how it feels to paint, to lose myself in my work, only to have it torn to shreds by critical words. Especially from someone I thought I cared about, who I thought cared about me.

My stomach clenches, and I look at the clock again. I'm out of time.

I burst through the garage door with one hand covering my eyes, making as much noise as possible to warn Winnie and James. From between my fingers, I see them pull apart, looking flushed but blissfully happy.

I'm shocked into stillness by the sight of James Graham actually smiling. *Wow*. I'm floored less by how handsome he is and more by the intense stab of envy I feel.

That. I want that.

Maybe without the cat in a bow tie.

Wait—why is there a cat in a bow tie?

"Are y'all done making up and making out yet?" I ask, grinning.

James chuckles. And looks at Winnie both like he wants to completely consume her and die fighting to protect her.

There's that stomach squeeze again.

Maybe it's an ulcer.

"No," he says, as Winnie says, "Not even close."

Disgustingly adorable.

"Yay! I'm so happy for you!"

"Then why don't you uncover your eyes?" Winnie asks.

"Right." I drop my hand. "I can be happy for you while also not wanting a front row seat to all this ..." I'm not about to mention the sexual tension hanging like a fog between them. "*Anyway*. I'm really sorry to do this right now, but I need to borrow your muscles and your truck. And since you and Winnie are officially back together, I can ask, right?"

James narrows his eyes at Winnie. "Are you just using me for my truck?"

"And your muscles," she deadpans.

I don't have time for their flirting and banter, so I clap my hands before they start kissing again.

"Great. I've got three big canvases that I need to get downtown to the gallery. Like, *now*."

———

My friends have entirely too much confidence in me. Too much unconditional love. Too much faith.

It's why I'm sitting alone on the sidewalk. Winnie and James helped unload and then left, so sure I wouldn't need help getting back to the studio with my paintings.

Paintings Mr. Silver dismissed after examining them with a pinched expression for less than five minutes.

One dimensional, he said. *Uninspired. Amateur.*

It's the last one that has me blinking back tears, wrapping my arms around myself.

I should text someone. James and Winnie can't be too far. But I want to give them a moment to enjoy finding their way back to each other. Mari's at the diner, dealing with the dinner rush, and Big Mo will be at the grill. Lindy and Pat are my best bet—just a block or two away and with Pat's truck.

I just need to pull myself together. I shiver. If I don't freeze first.

The door opens beside me before I can even think about hiding, and then Mr. Silver is assessing me, the same way he did my paintings. I know how I look: my hair knotted in a messy bun, my coveralls paint splattered, my feet bare.

Because, yeah, I didn't happen to remember shoes. And Winnie and James were both too busy making googley eyes at each other to notice.

"Are you crying?" he asks, sounding as disgusted as he looks.

I almost laugh. "Maybe."

He frowns down at me, while I wipe my eyes. "You must have a thicker skin if you think you can make it."

Now, I do laugh. "Believe me, I've tried to grow one."

My skin is rice-paper thin. Easily torn. Totally transparent. And no amount of self-talk or podcasts on bettering myself have made it an iota thicker.

Mr. Silver's gaze snags on my feet, which are numb. My toes are practically curled back into myself.

"You have no shoes?" He seems surprised. Did he really not notice? I honestly thought my disheveled appearance was part of the issue. For all the talk about artists being wild and free, you still need to be professional in professional settings. Like him—in a crisply tailored suit.

"I forgot," I say, feeling lame as his frown deepens.

I hear the engine of a truck before I notice the lights cutting through the darkness. A familiar truck pulls up to the curb, and my stomach sinks.

Not now.

Mr. Silver glances at Chevy as he climbs out of the driver's side. "Do you know this man?"

I nod, and this seems to be enough for him.

"Come see me tomorrow. No paintings. Just you. And wear shoes."

I'm still blinking in shock as he stomps away on expensive shoes, leaving only the man I've tried so hard not to fall in love with for basically as long as I can remember.

"Hey. You look like you could use a lift."

His smile is easy, but as always with me and only me, guarded. As if he knows just how I feel and doesn't want to lead me on. How can he not know? My thin skin doesn't hide my emotions either. Everything goes straight in and out like a sieve.

"Yeah, I could use a lift back to my studio. If you don't mind."

Chevy offers me a hand, and I let him pull me to my feet. He lets go almost immediately, sliding his hands casually in the pockets of his jeans.

He looks … nice. I mean he always does, but he looks like he dressed up for something. Or *someone*. *Oh, please, don't let it be a date.* I glance at the truck again, relieved to see the cab is empty.

"Well, let's get these loaded up before you freeze in your bare feet, Tiny."

I bite my lip, turning toward my painting so he doesn't see the smile I'm trying to hide. Every so often, Chevy calls me Tiny. Partly because I'm five-foot-two. And I think because of my full name, Valentina. Everyone calls me Val, but when I first met Chevy, a handsome, flirtatious boy a few years older, he said he was going to call me Tina. It morphed into Tiny, and I don't hate it.

I actually pretty much love it.

As sad as it is, I'll take even the smallest thing Chevy is willing to give me. Because I know this small thing is all I'm ever going to get from my best friend's brother.

Unless …

I watch as Chevy loads the paintings up in the bed of his truck, then opens the door for me. "Hop in, Tiny. Let's get you home."

I stare at his face a beat too long. Chevy's smile is friendly, nothing more. The physical distance he keeps sends signals that scream PURELY PLATONIC.

And maybe it's the raw emotional state I'm in after dealing with Mr. Silver, but some part of me has had ENOUGH. Before I climb into the cab, I step wayyyyy up on my tiptoes and press my lips to Chevy's cheek. I linger, letting his sandpaper stubble scrape my tender skin.

He has completely frozen, like my kiss is some kind of reverse fairy-tale magic, turning the prince to stone rather than waking the sleeping princess.

"Thanks, Chevy," I whisper, my lips brushing his jaw. I trail one hand up his arm, stopping at his shoulder and giving him a quick squeeze before I lose all my courage and hop in the car.

He stands there, long enough for me to buckle in. When I glance over, his jaw is slack, his eyes blinking rapidly.

I did that. I DID THAT!

I bite my lip, and the movement attracts Chevy's gaze. His jaw snaps closed, and he slams the door, walking the long way around the back of the truck like he needs the recovery time.

If I let it, the status quo will just keep status quoing along, and Chevy and I will keep being what we are to each other. Friends, with the whole friend of sibling thing thrown in.

Unless … I decide I'm tired of waiting and hoping and pining and decide to finally—FINALLY—go after what I want.

———

Don't miss Chevy & Val's story: The Pocket Pair.
Grab it HERE- https://emmastclair.com/chevyandval

A Free Sheet Cake Novella!

I've got a special FREE Sheet Cake novella for you! This one takes place between The Pocket Pair (book #3) and The Wild Card (book #4) but will act as a standalone.

There are minor spoilers… but if you're okay with that, you can sign up here! Read it now at https://emmast clair.com/ante

A NOTE FROM EMMA

Ahhhhh… another finished book!

While I do a lot of writing alone—or at a coffee shop or in the gym or somewhere public ignoring everyone else—I feel like it's a joint effort.

Because I'm always thinking of YOU, reader.

Writing is a weird work in that way. Creative work is work … and it's also play. It's individual, yet in some ways, it feels collaborative.

I write knowing you're going to be reading. I want the characters, the story, even the sentences and words to DELIGHT you. And I hope this book has done that.

I love James and Winnie. I had so much fun writing the two of them. Though I married a total cinnamon roll, I do love grumps. And while for some people, the grumps can be a bit, well, GRUMPY, I love peeling back the layers to see why they are the way they are. I also love it when they're gooey and soft just for HER.

As for some of the true or true-ish things in the book…

I had a blast going to the awards ceremony of the Texas

Craft Brewers Conference and getting to wander around asking questions of the vendors.

And yes—it was a LOT OF FLANNEL. I exaggerated too, of course, but aspects of the conference were based in reality.

I give Brian of Hardywood Park Craft Brewery a nod in the acknowledgments, but he helped so much with a lot of information that didn't make it onto the page (lest I put you to sleep) but was very helpful in thinking about the story and what James needed to do to start up his business.

For the record, I have nothing against clowns (teenage or otherwise) and also am wearing leggings as I type this, so no judgment there. Though I'm wary of multi-level marketing after joining like ten of them. (No kidding—pretty much the ONLY thing I haven't tried selling is leggings.)

Though roller derby didn't figure much into this book with Winnie's background, I did play derby off and on for nine years, coaching when I was pregnant or recovering from babies. I miss those days! It's an amazing sport, held together by the passion of the skaters, who basically have to treat it as a part-time job they pay to do.

I am not a poker ace like Winnie, though I love to play. (Eric and Lorin—miss poker at your place!) Each of the Sheet Cake books will have a poker game (or two) and a title that fits somehow thematically with the book itself.

One incident from this book that had a very real basis in my memory relates to King the turkey. When I was in high school, our church youth group had a breakfast before school. At Thanksgiving, we did turkey bowling (with frozen turkeys being hurled at cans of pumpkin stacked like bowling pins) and a REAL turkey given as a prize to the student who brought the most friends.

I REALLY wanted the turkey, but came in second place. In any case, at some point during breakfast, the turkey was set free and flew around the room, landing on tables and knocking over cereal and milk. We also put a hole in the wall with the frozen turkey bowling. Thanks for the inspiration, Pete Bowell (now of Hope Church in RVA).

Readers, thank you.

Thank you for making this job the best one ever. I appreciate all the support. With every book I launch, I have been so fortunate to have so many people cheering me along, reading, and sharing the love of these books.

I'd still write without you... but I wouldn't enjoy it as much.

I can't wait to get back to Sheet Cake with and write Val and Chevy's story!

GRAB IT HERE! https://emmastclair.com/chevyandval

ACKNOWLEDGMENTS

I have to say a huge thank you to a handful of wonderful people who helped with this book! Thank you so much to Stephanie of Alt19 Creative for the covers of this series. I LOVE them. You are amazing.

I'm also thankful to Brian of Hardywood Park Craft Brewery in Richmond, Virginia for talking to me about all of my brewing questions. (And a big thanks to Jenna for connecting us!) Can't wait to come out and have a drink this summer!

A special thanks to Jenny Proctor for being my critique partner and making my stories better. Always. Also, for listening to my ridiculousness and taking me down off all the ledges.

And a huge thanks to my early readers who gave feedback and caught typos: Jill, Ruth, Rita, Jody, Marsha, Vivian, Denice, Donna, Cait, Lyn, Marti, & Sandy. (I'll add a thank you generally to anyone I might have missed in this list. I try to keep track, but sometimes I miss people.) You guys rock!

Thanks to Jason Bradley for the proofing and edits! No more eyeballs will be landing on people. Well. Not TOO many eyeballs… ;)

WHAT TO READ NEXT

The Appies
Just Don't Fall- Emma St. Clair

Absolutely Not in Love- Jenny Proctor

A Groom of One's Own- Emma St. Clair

Romancing the Grump- Jenny Proctor

Runaway Bride and Prejudice- Emma St. Clair

Love Stories in Sheet Cake
The Buy-In

The Bluff

The Pocket Pair

Sweet Royal Romcoms
Royally Rearranged

Royal Gone Rogue

Love Clichés
Falling for Your Best Friend's Twin

Falling for Your Boss

Falling for Your Fake Fiancé

The Twelve Holidates

Falling for Your Brother's Best Friend

Falling for Your Best Friend

Falling for Your Enemy

Oakley Island (with Jenny Proctor)

Eloise and the Grump Next Door

Merritt and Her Childhood Crush

Sadie and the Bad Boy Billionaire

Izzy and Her Off Limits Love

ABOUT THE AUTHOR

Emma St. Clair is a *USA Today* bestselling author of over thirty books and has her MFA in Fiction. She lives in Katy, Texas with her husband, five kids, and a Great Dane who doesn't make a very good babysitter. Her romcoms have humor, heart, and nothing that's going to make you need to hide your Kindle from the kids. ;)

You can find out more at http://emmastclair.com or join her reader group at https://www.facebook.com/groups/emmastclair/

Emma is represented by Kimberly Whalen, The Whalen Agency.

Made in United States
North Haven, CT
06 May 2025

68639648R00247